MW01146400

"People don't put in enough i
work hard and hope everyt
plan your short- and long-term career, which is why I recommend studying
Martin's Salesforce Career Playbook!"

—DAVID LIU, Salesforce technical architect, Salesforce MVP

"This book is the missing link. There is a ton of information available today for
individuals looking to improve their technical skills, but there hasn't been a
full resource that brings together all of the career paths available to new folks
entering the industry. This book is a game changer and should be required
reading for anyone looking to launch or grow a career within the Salesforce
ecosystem."

—SELINA SUAREZ, Executive director/founder, PepUp Tech

"I wish I had read The Salesforce Career Playbook six years ago when I did
my transition into the Salesforce ecosystem. There are two main reasons to
read this book: First, to get a broad orientation about Salesforce ecosystem
roles possibilities, including evolution and transition paths. Second, to hear
and relate to the 'Day in the Life' real stories told by real people."

—SERGEY ERLIKH, MVP and solution architect

"The Salesforce Career Playbook is spot-on. It demystifies all the available
options and helps clarify the right path. I love the advice from all the people
already working in Salesforce, from the nuts and bolts of landing the first job
to the high-level advice for finding the right trajectory."

—CHRISTINE MARSHALL, MVP and Salesforce administrator

"This book answers so many of the questions that I am asked on a daily basis,
and it will be my go-to guide for anyone looking to better understand the
Salesforce ecosystem, the roles, responsibilities, and opportunities. Whether
you are a newbie, a career-changer, or advancing in your career, this book will
help you find and take the next step."

—BEN DUNCOMBE, Director and Salesforce recruitment specialist
at Talent Hub, a Salesforce recruitment firm

"This book provides a much-needed framework to guide Salesforce professionals on how to best navigate their Salesforce career path. There's much more to being a successful Salesforce professional than simply accumulating Trailhead badges and Salesforce certifications. This book sheds light on some of the other critical elements (and skills) needed for career success."

—DAVID GILLER, Salesforce Consultant & Trainer, CEO at Brainiate

"This book is about finding your home in Salesforce—and not just any home, but the right home. It's about figuring out who you are as a person and making sure you align your career with what you want out of life."

—ANNA LOUGHNAN, CRM product lead, community group leader, Salesforce MVP

"An excellent read for those navigating their Salesforce careers! Packed with tips for positioning yourself and getting hired."

—STUART SMITH, Co-founder and director of SaaSpeople, a Salesforce recruitment firm

"This book should be required reading for anyone interested in starting or advancing their career in Salesforce. It gives a clear understanding of different paths that can be taken and tips, tricks, and steps needed as you work through increasing both your technical and soft skills."

—VICKIE JEFFERY, Salesforce MVP, technology manager, Ausure, one of Australia's largest insurance broking companies

THE
SALESFORCE
CAREER
PLAYBOOK

A practical guide for starting and advancing
YOUR CAREER on the **world's FRIENDLIEST *and*
FASTEST-GROWING** tech platform

MARTIN GESSNER

A CLOUDTALENT360 BOOK

ACKNOWLEDGEMENTS

Salesforce is known for its generous community, so it should come as no surprise that many people donated their time by providing stories and wisdom that shaped this book. A special thanks to Jim Bartek, David Beckham, Prolay Chaudhury, John Conway, Ajay Dubedi, Dominick De-Fazio, Ben Duncombe, Jordan Elkin, Andi Giri, Donna Hudson, Christina Ingersoll, Rob Kaplan, Berenike Kassab, Vamsi Krishna, Marc Lester, Neal Lightfeldt, Christine Marshall, Pat McClellan, Numaan Mohammad, Natalya Murphy, Lorna O'Callaghan, Veronika Peycheva, David Scullion, Ken Seaney, Carlos Siqueira, Yelena Slobard, Santosh Kumar Sriram, Matthew Sutton, Evan Sveum, Jayant Umrani, Julian Virguez, Ashley Wagner, and Aymeric Zito.

I also want to thank the people who took time to review the book and provide feedback, including reviewers, including David Liu, David Giller, and Sergey Erlikh, and Jocelyn Baker, who helped guide the process of writing a book.

And finally, thank you to the many people who contributed by answering my survey.

TABLE OF
CONTENTS

INTRODUCTION

The commonly cited statistic is this: Upon graduation, 65 percent of the children who entered primary school back in 2016 will hold jobs that have not yet been invented. And if the disruption that has already occurred in industries across the board is any indication of what is to come, these jobs will be technology-centric.

Yet, a gap in many industries exists between what people are being trained to do and what the workforce will be demanding in the years to come. In fact, in the United States alone, the U.S. Bureau of Labor Statistics estimated that of the 1.4 million newly created computing jobs in one year, only 400,000 people graduated with the computer-science degrees necessary to fill these jobs.

A career in Salesforce bridges that gap. Over and over, what we hear from people who have successful Salesforce careers is this: Though Salesforce careers are appealing to people with a technology background, you do not need a background in technology to be successful in Salesforce. Regardless of whether you have spent years studying computer sciences or coding, you can ride the wave of disruption, and either change the direction or your career or enter the workforce in a relevant, technology-centric career.

In the transportation industry, ride-share services such as Uber and Lyft disrupted taxicabs; in retail, online shopping has threatened brick and mortar stores; in education, online degrees are replacing a noticeable percentage of traditional degrees; in accounting, artificial intelligence is taking the place of manpower; I could go on and on.

Like any career in technology, working in a Salesforce role requires a variety of skills, both technical and non-technical, depending on the position. You may have already picked up some of these skills during the course of your education and prior work experience. If you need to learn and add to your skills, Salesforce's robust training tools can teach you, and many of these tools, such as Trailhead, are available at no charge.

Indeed, Salesforce offers multiple career paths, depending on your career choice, all of which position you for an in-demand job at one of a variety of careers with an average salary generally ranging from USD $60,000 to $120,000 for a Salesforce administrator position, all the way up to USD $125,000 to $170,000 for a senior Salesforce architect.

This book is a resource for people of all different backgrounds. It explains the career options and roles for those who **do** have a background in technology and those who **do not.** If you are in doubt that you, too, can pursue a career in Salesforce, consider this: The Salesforce platform was established as click-friendly instead of code-friendly. Yes, skilled coders love the platform, but so do non-coders as it enables users to develop apps and customize the platform by way of configuring instead of coding. This draws people from various backgrounds. General business consultants, educators, biochemists, retailers, and hair stylists are just a few of the professionals who have transitioned into Salesforce careers, which are equally appealing to young adults coming out of high school or college, forty-somethings transitioning into new careers, and those coming out of retirement to pursue a job about which they feel passion.

Jobs in Salesforce are heavily in demand, with 300,000 new job openings in the current year alone and an estimated 3.3 million jobs within the next two years. Salesforce has 19.5 percent of the market share in CRM software, which is more than double its second-place rival. It is expected to double its revenue within a four-year period, so the growth in jobs will not be slowing down anytime soon.

> *I have seen so many people create opportunities to travel globally and see the world because Salesforce was their career path. In a way, Salesforce is the same wherever you go. If you can communicate in the language of Salesforce, you can work anywhere because your skills will be in demand all over the world.*
>
> **—Ben Duncombe**
> **Director of Talent Hub, a Salesforce recruitment company**

The expanding job opportunities available within Salesforce run the gamut and include:

- Salesforce administrator careers.

- Business analyst or project manager careers working for companies big and small that use Salesforce.

- Developer careers for those that are more technical and who like to customize and develop solutions in Salesforce.

- Architect careers whereby Salesforce specialists design solutions before they are implemented.

- Consulting careers in which Salesforce professionals help implement and customize Salesforce to deliver technology solutions to clients.

- Careers working as entrepreneurs, which could include owning a consulting firm, becoming a freelancer, or developing an app for the AppExchange.

- From 2019 to 2020, Salesforce grew its workforce from about 35,000 employees to about 50,000 employees, making it an attractive organization for developing your career.

As for me, the author of this book, I spent ten years working in various Salesforce roles, including business analyst, project manager, consultant, and solutions architect. Along the way, I have earned twelve different certifications to move up the career ladder. Currently, I run a company that has helped thousands of people learn Salesforce and prepare for certifications.

Through my work, I have been fortunate to meet people from around the globe, some of whom are beginning their careers in Salesforce and some of whom are advancing or changing the direction of their Salesforce careers as they learn more and more about the various Salesforce opportunities.

What I have come to realize is this: The Salesforce ecosystem is analogous to the job market as a whole. There is a little something for everyone if you know where to look and how to position yourself. Regardless of whether you have a master's degree in information technology or no formal education beyond eighth grade, you can earn a more-than-competitive wage and move up the ladder in a Salesforce-related career. The same is true for homemakers and businesspeople, techies and non-techies, artists and academics. You name it, and I have seen someone thrive.

However, what is true in the traditional job market is also true within Salesforce: Not all jobs are for everyone. While some people prefer defined job duties, others would wither away if they performed the same job functions day after day. Some have a high tolerance for change and risk; others prefer stability. Some of us thrive as entrepreneurs while others prefer the security of more traditional jobs.

The Salesforce Career Playbook explores the different options and career paths within the Salesforce ecosystem so that you can align your strengths and needs with a career that is right for you. After all, you will have a more successful, fulfilling career if you are allowed to bring your strongest talents to work each day. This book can be useful if you are new to the Salesforce world or if you have already started your Salesforce career.

It answers three big questions:

1. "What are the careers and roles available if I am new to the Salesforce world?"

2. "What are the career paths available to me if I'm already working in a Salesforce role and would like to develop and grow my career?"

3. "Most of all, which of these paths is best suited to my personality, skills, and lifestyle preferences?"

In any case, the mission of this book is that you walk away knowing your next best step for pursuing a meaningful career in Salesforce.

PART ONE

OVERVIEW OF SALESFORCE ROLES

Let there be no doubt: Salesforce jobs are in demand. Over the next few years, the expansion of the Salesforce ecosystem is expected to result in the creation of 4.2 million jobs worldwide.

What exactly are the jobs in the world of Salesforce? Firms have varying names for different positions within their specific ecosystems, making it impossible to cover every single job out there. This book covers the five roles that come up most often on job boards. Each role will be described in full in one of the five chapters of this section.

- **Chapter One: Administrator**
- **Chapter Two: Developer**
- **Chapter Three: Business Analyst**
- **Chapter Four: Consultant**
- **Chapter Five: Architect**

Salesforce Developer
Average Salary

$124,944

Salesforce Administrator
Average Salary

$62,000

Salesforce Business Analyst
Average Salary

$100,000

THE SALESFORCE ECOSYSTEM

Salesforce Consultant
Average Salary

$102,687

Salesforce Architect
Average Salary

$142,242

In Part One of this book, we will cover each of these roles, as well as:

- The average annual salary and salary range,

- The job description,

- The technology-related requirements necessary for the job,

- The general business and "soft" skills necessary for the job,

- Tips for obtaining a job in each of these roles, and

- A day in the life of someone working in each of these roles.

In the world of Salesforce, "soft" skills are just as important as technology-related skills. Employers look for both.

Soft skills are the unquantifiable attributes that enable an employee to work with others, manage stress, and persevere in the face of obstacles. Soft skills include communication skills, collaboration, conflict-resolution skills, and agility. Salesforce delivers three updates a year packed with new features, so the abilities to continually learn, think critically, be curious, and teach others are valuable.

These are skills that are not traditionally taught in formal education but can make or break an employee.

Technology-related skills (which fall under the category of "hard skills") are the tangible, quantifiable, technical skills required to complete a job. They are task-specific, and they are traditionally taught through formal education, certification programs, and on-the-job-training.

In the Salesforce world, the technology-related skills required vary greatly depending on the role. However all roles require a logical mind, analytical thinking, attention to detail, and problem-solving skills. The driver for implementing Salesforce is often a company's desire to improve and automate business workflows, so the skills of understanding and designing business processes are important.

Obviously knowing Salesforce inside and out is required, together with the ability to configure and enhance applications built on the Salesforce platform. Developers need software development skills to design, develop, and test code. As the Salesforce platform has evolved, so has the technology complexity, requiring developers to be strong at coding in multiple languages used in the platform, such as Apex and JavaScript.

CHAPTER ONE:
Salesforce Administrator

A Salesforce administrator is responsible for maintaining the Salesforce system's functionality after it has been implemented in a company. Not only do administrators manage the day-to-day tasks related to using Salesforce, but they also solve user problems and requests, train employees on using the system, and extend the existing functionality of the platform as the business changes, evolves, or expands.

Average Salary of a
Salesforce Administrator in the United States:
$62,000

The salary of an administrator in the United States generally ranges from $60,000 to $120,000.

These figures are an average of an aggregate of sources. At the time of this writing, Mason Frank reported a low-end salary of $100,500 for junior administrators and a high-end salary of $110,000, with salaries ranging to $126,000 for senior administrators. Salesforce reported the average salary to be $95,000. Neuvoo reported that entry-level positions might start at $48,750 but average salaries are $94,951. ZipRecruiter reported $88,146 as an average salary with salaries as low as $36,000 and as high as $140,500 and most often ranging between $65,000 and $107,000. Indeed reported $87,744 as an average salary. Glassdoor reported $87,292 as an average salary, with salaries ranging from $62,000 to $117,000.

In small firms, the Salesforce administrator might be the sole employee with Salesforce knowledge, meaning that the job description might include some tasks that, in a larger firm, would be delegated to other roles, such as a business analyst, project manager or developer. Small firms, after all, require employees to wear more hats. In larger firms, though, the administrator might work with a team, including developers, business analysts, project managers, or architects, as well as specialized administrators. For instance, a large company might have a sales administrator who works with the company's sales representatives, as well as a marketing administrator and a customer service administrator, both of whom work on a specific aspect of the company's functions.

With this in mind, remember that this book does its best to describe roles consistent with industry standards, but job duties will vary from company to company.

Admins end up wearing two hats: One is the break/fix hat, which is a little like being the ticket-taker at the butcher counter. Your mindset is: "Who is next? Someone wants this, and they want it right away, so I need to get it done and move onto the next thing."

Normally, your job is to get it done that day, and the job is simple: Add a new value on a pick list, turn off a user who is departing, or add a user who is onboarding.

The other hat is project-based. Admins are usually involved in projects that can move the needle for the company or for a department. This is usually more fully scoped with a timeline and a sandbox from which you give demos, solicit feedback, and make changes.

If you are a good admin, you are also involved in training once these projects are complete and implemented. Preferably, you are prepared to teach the users because the very nature of the project was to move the needle.

—Rob Kaplan
Senior consultant and engagement manager,
and previous administrator

JOB DESCRIPTION

A Salesforce administrator is often a combination of a number of roles, including project manager, business analyst, process improvement manager, support analyst, and system administrator. Administrators spend much of their time supporting users, answering day-to-day questions about the platform, troubleshooting, configuring the system, and training users. Their job description includes:

- User administration

- Data gatekeeping and security

- Data management

- Responding to user questions and requests

- Automating processes

- Creating reports and dashboards

- Training

- Project management

- Staying current

User Administration

A Salesforce administrator is the gatekeeper to the Salesforce org and creates user accounts, updates and removes users when employees leave or change positions, and helps users with password and access problems. By assigning and configuring profiles and permission sets, an administrator also ensures users have the necessary role-specific permissions.

Data Gatekeeping and Security

A Salesforce administrator is the data guardian, protecting access and making sure that all users—internal and external—have access to and see only the data that they need. An administrator also understands and configures the powerful array of data-access and security mechanisms, including profiles, roles, sharing rules, and field-level security.

Data Management

No system is useful unless it has clean, reliable, accurate data that users can rely upon. Using data import tools, a Salesforce administrator imports data into the org. The administrator also monitors data to prevent it from being neglected and becoming stale.

An administrator also monitors the quality of the data and identifies when data is duplicated, and when it needs to be cleansed, updated, or merged. An administrator uses data management tools to correct issues of quality.

As well as ad-hoc data imports, Salesforce often has data feeds and other integrations with both internal and external systems. When no technical resources are available, an administrator monitors and manages data integrations and associated tools.

As a solo administrator, every day is an adventure. I have quarterly projects or rollouts that I am always working toward, but at least fifty percent of my day is spontaneous. From bug fixes to feature requests and ad hoc training: I always have the opportunity to do something new.

—Daymon Boswell
Administrator

Responding to User Questions and Requests

Users who have adopted Salesforce and are engaged in the platform are full of questions, and they often have requests to change or improve their configuration. An administrator spends time answering questions about the system, resolving issues, and responding to requests for changes and enhancements. An administrator is also proactive in gathering feedback from users and seeking ways to improve the system.

An administrator uses the power of the "clicks-not-code" platform when implementing changes and enhancements to enable features and configure objects, fields, formulas, page layouts, record pages, record types, workflows, processes, flows, and more, surprising end-users with the agility and speed with which robust solutions can be developed.

When a request needs programmatic customization, an administrator evaluates, scopes, and coordinates the implementation of development requests with a Salesforce developer.

In the Words of a Salesforce Administrator...

I have one consistent goal: Continuously identify ways to solve users' problems. I can do that a number of ways, but several top the list:

1. *Ensure data integrity in order to develop and sustain users' confidence in the system;*

2. *Maintain a continuous dialog with users to find and resolve pain points through new features/applications;*

3. *Continuously look for opportunities to streamline and automate processes within the company.*

Automating Processes

Salesforce is used to support and improve sales, marketing, service, and custom business processes. The administrator works with stakeholders and subject-matter experts to identify and improve business processes that can be configured to run on Salesforce.

Salesforce provides an ever-expanding army of tools to allow an administrator to become a process automation hero. The administrator understands and configures the process automation tools, including workflow rules, flows, and approval processes.

Creating Reports and Dashboards

Salesforce provides powerful analytical tools, including reports and dashboards. The administrator can use these tools to create useful insights and metrics for the business, or to help users create and troubleshoot their own.

Training

An administrator often develops training materials and trains groups or individual users. New features are added with each release, which often requires user-training.

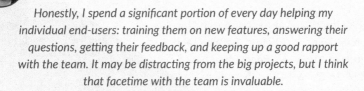

Honestly, I spend a significant portion of every day helping my individual end-users: training them on new features, answering their questions, getting their feedback, and keeping up a good rapport with the team. It may be distracting from the big projects, but I think that facetime with the team is invaluable.

—Emily Duncan
Administrator

Project Management

A Salesforce administrator is often responsible for implementing new features and functionality, managing the implementation of Salesforce in a new part of the business, and working with developers, AppExchange vendors, and other third parties to complete a project.

Staying Current

With three releases a year and Salesforce's frequent acquisitions of businesses that offer complementary functionality to Salesforce, the world of Salesforce is constantly changing. An administrator needs to keep up-to-date with Salesforce releases to understand what is new, what is changing, and what might need to be reworked as a result of the changes.

TECHNOLOGY-RELATED JOB REQUIREMENTS

The requirements for being hired as a Salesforce administrator often include:

- Salesforce Administrator certification.

- Depending on the organization and which Salesforce functionality is used, additional certifications, such as Sales Cloud and/or Service Cloud.

- Strong Salesforce platform knowledge, with the proven ability to configure and customize Salesforce declaratively (using point and click customization) and utilize process automation tools.

- Knowledge and experience with data management, data validation tools, data analysis, and creating reports and dashboards.

A big difference exists in what a Salesforce administrator can be asked to do, and that depends on how big the firm is. If you are the only administrator, you are asked to do it all.

When you are the only admin, you have to have all of the skills. You have to be a people-person because you are going to be interacting with stakeholders a lot. You have to be technical enough to speak the lay person's language and describe the technical requirements.

It is all on you, and everyone is going to come to you. You will be the point person for the employee with the deepest technical problem as well as the most mundane problems, like getting locked out of accounts.

And you will be interacting with users all the way from high-level executives all the way down to the interns.

In any situation, it all depends on you. When you take time off work, the job will come to a complete halt because no one is there to back you up.

Point being: It ends up being a lot of pressure, and some people really like that. It truly is a lot of variety, and it is a way to learn a little bit about everything. But, you need to be aware that there will be a great deal of pressure put on you, not only when you are taking time off, but also if someone needs you after hours. You are literally the whole solution.

But it's a great way to start out because you will learn a lot being thrown into the deep end. You will learn how to find answers for yourself, and you will develop connections with all of the critical websites and resources that have answers.

—Nick Liechty

Salesforce operations manager for a cyber-security company with 2,000 employees, 1,700 Salesforce users, and a dozen Salesforce professionals, which include administrators, business analysts, and developers.

GENERAL BUSINESS AND SOFT SKILLS

Along with technology-related skills, employers also search for general business and soft skills, such as:

Communication

Administrators need excellent verbal and written communication skills to help train employees, resolve user issues, and communicate needs to developers. Much of an administrator's time is spent in meetings and working one-on-one with users, so employers search for administrators who are high-caliber communicators.

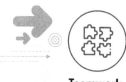

Teamwork

Administrators need strong teamwork and stakeholder engagement skills as they are asked to customize Salesforce to meet user needs, so they need to have a desire to serve the needs of a variety of business types, from salespeople to executives. Because they pass along more challenging customizations to developers, administrators must be willing to work with technical teams to advocate for non-technical end-users.

Strategic thinking

Administrators need the ability to think strategically, aggregate resources, and problem solve. On a daily basis, administrators are faced with a variety of troubleshooting tickets and user requests. They must, then, be able to prioritize, manage time, and find answers.

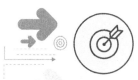

Action-orientation

Administrators should have a strong instinct for action, ability to organize, and aptness to self-start. Administrators serve as a support function; the more willing they are to take the initiative, the better they can support users.

Project management

Administrators should have excellent project management and presentation skills as they are required to manage multiple facets of a project and communicate progress to end-users, team members, and superiors. As projects progress, and as new functionality is implemented, administrators train end-users.

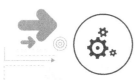

Operational acumen

Administrators should have a strong understanding of business processes related to sales, marketing, customer service, and operations. To implement Salesforce within an organization, a Salesforce administrator needs to have (or gain) deep and detailed knowledge of how a company operates so that it can assist users in best integrating Salesforce into the company's operations, train users, automate the company's processes, and solve business problems.

> *To show empathy, to ask questions but also to listen, and to then drive engagement are really important for an administrator.*
>
> ## —Ben Duncombe
> **Director of Talent Hub, a Salesforce recruitment company**

Although getting a job with no related experience can be difficult, Salesforce reports that about 39 percent of the jobs posted for Salesforce administrators are entry-level jobs.

TIPS FOR JOB-SEEKERS

If you are interested in starting a career as a Salesforce administrator, consider the following tips for landing your first job.

1. **Obtain your Salesforce Certified Administrator certification and complete Trailhead badges.**

Although neither a certification nor Trailhead status will guarantee you a job, they will demonstrate that you have a baseline of knowledge. Increasingly, certification is a requirement for an administrator role.

2. **Build an app. Use your work or personal life as inspiration for creating an app that you can build to showcase your knowledge and skills.**

Then, put the app on your résumé or curriculum vitae (CV), and demo it during your interviews. By doing this, you can demonstrate your Salesforce skills, and you can also demonstrate some of the softer skills needed for administrators. You can tell a story of how you identified a need and built an app to solve a problem, showcasing your strategic thinking, action-orientation, and operational acumen.

3. **If you do not have on-the-job Salesforce experience, look for opportunities to volunteer at a nonprofit or volunteer organization.**

You could even look for opportunities in a nonprofit where you could implement Salesforce yourself or form a team with people more experienced and learn from them. I recently volunteered at my local dog shelter and noticed the systems were very old. I talked to the manager about implementing Salesforce to quickly improve their processes and modernize the user experience. Through its Power of Us program, Salesforce provides ten free enterprise licenses to nonprofits. A volunteer could implement it for the nonprofit and gain experience in the process.

4. **Get involved.**

Attend Salesforce events, like World Tour and Dreamin. Get involved in the online Trailblazer community and join online collaboration groups. Complete superbadges. Go to user group meetings. You could meet someone who knows of an opportunity, paid or unpaid, that could help you.

5. **Consider how you could differentiate your Salesforce knowledge from other people seeking administrator roles.**

Align your interests with demand. For example, if you are interested in service, consider building upon your Salesforce Certified Administrator certification with the Salesforce Field Service Lightning Consultant credential, as Field Service has been one of Salesforce's fastest-growing products.

Day in the life: -
CHRISTINE MARSHALL

Christine Marshall is a solo administrator who works in Bristol, a city on the River Avon in the southwest of England, for a global engineering firm with headquarters in France and offices in the United States, Canada, India, and Europe.

Christine's company uses Sales Cloud to manage the sales process from lead to deal and to ensure proactive account management. Salesforce is pivotal to this global company, aligning more than eighteen different legal entities within the company, and creating a collaborative approach to sales.

Christine's role initially sat within the sales function, but it was moved to the IT department in 2019. She has two direct line managers: the head of business core solutions based in India and the IT director for the UK. Overall, her role rolls up to the company's CIO, based in Germany.

Christine maintains that the life of a solo admin is never lonely, despite not having a team. On a day-to-day basis, she handles user support, collaborates with her global super users, and is in constant contact with the senior leadership team, either directly or via a steering committee.

Christine is a Salesforce MVP, runs the Bristol Salesforce admin user group, and writes a blog, The Everyday Admin.

8:00 a.m.
Christine starts her day by checking for any requests that might have come in from users overnight. She notes high-priority requests to be tackled immediately, and she flags and schedules everything else using "Cases" in Salesforce. Christine encourages her users to request support via a help button on the Salesforce home page that logs a case directly in Salesforce; this helps her more easily stay on top of her work and prioritize issues. This morning, she is making some urgent changes required to a dashboard that will be used in a key sales meeting later today.

10:00 a.m.

Christine meets with the team in India, including her boss and developers, to discuss new features, progress, and goals. Today, they are discussing the successful rollout of Single Sign On and planning their next project, Lightning for Outlook.

11:00 a.m.

With an ever-growing number of Salesforce users, Christine is tasked with onboarding new departments and business units. She plans their migration from legacy platforms to Salesforce, including development, data loading, and training. Today, she is designing and building a new app for a "satellite" company that, although owned by the company, operates independently. It is important that Salesforce is set up to reflect their own brand identity and individual sales process.

Noon

Christine tries to get out for a brief walk at lunchtime, but she often works through. As the only administrator with a global user base of 300+ sales employees, she juggles multiple requests from users in different time zones. Today, she gets a request from a new user whose transition to Salesforce has prompted the group to examine their data—and they have discovered it leaves a lot to be desired. Christine is supporting them by cleansing and mass-updating data using the Data Loader. Through the use of features such as Einstein Opportunity Scoring, plus Christine's own data quality fields, users find that Salesforce can easily help them identify poor quality data or records that need urgent attention.

12:30 p.m.

The afternoon is reserved for requests from users in the UK and Europe, as well as training new users in these areas. Today, she is training a new employee from the London office who will become a super user.

Typically Christine will train all users for America, Canada, India, the UK, and Ireland. Super-user training is more intensive as it requires in-depth training on reporting and dashboards. As well as initial training, Christine posts frequent tips and tricks via a Chatter group and training videos her users can utilize at any time.

2:00 p.m.

Christine tries to reserve time in the afternoons to take action on any customization and enhancements. She also uses this time to research potential products or apps from the AppExchange that might meet her requirements. For all projects, she acts as the business analyst, project manager, technical lead, and trainer. Christine is a huge fan of the AppExchange and often uses new apps to enhance Salesforce. In particular, she loves Field Trip for finding unused fields and Graphics Pack for images she then uses to create highly visual formula fields, such as a data quality score.

3:00 p.m.

As users in the United States and Canada begin their workdays, Christine transitions her focus to helping these users with requests and training. Today's request is from an American user; the user works in sales administration and would like Christine to show her how she can create reports of open opportunities and subscribe to them on behalf of herself and other sales team members.

3:30 p.m.

A great Salesforce administrator needs to be proactive, so Christine makes time to review her Adoption and Housekeeping dashboards. She monitors logins, usage and data quality, then flags any concerns before they escalate.

Recently, Christine noticed that the data quality of accounts was looking very poor. Around one-fifth of all accounts were created without a billing address, website, or phone number. This meant that duplicate accounts were easily being created, despite having duplicate and matching rules enabled in the system. To resolve this, Christine made certain fields required and created a validation rule to ensure users enter a billing address.

4:30 p.m.

Getting support and learning to delegate is key for a busy solo administrator. Christine meets with her super user group to get feedback, define enhancements, and prioritize enhancements. Every eight weeks, Christine also meets with a steering committee to set very high-level business objectives that can be supported by Salesforce. The most recent objective is to complete onboarding of all businesses within the company, then to create reports and dashboards to track key performance indicators. Once all areas of the business are using Salesforce, the company will finally have a complete 360-view of all customer activity across the globe.

CHAPTER TWO:
Salesforce Developer

Salesforce developers design, develop, and implement customized solutions on the platform. These are the people who are responsible for creating and supporting programmatic solutions, for integrating other platforms with Salesforce, and for troubleshooting advanced technical issues. They are skilled with computers and have knowledge of coding.

Average Salary of a
Salesforce Developer in the United States:
$124,944

The salary of a
developer in the
United States
generally ranges
from $87,000-
$157,000.

These figures are an average of an aggregate of sources. At the time of this writing, Mason Frank reported a low-end salary of $114,000 for a junior developer and a high-end salary of $144,500, with salaries ranging to $162,500 for senior developers. Neuvoo reported the average U.S. Salesforce developer's salary to be $130,000, with entry level positions starting at $79,201. Salesforce reported an average salary of $125,000. Glassdoor reported salaries ranging from $87,000 to $157,000, with an average salary for a senior developer around $119,542. Indeed reported $115,861, and ZipRecruiter reported salaries as low as $48,000 and as high as $174,500, with the majority of salaries ranging between $92,000 and $135,000 and an average salary of $114,763.

In a small firm, an administrator might double as a developer. Alternatively, in a small firm, a developer might not exist. Rather, the company might hire a consultant to tackle any development projects beyond the in-house staff's know-how.

In a larger firm, the roles are separate and distinct. Whereas administrators manage the day-to-day use of Salesforce, developers manage all technical aspects of Salesforce and build functionality within the platform using their Apex, Visualforce, and Lightning coding skills. When customization is complete, developers hand it off to others in the team to implement and manage the functionality developed.

Using the analogy of a home, the developer is the person who builds custom complex features of the home whereas the administrator is the head of the household. The developer works in the background, whereas the administrator tends to be front and center with direct customer and/or end-user interactions.

JOB DESCRIPTION

The role of a developer will differ from company to company, but will typically involve some or all of the following:

- Developing customized programmatic solutions to meet requirements and support business processes.

- Developing and supporting integrations between Salesforce and external systems.

- Collaborating with project team members to design, develop, test, and deploy functionality as part of projects, which includes meeting with end-users and managers to determine project specifications related to user interface, customized applications, and integration with other software.

- Working with the administrator on development issues related to maintenance of the platform and support of users.

- Providing internal technical support related to the Salesforce platform.

> *For us, the biggest gap or challenge in the market is in finding good senior developers. Everyone wants a developer. That's just where the most demand is. Salesforce partners need developers. Salesforce end-users need developers. Salesforce product companies need developers. Like I said, everyone needs developers.*
>
> **—Ben Duncombe**
> **Director of Talent Hub, a Salesforce recruitment company**

TECHNOLOGY-RELATED JOB REQUIREMENTS

Aside from some architects, developers are usually the most technical professionals within the Salesforce ecosystem, and they should have a significant knowledge and experience in technology, which could include:

- Salesforce certifications, such as App Builder, Platform Developer I, or Platform Developer II.

- Additional certifications depending on functionality a company has implemented, such as Community Cloud, CPQ, or Field Service Lightning.

- Salesforce Platform development experience using Apex, SOQL, SOSL, Visualforce, or Lightning Framework.

- Experience with web technologies, including HTML, CSS, XML, JSON, and JavaScript.

- Experience working with REST and SOAP APIs.

- Experience working with integration and middleware tools, such as MuleSoft.

- Working knowledge of Agile delivery and scrum framework.

- Bachelor's degree in computer science, engineering, or a related field.

I went to business school, so this is a whole new world for me. I remember being so scared when I was interviewing with banks and businesses, but now that I have become a developer, I feel freedom that the world is mine. I think that is because of the nature of the market, being in this community, and being a developer.

There are so many companies that need good development, and there are not enough developers. As long as you understand that, you should not ever walk into a situation thinking you need the company more than they need you. If you are a good developer, in the end, they need you more.

But be aware that soft skills will not get you there alone. It is important to have a good foundation and proof that you are a good worker—that you are the value that you are trying to present yourself as. I find that many companies have been through previous developers, and they are not happy with the quality of work these developers provided.

If you can prove quickly that your quality of work is exceptional and that you are willing to do what needs to be done, then you should feel freedom that the world is yours.

—Dominick DeFazio
Developer and chief technology officer

GENERAL BUSINESS AND SOFT SKILLS

Along with technology-related skills, employers also search for general business and soft skills, such as:

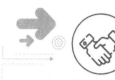

Communication and negotiation

Oftentimes, users of Salesforce will ask developers to provide specific solutions when better solutions might exist. As such, developers must be capable of interpreting requests, discovering the underlying logic for the request, and presenting alternative solutions.

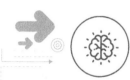

Solutions-orientation

On the other hand, users might also be faced with problems for which they have no solution. Developers, then, must be problem-solvers who can brainstorm for various solutions to meet a business goal.

Agility and coachability

Salesforce releases updates every quarter, so developers should be willing to learn new material and adapt their techniques, applications, and customizations accordingly.

Team mentality

A developer's job is to help enhance the productivity and efficiency of the team by automating tasks or creating structures to facilitate jobs. As a result, they must be invested in the larger goals. The best developers do not simply develop; they understand the varying perspectives of different stakeholders within an organization.

Commitment to learning

Because Salesforce releases updates quarterly, a developer can never claim to know everything there is to know about Salesforce, so following and learning Salesforce's new product releases and technical capabilities is part of the job.

The best parts of my day are breaking down problems and being challenged to find solutions.

—Jorge Luis Pérez Pratt
Developer

Though many employers look for experienced candidates, Salesforce reports that about 18 percent of the jobs posted for Salesforce developers are entry-level jobs.

TIPS FOR JOB-SEEKERS

If you are searching for an entry-level job as a Salesforce developer, consider the following tips:

1. Be familiar with and prepared to discuss Salesforce development best practices.

Companies often have had bad experiences with code that was not created in accordance with best practices, which led to costly revisions, wasted time, and duplicated work. Establish yourself as someone who cares not only about developing a solution, but also about solutions that are high-quality and in accordance with Salesforce's best practices.

2. Look for outside mentors or people in your organization who can review your code.

Having a more experienced person review your code is invaluable in terms of learning and improving your skills.

3. Get involved.

Attend Salesforce events, like World Tour and Dreamin. Get involved in the online Trailblazer community and join online collaboration groups. Complete superbadges. Participate in user groups. User groups will help you connect with people who can help you find employers, provide advice, or even give you a job opportunity.

4. Showcase your skills by building an app or Lightning component and listing it on the AppExchange.

Numaan Mohammad, a developer working in Canada, developed an app that helps view, filter, and export Big Object data. Creating the app helped Numaan build connections, which he believes helped him secure his latest job, which gave him an exciting opportunity to travel from India to Canada.

5. Be ready to talk through examples of challenging requirements and how you solved them.

Although a developer is not typically business facing, communication skills are still critical. Talking through a challenge and your solution will demonstrate your problem-solving skills and help you differentiate yourself from other developers.

Day in the life:
DOMINICK DEFAZIO

At the time of this writing, Dominick DeFazio was the lead developer for a recruiting company in New York City. To implement the recruiting process, the company used a managed package called Bullhorn for Salesforce. The company had Sales Cloud and Community Cloud, as well as numerous integrations with Microsoft products and Amazon VMs. Many features needed for recruiting were missing from the managed package (such as invoicing, timesheets, and search), so custom code solutions fill in the gaps. Dominick reported directly to the CTO and commonly met with the managing partners and executive team in order to understand development priorities.

At the time, Dominick also had a contract job with a non-profit philanthropy/impact-investing company, where he was moonlighting. Dominick later left the recruiting company to work full-time for the non-profit.

This is a day in the life of Dominick DeFazio while he was working full-time for the recruiting company and moonlighting for the non-profit company.

7:30 a.m.

Dominick's early hours are spent working from his apartment for his contract job. This work is for a small company where Dominick wears many hats. He helps with email marketing, development, technical strategies, and database management. Though the company does have an operation of Salesforce, he helps with the many moving pieces of a small and growing company.

Today, he is working on multiple key projects. He continues to improve invoicing and payroll processes with further automation. Much of his work is centered around rebuilding and enhancing existing features and applications. This includes an applicant tracking system, search and match, and productivity task lists. He is increasing search capabilities by establishing a SQL résumé database dynamic search that returns results to Salesforce.

10:30 a.m.

Dominick rides his bike ten blocks to the downtown office in New York City. His employer, a recruiting company, does not mind that Dominick comes in late because he has worked hard and cemented his role as the lead developer. His first duty for the day is to get a cup of coffee and meet with the morning team to discuss where he is with the projects, give updates and demos, and solicit feedback. Today, he is working on a new applicant tracking system to replace the kanban-style interface that came with the recruiting managed package. The ATS is a massive undertaking, requiring over a dozen components nested into each other. It includes interview scheduling, mass emailing, kanban stage tracking and editing, and intra-team notification systems.

11:30 a.m.

Dominick takes an hour lunch break with his team, leaving the office to have lunch in the city.

12:30 p.m.

Dominick has anywhere from ten to twenty projects at any given time, particularly for the back-office team working with invoicing and payroll. After lunch, he grinds away for a solid four or five hours on a chosen project based on coming deadlines and a project showcases. Today he's working on a click-and-drag HTML table that will serve as a scheduler for interviews. It resembles a calendar but allows for quick availability for information input. It's built for users, by users, so as to replace complicated email chains.

"As a developer, the only metric I have for myself in terms of performance is how quickly and proficiently I build Grade-A applications, so getting on my computer and not being distrubed for four or five hours is the most important part of my day. I code as long and as hard as I can."

Grade-A applications can be measured on two fronts: 1) by quality of code, and 2) by quality of UI/UX. Efficient, clean, and well-labelled code is extremely important when building for over 200 users, as any bugs will almost immediately be found. For larger applications, feature-based quality unit tests prevent faulty updates. On the front end, applications should look and feel great. Enabling the recruiter to do their work faster and easier than before is Dominick's main goal.

Main challenges include the need for components that don't exist in the Lightning Component Library (such as multi-select drop downs, lookup inputs, calendars), avoiding governor limits, and avoiding long server calls that hold up front-end functionality.

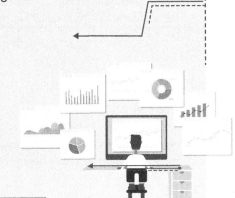

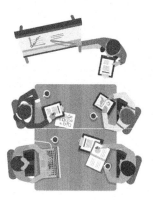

4:30 p.m.

Occasionally, Dominick is pulled into another meeting to discuss ongoing projects. Today, he is meeting with the COO and the CFO to review current issues with invoicing automations and potential fixes. New clients requested new invoicing grouping structures, requiring code to be flexible. The company's community portal is buggy and outdated, and needs to be replaced with a Lightning community.

Invoice email automation is working and is ready to be expanded from weekly invoices to include monthly and bi-monthly invoice split types.

5:00 p.m.

Dominick rides his bike to the gym for his daily workout before eating dinner. Keeping fit is vital to maintaining focus and energy throughout the workday. He rock-climbs at a gym in Queens, attends yoga classes, and runs along the East River. Rock climbing gives him strength and provides a unique dopamine rush after each completed route.

Running and yoga allow him to de-stress and brainstorm new avenues to pursue in projects. Body equilibrium is important to Dominick, and he has found that he is twice as productive when he is in shape.

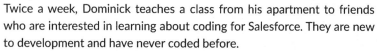

7:00 p.m.

Twice a week, Dominick teaches a class from his apartment to friends who are interested in learning about coding for Salesforce. They are new to development and have never coded before.

The class is focused around teaching core skills in Salesforce development in order to prepare them for a developer career. Dominick plans each class the day before.

The advanced class has a project that continues over the weeks and generally is similar to something Dominick is doing at work, so it closely reflects real work. For the novice class, he teaches basics of coding all the way through Apex and triggers, then to lightning component development.

Three of his students have secured careers as a result of participation in class. Students who excel in class and get their certification are either placed on Dominick's team at the recruiting company or work with him on contract work for NEXUS. This gives them initial experience that is vital to securing their next job.

8:30 p.m.

Dominick spends another two or three hours each night on contract work. Today, he is completing an email marketing campaign to advertise an upcoming summit. Outreach is conducted through list emails and campaigns via Sales Cloud. He also upgrades object structures, provides administrator services, and builds custom components for the small eight-person team.

CHAPTER THREE:
Salesforce Business Analyst

A Salesforce business analyst is often involved in every step of a Salesforce project or functional enhancement, from identifying requirements, solution design, coordinating with developers, implementing, testing, and training users. In addition to general IT business analyst skills, a Salesforce "BA" is a specialist who understands the capabilities of the Salesforce platform and the business processes that it supports.

THE THREE LAYERS OF A BA'S SKILLS

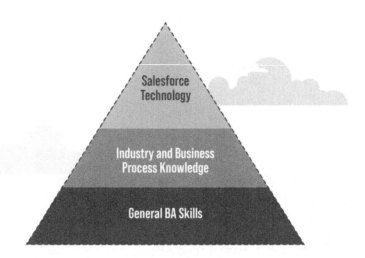

Three layers exist to a Salesforce business analyst's skills. The fundamental layer is general BA skills, which is a requirement for any job as a business analyst. Next, a Salesforce business analyst will have an easier time securing a job if the analyst has domain knowledge in the industry—for instance, financial services, insurance, or manufacturing—and understands the business processes of a particular organization. Though industry knowledge is helpful, it is not necessarily required. The top layer, though, is knowledge of the Salesforce platform, and this layer is a necessity for anyone pursuing a role as a Salesforce business analyst. This layer allows the analyst to effectively recommend solutions that can be enabled by the platform.

The role of a Salesforce-specific business analyst is the same as it would be for any other IT business analyst: Identify needs and recommend solutions to bridge the gap between current business processes and the desired state that will improve outcomes and help meet objectives.

The analyst is responsible for understanding not only the capabilities of Salesforce, but also the various business processes at play within an organization. Although Salesforce can be used to enable a wide variety of business processes, it is typically used in marketing, sales, and service processes. As such, a Salesforce business analyst is expected to have a working knowledge in one or more of these areas in terms of understanding both business process as well as the features that Salesforce offers that can enable them.

Average Salary of a
Salesforce Business Analyst in the United States:
$100,000

The salary of a business analyst in the United States generally ranges from $80,000 to $120,000.

These figures are an average of an aggregate of sources. In late 2019, Neuvoo reported the average U.S. salary to be $105,042. Indeed reported $104,849. Salesforce reported $104,000. ZipRecruiter reported $103,126, with salaries as low as $49,500 and as high as $170,500, with the majority of salaries ranging between $82,500 and $120,000. Glassdoor reported an average salary of $83,431, with salaries ranging from $57,143 to $113,780.

A dedicated business analyst role is typically reserved for large end-user firms. At a smaller to mid-size firm, an administrator or project manager may wear multiple hats and also act as a business analyst.

The business analyst is one of multiple Salesforce resources working on a project team. Whereas the administrator on the team manages the day-to-day use of Salesforce, the business analyst is tasked with understanding the business, documenting needs, overhauling processes, and ensuring solutions are delivered to meet stakeholder needs.

Importantly, the analyst needs to know that the solutions being asked for by the end-users are not always the best or most efficient solutions for addressing that need. Because the end-users are not the Salesforce experts, they will not know if a better solution exists.

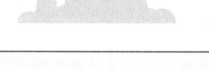

As a business analyst, I focus most of my time on gathering information about what the client needs and working with the development team to make sure those needs are met. When I worked as an administrator for a firm of more than one-thousand users, I was actually doing the builds, and the testing, and the deployments. That's the big difference.

—Yelena Slobard
Business analyst for a medium-sized consulting company

JOB DESCRIPTION

The role of a Salesforce business analyst will differ from company to company, but will typically involve some or all of the following:

- Identifying and documenting needs
- Analyzing business processes
- Defining requirements
- Recommending solutions
- Validating solutions
- Configuring and coordinating solution development
- Coordinating user-acceptance training
- Training end-users

Identifying and Documenting Needs

A business analyst is responsible for collecting and organizing needs, is-sues, and requests via interviews with users, questionnaires, meetings, observations, workshops, brainstorming sessions, and use cases. Require-ments-gathering is one of the most important things—if not the most im-portant thing—that a business analyst does.

 ## Analyzing Business Processes

A business analyst will understand current-state business processes and analyze how they can be improved to meet business needs and objectives.

 ## Defining Requirements

An analyst generates a list of requirements from users and stakeholders. A good business analyst is also skilled at documenting and keeping infor-mation organized. Requirements are then turned into a document or user story that describes business and functional requirements. In addition, the business analyst needs to consider other aspects of a solution, including data migration and integration requirements.

 ## Recommending Solutions

The analyst is responsible for knowing how the capabilities of the Sales-force platform can be used to enable the future-state business processes and recommend appropriate high-level solutions. The solution the cus-tomer is asking for is not always the best or most efficient way to solve the problem, but the customer will not know if there is an easier way to address their need. The business analyst works with a solution architect (if the role exists at the organization) to translate functional requirements into the most appropriate technical solutions.

Validating Solutions

The analyst reviews and validates the potential solution with the stakeholders, often using tools such as user stories and wireframes. User stories are used in the Agile methodology to document use cases that describe, in story version, requirements and how a process will be used. Wireframes are sketches or mockups of the screen layout and are used to visually communicate and validate how a Salesforce screen will be used in the solution.

 ## Configuring and Coordinating Solution Development

When a business analyst fills multiple roles, the business analyst may also be responsible for configuring part or all of a solution in Salesforce, particularly when the solution can be achieved using declarative capabilities of the platform. When a solution requires a developer or involves an outside vendor, the business analyst will communicate requirements and validate solutions before they are shown to end-users, acting as a representative for the business requirements. When solutions are ready, the business analyst may participate or run system demonstrations to end-users.

 ## Coordinating User-Acceptance Testing

When a solution is ready to be tested by end-users, the business analyst often ensures the solution is ready to be tested, facilitates testing sessions, answers questions, documents issues, and communicates with the technical team to get the issues resolved and retested.

 ## Training End-Users

With the knowledge of the business requirements, business process, and system solution, a business analyst often trains end-users when a solution is implemented.

TECHNOLOGY-RELATED JOB REQUIREMENTS

As a business analyst bridges the gap between IT and non-technical end-users, the analyst must be capable of communicating in two languages: first, in technical terms with the IT department, and, second, in layman's terms for end-users. Because an analyst is the bridge between the business and IT side, business analysts need a combination of business skills and IT skills.

> *I have always found that I span the bridge between technical and non-technical really well. I can understand the developer's requirements, elicit the businessperson's requirements, and explain to each person how these components mesh together.*
>
> ## — Yelena Slobard
> **Business analyst for a medium-sized consulting company**

These skills will vary from job-to-job, but technology-related skill requirements often include:

- Demonstrated knowledge and experience of the Salesforce platform capabilities, in particular Sales, Service, Community, and Marketing Cloud.

- Demonstrated knowledge of the Salesforce declarative platform capabilities, including process automation tools, and the appropriate use of programmatic customization.

- Working knowledge of Agile delivery and scrum framework

- Salesforce certifications, specifically Administrator, Sales Cloud Consultant, Service Cloud Consultant, Community Cloud, and Marketing Cloud Consultant.

GENERAL BUSINESS AND SOFT SKILLS

Along with technology-related skills, employers also look for business analysts with related general business and soft skills, which could include:

Confidence

Business analysts must be able to defend best practices for meeting goals and remain steadfast in making sure that a system configuration is justified by a business need.

Communication

Business analysts must be able to tailor their vocabulary when speaking to different stakeholders, including end-users, IT, and executives. Business analysts often meet with end-users who do not know what they want, or who are unable to articulate what they want. This requires excellent communication skills on behalf of the business analysts, who might need to ask probing questions or change the communication style.

Facilitation

In the words of Donna Hudson, a business analyst at a consulting company, *"Business analysts are trying to get a group from one place to another place, so when conversations start to veer off track, you have to gently nudge people back into focus and back on that path."*

Elicitation

Business analysts are charged with listening and extracting small bits of information that might be key to a business solution.

Problem-solving

Inevitably, a new process will present challenges or create problems that need to be addressed. The analyst is responsible for revising solutions as issues unfold.

Patience

Remember that business analysts work with non-technical end-users, some of whom require multiple sessions before the technology "clicks." The best business analysts can keep frustration at bay and remain calm and composed while training end-users.

Sometimes during a training session, you have to go through the material several times before it clicks. There are times when, behind the scenes, I am covering my face and thinking, "Oh no. I have said this three times." But I never let the client hear that. It's not the client's fault. It's the consultant's job to say, "No problem. I'll spend as much time with you as you need."

— Donna Hudson
Business analyst for a consulting company

Though many employers look for experienced candidates, Salesforce reports that about 23 percent of the jobs posted for Salesforce business analysts are entry-level jobs.

TIPS FOR JOB-SEEKERS

To present as a strong Salesforce business analyst candidate, consider the following tips. These Layers are:

1. ### First, be honest with yourself about your strengths and interests.

Consider whether you prefer understanding how a business process works and whether you enjoy dealing with people. Can you effectively run meetings and workshops with conflicting priorities and various stakeholders? Or, would you rather be developing solutions? If you would rather spend your time on the technical side, a different role may be more suitable for you.

2. ### Remember that there is no one-path-fits-all.

Some analysts have a business or IT background. You could also navigate your way into a business analyst role after being a Salesforce administrator or a general IT business analyst, or after having a customer-facing sales or service business role.

3. ### Demonstrate your competence in the three layers.

These three layers are: 1) general business analyst skills, 2) industry or business process knowledge, particularly in sales and marketing processes; and 3) knowledge of the capabilities of the Salesforce platform.

4. Relate your understanding of functional capabilities to marketing, sales, and service processes.

For example, be ready to talk through how the sales stages of an opportunity can be configured to support customized sales processes. On the service side, know how support processes can be configured to support the lifecycle of cases and how case-automation features can fulfill requirements.

5. Be prepared to explain transferrable skills.

You may have not had the title of a business analyst, but perhaps you did fulfill a number of the responsibilities, such as managing stakeholders, gathering requirements, facilitating workshops, improving processes, documenting, designing solutions, implementing CRM, or training users.

6. If you have previous experience and want to become a Salesforce specialist, consider obtaining the Admin certification.

This will demonstrate that you have knowledge of the fundamentals of the platform. A further certification, such as Sales Cloud Consultant, Service Cloud Consultant, or Marketing Cloud Consultant will be helpful to further demonstrate expertise.

7. Be ready to discuss examples of identifying opportunities and implementing process improvements.

This is particularly relevant if you have worked in a customer-facing role in sales or service. Also be ready with examples of your communication, facilitation, and negotiation skills that you have developed in your previous roles.

8. Think in terms of processes first and solutions second.

If you have a technical IT background, resist the temptation to jump to solution mode and discuss Salesforce functionality before understanding business needs.

9. Be prepared to answer the basic questions about how you would perform as a business analyst.

Think about the answers to these questions: How would you go about meeting with stakeholders? How would you ask questions to understand needs and elicit requirements? How would you run workshops to understand business processes and challenges?

10. Gain experience at your current job, if possible.

If you work for a large company that already uses Salesforce, build up your experience and portfolio by looking for ways to get involved in Salesforce-related projects even if this means volunteering your time beyond your current role.

11. Get involved.

Attend Salesforce events, like World Tour and Dreamin. Get involved in the online Trailblazer community and join online collaboration groups. Complete superbadges. Go to user group meetings. You could meet someone who knows of an opportunity, paid or unpaid, that could help you.

12. Brainstorm ideas on how you could promote yourself even before an interview by providing an example of your skills.

For example, you could record a video that showcases your ability to understand a list of mock requirements and how you would recommend meeting the requirements in Salesforce, even going so far as to show a configured Salesforce feature.

Day in the life:
DAVID BECKHAM

David Beckham is the senior lead Salesforce business analyst for Thryv (formerly known as DexYP), a software company that uses Salesforce as their system of record for sales and service to sell advertising and SaaS solutions to small- and medium-size businesses. His primary responsibility is supporting the company's sales users in pre-sales processes using Sales Cloud. He reviews requests and requirements to help the sales teams be more productive and ultimately improve sales results. His job duties include the design of solutions, which consist mostly of configurations and process. David is also responsible for using Salesforce DX to migrate changes to the company's quality-assurance environment for testing. In short, he helps manage the design and the solution all the way to production.

David has five certifications in Salesforce—Administrator, Advanced Administrator, Application Builder, Sales Cloud Consultant, and Service Cloud Consultant—and has been working with Salesforce now almost ten years. For the past 23 years, David has been in sales and sales operations with the same company, surviving several buyouts and mergers. He attributes this to his Salesforce experience, which gives him the ability to adapt and remain relevant to his company.

"When I say I love my job, I mean it. I really do love what I do," he said. *"I enjoy every aspect of my job from working with sales to creating solutions for their issues to trouble-shooting problems that our teams face. The day is always interesting and can be calm to crazy depending on what is going on."*

6:00 a.m.

David wakes up, eats breakfast, showers, and has his morning coffee before making a thirty-second commute to his home office.

David started working from home about five years ago and finds that he is more productive and has more balance. Whereas others might get distracted by personal activities while working from home, David said he is able to focus on work.

(That said, every other month, David spends a week at the company's home office in Dallas, Texas, to meet with teammates and collaborate on large projects. This is a great time to reconnect with old work friends, meet new ones, and put a face to the names that he works with on a daily basis over the phone.)

6:30 a.m.

He starts the workday reviewing any story-related emails that come in overnight from the offshore teams. (Think of "stories" as case studies that describe the type of person using Salesforce, what they need to do, what the business requirements are, and why they need these requirements.) His company has system releases every three weeks, and at any time, David will have stories that the team is working on. For instance, David recently created a new process builder that updates a field on leads to show when a lead was last assigned to a sales rep. Today, David receives an email from the offshore team that conducts quality assurance testing on the new update. The team has found a bug in David's update. He spends the morning making sure this bug is fixed, and all of the other story-related emails are addressed.

7:00 a.m.

After reviewing his emails, David takes his dog for a thirty-minute walk, which is one of the perks of working from home.

"My company cares about their employees and encourages us to stay healthy," he said.

7:30 a.m.

With the dog walked, it is time to start the real work. Most days, David has at least three to four conference calls, so he plans his work around these meetings. His first call is with quality assurance team for their daily triage calls. The daily triage calls allow the team to discuss current issues within the production org or in the quality-assurance orgs that the company is testing. The team talks about any open bugs or problems they are facing to help reach a faster resolution. David uses his skills and knowledge of Salesforce to help diagnose an issue related to Salesforce. At the end of the call, the team gives commitments for making updates so they can keep their teams moving forward with development and testing.

8:30 a.m.

David has ninety minutes before his next meeting, so he works on a development project, making sure he is ready to demo a new feature. Today, he is working on a new object called Client Jacket, which holds relevant information that is specific to each client. The object works with contacts, leads, and accounts and has many features that use workflow rules and process builder.

(Other days, he could be working on projects such as simple page layout changes, new fields, or process updates.)

10:00 a.m.

David's second meeting of the day is with the company's Lightning triage team. In the most recent merger, two companies were combined, including two Salesforce instances plus all the processes and products of each company.

The new company moved all of these to one Salesforce instance and one set of processes.

Simultaneously, the company started using CPQ and moved its organization to the Lightning Experience user interface. This was a major undertaking that took the better part of last year to complete.

Today, David is having a daily meeting to discuss issues that are a result of this major change so a course of action can be determined. During the call, they not only identify issues to be fixed, but they also assign the correct team to resolve the issues. David is currently addressing page-layout fixes.

When the team migrated its org to Lightning, some of the Classic page layouts had far more information than was needed by sales. David needs to update leads, opportunities, and accounts for the outside sales team, reducing the fields so that the pages work better on desktop and mobile and provide a better user experience and faster adoption of Lightning.

11:00 a.m.

Part of David's job is to work on designs for the company's epics. ("Epics" are detailed bodies of work that describe and encompass a change or group of changes that can involve multiple teams. As described earlier, "stories" feed into epics and provide user experiences related to an overall epic.) After sitting through a requirement meetings to collect all issues, he writes up the design, reviews the story points he has for each sprint, and determines if he needs to hand off any work to a developer or junior administrator.

David is responsible for all pre-sales activity in Sales Cloud that can be done with configuration and process. Today, he is working on the addition of a new object called Client Jackets, which tracks important client information, starting when the client is a lead and migrating to conversations and securing an account. David is doing all this through configuration and process builder.

When the changes or epic includes any work that does not fall under "configuration" (such as Triggers and VisualForce pages) David calls on a developer.

Handing off work to a developer or junior administrators does not relieve David of the story. As the senior lead business analyst, David is responsible for the development of the story, so he has to review and approve the junior administrator's or developer's work.

As senior lead, he is also responsible for training and developing junior admins and users when needed with the goal of creating self-sustaining functional users.

12:30 p.m.

David holds his "office hours" during his lunch break. He uses this time to study or help other users with issues they are having. Today, none of the sales teams or leaders come to him with questions, so he spends his time working on Sales Cloud-related trails in Trailhead. David is studying for his next certifications—Sales Cloud Consultant and Service Cloud Consultant. David acknowledges that experience is the biggest factor in a successful career but that earning certifications is the best indicator that a person is committed to learning and improving.

1:00 p.m.

Another meeting: This one is a grooming call for up-coming stories and epics that his team is responsible for. ("Grooming" describes how a team discusses what is being asked in an epic. During a grooming call, team members discuss the requirements and ensure they have all the details necessary to complete the design.) During this call, David outlines what he understands the issues to be and allows the project managers to fill in any details that he needs so that he can work on the design.

1:30 p.m.

After the grooming calls, David must start reviewing his new projects. He completes research as needed on the issue. He will review the project from start to finish to see where the gaps are and then use Salesforce resources to fill in where he might have questions. Once he has his research, he writes up the design document so the plan for his design can be discussed in the JAD sessions every two weeks. This is where David reviews his design with other developers to ensure that all aspects of the request are being met. Once he gives his design overview, the project managers and developers sign off so work can begin.

3:00 p.m.

Today is Thursday, and on every other Thursday and Friday, the company has demos whereby the team shows the work it has completed so that it can be handed to the quality assurance (QA) teams.

Today, David is showing a demo of the new Client Jacket created and the email notification that it creates when a user creates a new jacket.

From there, David will work with QA to fix any bugs that come up during testing, to release the changes, and to validate the updates and close out the stories.

4:00 p.m.

The teams are using Salesforce DX to push changes from their dev/ scratch orgs to their quality assurance environments for testing. This is a new change in process; they used to push their changes to their offshore teams to move them from development sandboxes to testing environments. David spends thirty minutes receiving additional training on Salesforce DX, specifically so that he can become an expert in GitLab and VS Code and push changes in DX himself.

"My job is to always be learning," he said.

4:30 p.m.

It's time to close shop for the day. Before ending the workday, he ties up any of the day's loose ends, answering important emails, and scheduling or delegating tasks that came up for the day.

CHAPTER FOUR:
Salesforce Consultant

Salesforce consultants help customers implement or improve their use of Salesforce. Consultants can work as employees at consultancy firms, they can be entrepreneurs who own a consultant firm, or they can be freelancers hired by one client at a time. This section is about the most common type of Salesforce consultant: a consultant who works as an employee at a consultancy firm. (If you are interested in becoming a freelancer or opening your own firm, see Chapter 10.)

Consultants are employees of consultancy firms that are hired by businesses who are outsourcing some or all of their Salesforce needs. Consultants help define their clients' business requirements, customize Salesforce platforms accordingly, and enable end-users to become more efficient via Salesforce tools. In other words, they help clients implement and optimize Salesforce to improve business outcomes.

Average Salary of a
Salesforce Consultant in the United States:
$102,687

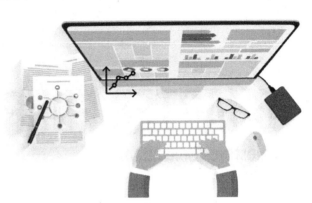

The salary of a
consultant in the
United States
generally ranges
from $82,000 to
$127,500.

These figures are an average of an aggregate of sources. In late 2019, Neuvoo reported the average U.S. salary to be $120,000, with entry-level salaries beginning at approximately $75,210. ZipRecruiter reported an average salary of $109,482, with salaries as low as $51,500 and as high as $211,000, with the majority of salaries ranging between $82,500 and $127,500. Salesforce reported an average salary of $95,000; and Glassdoor reported $86,267. Payscale reported that an entry-level consultant (defined as having less than one year of experience) will earn an average of $60,940 whereas an early-career consultant (one to four years of experience) earns an average of $75,841. Upon reaching mid-career (five to nine years of experience), a consultant can expect to earn around $94,700, and experienced consultants earn around $109,055.

Consultants need both functional and technical skills. They not only facilitate workshops to identify, capture, and translate key requirements into Salesforce solutions, and later to train users, but they also design and implement these solutions. The role of a consultant is similar to the business analyst role we described in the previous section. The difference is that a business analyst works with internal customers in an end-user organization, and a consultant works for a consultancy on projects with external customers, often working with multiple customers at the same time.

Consultants work on a project basis. They can be role-specific or industry-specific. For instance, there are consultants who are specialists in such areas as sales, customer service, or marketing. Some specialize in solutions for specific verticals, such as financial services, retail, or manufacturing. Some are generalists whose knowledge of Salesforce is so broad that they can customize solutions for most any industry.

When you are in a customer-facing role as a consultant, you must be able to wear the hat of a business analyst, which means you have high listening-comprehension skills and can translate requirements to the team that needs to deliver. You are client-facing, so your communication skills need to come first.

— Andi Giri
Managing director of Softsquare, an IT consulting firm

Generally speaking, consultants:

1. Start by eliciting information from the client so that they understand the business challenges and can align solutions accordingly.

2. Design a solution for the client to approve.

3. Develop the solution, once approved, and usually with the help of Salesforce developers.

4. Deliver the solution.

5. Train end-users.

I used to be an admin, but one of the reasons I went to work as a business analyst at a consultancy firm is because I wanted something new every day. I have about ten projects going on right now, so I am working on CPQ projects, service projects, and a Lightning transition. I have a new challenge and something new to think about every day.

— Yelena Slobard
Business analyst for a medium-sized consulting company

JOB DESCRIPTION

Though a consultant's job will vary based on the employer's needs, a Salesforce consultant's job might include:

- Working on proposals, creating high-level estimates, creating demonstrations for sales, and presenting to potential customers.

- Facilitating workshops to identify, capture, and translate key requirements into Salesforce solutions across sales, service, and marketing processes.

- Mapping business processes.

- Managing the client relationship, which includes resolving conflicts and establishing expectations.

- Developing solution designs.

- Configuring solutions.

- Working with technical developers to implement any customizations that involve code or integration.

- Migrating existing data.

- Developing and providing training.

If you are a Salesforce administrator or developer who works directly for a company, eventually you get comfortable with this organization and your work cadence. You know the company inside out, and you become well-positioned to make adjustments and propose new features as the company grows.

Moving to a consulting company requires a different pace. For each project, you are working with a different customer and potentially a different industry, perhaps an industry you have never worked with in the past. You might not be familiar with their lingo or their processes. You will be out of your comfort zone.

Depending on the size of the company, you might talk to a team of business analysts dedicated to this project, or you might work directly with senior stakeholders and executives who are driving the initiative.

No matter the company, you need to learn how to quickly understand what they are going through, how it impacts their business and their people, to design the right solution that can solve their issues in accordance to the level of transformation they can take on. Sophisticated technology is pointless if not adopted widely.

As Salesforce consultants, we are in the technology industry, but at the end of the day, what we deliver is change.

— Aymeric Zito
CEO of ProQuest Consulting

TECHNOLOGY-RELATED JOB REQUIREMENTS

Consultants need to have both functional and technical skills, including:

- Hands-on experience with Salesforce, similar to the technical skills necessary as an administrator. In fact, if you have ever worked as an administrator, you were a consultant. The only difference is that you were an *internal* consultant.

- Data gathering and analysis.

- Experience of the AppExchange and commonly-used Salesforce apps.

- Project management.

- Salesforce certification(s), the most important being Salesforce Administrator, but the more the better.

Think of the consultant like you would think of the COO. The consultant needs to think: How is my client's business going to operate? So that they can advise automation, consultants need to think through the entire business process, starting with the process of getting a lead and continuing through converting that lead into a client. The ability to think through all those steps in the operations of a business sets consultants apart from admins, developers, and the rest of the people on the team. Consultants need to dig into business analysis and understand what can be done in marketing, in sales, in operations, in field service, and in finance. Importantly, they have to know enough to advise a CEO and say, "You can automate this process and save six figures over here." Having that experience to guide executives through digital transformation is one of the hard parts of the consultant's role.

So what do consultants need? They need to understand business processes. They need to be able to get in front of a room of people and convince them to make a change, and they need to be able to clearly communicate the impact of that change. They need to think deeply and holistically.

Consultants are responsible for both the strategy and the implementation, so they also need to know the right questions to ask, where to look for the answers, and have that next level of expertise in terms of anticipating what can go wrong and having a plan for keeping the project on the rails.

— Jim Bartek
CEO of Growth Heroes, a boutique consulting firm

GENERAL BUSINESS AND SOFT SKILLS

In addition to technology-related skills, Salesforce consultants also need general business and soft skills, which might include:

Agility

Because consultants work on multiple projects at a time with a number of different clients who have their own unique personalities, business models, and challenges, consultants need to be able to work under a variety of conditions. Beyond that, consultants will have multiple clients at a time and need to have the flexibility to shift gears quickly so as to jump from one project to another.

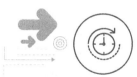

Time management

Consultants manage and prioritize multiple projects. Because consultants have multiple clients, travel might also be involved, be it across the city, across the country, or across the globe to work as short-term employees at a firm while implementing Salesforce. This adds a layer of complexity to time management.

Patience

Consultants work with clients who have a variety of personalities. Some have strong technical skills while others need tremendous hand-holding.

Conflict resolution

As with any new endeavor, various stakeholders may have competing goals. Consultants need to understand these different viewpoints and provide solutions accordingly.

Communication

Consultants need to be capable of eliciting information, running workshops, and explaining goals. Because consultants are responsible for solving problems, they need strong communication skills so that they can truly understand the problems.

Confidence

Consultants work with a variety of people, including CEOs. As well, they often stand in front of crowds to defend a business solution.

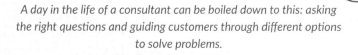

A day in the life of a consultant can be boiled down to this: asking the right questions and guiding customers through different options to solve problems.

— Aymeric Zito
CEO of ProQuest Consulting

About 27 percent of the jobs posted for Salesforce consultants are entry-level jobs.

TIPS FOR JOB-SEEKERS

If you are interested in pursuing a career as a Salesforce consultant, consider the following tips:

1. Practice and improve your presentation skills.

In interview and hiring situations, consultants are often provided with a scenario and asked to present a solution. Consider that this requires both a written presentation in the form of a slide deck or a drawing on a whiteboard, as well as a verbal presentation that requires explaining the thought process and communicating the process of arriving at a solution.

2. Practice and improve your problem-solving skills.

Know that interviewers are looking for an organized approach to solving a problem, and you might be presented with a problem that is not Salesforce related. Ajay Dubedi, the CEO of Cloud Analogy, sometimes presents candidates with a matchstick puzzle. He is not interested in how fast the candidate solves the puzzle, or even if the solution is correct. Instead, Dubedi wants to understand the thought process and approach the consultant uses to arrive at the solution.

3. Collect examples of how you have effectively engaged with stakeholders at different levels in an organization.

As a Salesforce consultant, you will be required to present at different times across the entire customer-engagement cycle. This includes sitting in on pre-sales meetings with senior management, running workshops with operational management, providing regular demonstrations with product owners, and training end-users.

4. Highlight your advanced and consultant level certifications, as well as your plans for obtaining additional certifications in the future

The quantity and type of certifications that individual consultants hold contribute to the innovation points that a consulting firm can earn through Salesforce's consulting partner program. Your certifications will be added to your employer's points, and they will be welcomed! At the time of writing this book, advanced and consultant certifications, such as the Salesforce Platform Developer II credential and the Sales Cloud Consultant, are worth three times as much as the Certified Salesforce Administrator or the Salesforce Platform App Builder certifications.

5. Be sure that you can demonstrate that you are up-to-date with the breadth and latest capabilities of the platform.

This means staying curious and going through the notes every time Salesforce has a new release. A Salesforce consultant is a trusted advisor, so be aware of the features that Salesforce provides out of the box. For example, a customer may need to send surveys as part of its post service experience. In this case, you should know that one of the customer's options is to use Salesforce native survey functionality.

6. Get involved.

Attend Salesforce events, like World Tour and Dreamin. Get involved in the online Trailblazer community and join online collaboration groups. Complete superbadges. Go to user group meetings. You could meet someone who knows of an opportunity, paid or unpaid, that could help you.

When you are a consultant, you are also a salesperson to a degree. You are selling your vision and selling your understanding and knowledge, so you need to be able to listen, to question, and to engage.

— Ben Duncombe
Director of Talent Hub, a Salesforce recruitment company

Day in the life:
SANTOSH KUMAR SRIRAM

Santosh Kumar Sriram is a principal consultant for Australia's ProQuest Consulting, a platinum Salesforce provider and a national leader of Field Service Lightning and Consumer Goods Cloud. ProQuest Consulting specializes in delivering Salesforce solutions to businesses in a variety of industries, including solar installations, garbage management, nonprofits, and printing services (among others).

Santosh's role primarily includes overseeing projects' architecture, mentoring the consultants, handling pre-sales activities, and standardizing processes to drive operational efficiency. During his ten years in the Salesforce Ohana, he has earned fourteen certifications and become a Salesforce Certified Application Architect. His goal is to become a Certified Technical Architect.

"What makes ProQuest interesting is that it has the nimbleness of a start-up but processes and the methodology of a Big Four organization," he said.

Santosh and his spouse moved from the USA to Australia in September of 2018. They are enjoying the Aussie life, particularly the balanced work-life approach that ProQuest offers, giving them enough time to enjoy the country as a couple.

5:30 a.m.
Santosh awakens, freshens up, and drives to his F45 gym training center in Hornsby for his 6:00 a.m. class. After an intensive workout, he sips on a cup of Indian filter coffee. He quickly scans for sports news and checks his schedule so that he is mentally prepared for the day ahead of him.

7:30 a.m.

After showering and eating a light breakfast, Santosh takes a brisk five-minute walk to reach Waitara station on Sydney's North Shore railway line. The trains are generally crowded during peak hours. Santosh is lucky today: He finds a seat. This is Santosh's "me time." He spends the 45-minute train ride to the office reading non-fiction. He is currently halfway through *The Art of War* by Sun Tzu.

8:15 a.m.

Santosh's train arrives at the Wynyard station, and he takes a ten-minute walk to the office.

8:30 a.m.

First things first: Santosh skims through his emails and starts his to-do list for the day, which includes following up on emails and daily tasks. Then, he and a few of his peers walk across the street to Cabrito, a nearby coffee shop, where Santosh orders an extra-hot cappuccino and debriefs with his coworkers.

9:00 a.m.

Today is Monday, which is a special day for ProQuest employees. Sure, a few employees have the Monday-morning blues, but they quickly dissolve during the traditional Monday-morning company-wide stand-up. ProQuest is a firm believer in Agile practices and scrum ceremonies. The company not only delivers projects using these frameworks, but it also respects the same in organizational communication. Each morning, then, the team huddles and discusses the past week and celebrates great outcomes from teams. It also discusses the upcoming week's objectives. Santosh loves these sessions and makes it a point to actively participate, getting to know his coworkers and their projects well. Today, he discusses the Harry Potter-themed escape room he enjoyed over the weekend, and he pitches the idea of having a team escape-room event.

Of course, it helps that ProQuest serves breakfast, thanks to Georgia, the employee experience specialist who always goes the extra mile to make the team feel special.

9:30 a.m.

The most significant factor of scrum, said Santosh, is transparency. Daily, at 9:30 a.m., the teams at ProQuest have morning stand-ups with their product owners to provide daily updates. These stand-ups are fifteen minutes long. Because Santosh works on multiple projects at once, he moves from one stand-up to another. Santosh ensures that the updates are succinct and clear for the product owners to digest the update. As a part of his update, he also presents what the next steps are going to be and raises any red flags (which the ProQuest team calls "blockers). If the update is about user experience or custom developed screens, Santosh uses wireframes as a communication tool to ensure that the product owner can visualize the experience and make key decisions.

Today, Santosh and his team work on the wireframes of the public-facing community (portal) and its user experience so that the client has an understanding of how the screens are going to look.

10:00 a.m.

Handing off the technical work, and helping the team with architecture decisions and integration orchestration are some of Santosh's key responsibilities. He works with the rest of the team to streamline information, strategize for delivery, identify next steps, and identify issues to be fixed, as well as resolve any potential risks that come along with Salesforce's release management and metadata management.

10:30 a.m.

Santosh is currently working on a project for a company that leverages Salesforce Community Cloud, Field Service Lightning, Service Cloud, and Lightning Web Components. The project was kicked off about a month ago, and today, the team is meeting with the client to discuss certain requirements. ProQuest has a refinement session with the client whereby they go through the end-to-end flow with wireframes and epics.

The team catches a cab to the meeting and takes the iconic route on the Harbour Bridge overlooking the Opera House and the tall scrapers of the Sydney skyline that touch the blue sky. This refinement session lasts for an hour, during which time Santosh and the team walk the client through the story map, future process flow, and the first version of the wireframes. They gather feedback and confirm the modifications that were noted during the session. (After all, what's Agile without iterations and alterations?)

Santosh and the team take a cab back to the office.

Noon

Santosh arrives back at the office to find the kitchen busy and awaiting the weekly lunch 'n learn, which they call OneQuest. Kudos to Georgia, the employee experience specialist, who has ordered Thai curries, rolls, and special rice for the session.

At today's OneQuest, a senior functional consultant and Santosh's co-worker, Laura, and her team are sharing their stellar experience working for a client on Consumer Good Cloud. OneQuest is a critical get-together for the team. As the adage goes, sharing is caring!

After the presentation, the team thanks Laura and her team by sharing a giphy on Slack or posting "chatter thanks." Yes, ProQuest uses Salesforce to drive its own business!

1:00 p.m.

First on this afternoon's list is a "poker-sizing" session with a team that is building an installer portal for a solar panel company. The team has refined the epics (a.k.a., user stories) and walked the product owner through them.

Upon sign-off, Santosh's team "poker sizes." This activity consists of defining epic complexity and also detailed estimation alongside design discussions. Each requirement is discussed prior to sizing, and each of the team members individually and confidentially picks a point estimate for the feature.

After every estimator picks the estimate, all estimates ("cards") are then revealed at the same time. If all estimators selected the same value, then that becomes the point value of the feature. If not, the highest and the lowest estimators engage in a discussion to reach a consensus on the point value of the feature.

Santosh's key responsibility at ProQuest is to architect solutions and challenge the rest of the team in terms of performance, efficiency, and user experience driving a specific design decision.

3:00 p.m.

A prospect in Brisbane, a printer manufacturing company, is looking for an implementation partner to work on a Lightning Experience migration. Today, Hans, one of ProQuest's sales team members, is in Brisbane with the prospect and wants Santosh to hop on a virtual call to discuss strategy and approach.

Santosh is one of the operations team members who aids in pre-sales. During such opportunities, he shares his prior learnings, experiences, and recommends the approach and next steps forward. Santosh loves to virtually whiteboard. He sometimes also employs his signature excel-boarding to get the message across a virtual call. ("Excel-boarding" is the white-boarding equivalent on Excel.)

4:00 p.m.

The last hour of Santosh's workday is spent preparing for certifications, processing Salesforce release notes, or trying out new features to recommend to the team.

He loves this time, as this is the time where he learns the most. Santosh documents key features released by Salesfoce and the steps to mitigate future issues, if any, in the internal confluence pages (LMS) for the rest of the team to benefit.

By the time he is done, it is almost 4:45, and Georgia is asking the team to head over to King's Landing. (Did we forget to mention that the ProQuest team has named its meeting rooms after Game of Thrones locations?)

This month is "Office Olympics Month," where they have "minute-to-win-it" games. One of Santosh's favorite games is Office Tennis: The contestants are doubles partners and, using clipboards as racquets, rally a crumpled piece of paper back and forth before landing it in a basket on the opposite side of the room. Santosh said it is a great way to release the day's anxieties and blow off steam before heading home for some quality family time.

CHAPTER FIVE:
Salesforce Architect

Salesforce architects use their knowledge and experience to recommend and design end-to-end solutions to complex customer problems. You will find architects at larger organizations and consulting companies where there is a need to ensure that solutions are designed appropriately and that the company can scale for large numbers of users and data volumes. It is important to note that Salesforce will often be one component, albeit a central component, of a solution in an enterprise IT landscape. To be effective, therefore, an architect needs not only to be familiar with Salesforce, but also how Salesforce will fit in and integrate with the other systems in an organization. The position requires high-level knowledge of the complete set of Salesforce clouds, products, and features, as well as other commonly used technologies and systems used in a company (e.g., AWS, Active Directory, ESBs, ETL, APIs, SAP) to design appropriate solutions.

Average Salary of a
Salesforce Architect in the United States:

$142,242

The salary of an architect in the United States generally ranges from $125,000 to $171,000.

These figures are an average of an aggregate of sources. In late 2019, Indeed reported the average U.S. salary to be $120,952; Glassdoor reported $132,662; Salesforce reported $150,000; ZipRecruiter reported $150,099; and Neuvoo reported $157,500. Neuvoo reported entry-level salaries beginning at approximately $112,500 with most experienced workers earning up to $204,750, Glassdoor reported salaries ranging from $123,966 to $170,867, with bonuses and additional compensation averaging around $17,384. ZipRecruiter reported salaries as low as $103,500 and as high as $202,500, with the majority of salaries ranging between $128,500 and $171,500.

An architect will typically start by analyzing the organization's current architecture and determine a roadmap to reach an appropriate target state. This can involve simplifying the IT landscape by retiring legacy systems, evaluating applications for consolidation or replacement, and considering if and how the Salesforce platform can contribute. The architect will lead architectural discussions with senior management, contribute to discovery workshops, and make major design decisions. A Salesforce architect will often work with an enterprise architect to ensure the Salesforce solution is in line with the enterprise architecture and roadmap.

> *An architect needs the skills of a developer and an analyst. An archi-tect has to be capable of taking a couple of functional and technical concepts that lay at various levels and weave them together into a connected whole that makes sense to the customer and to the proj-ect team. An architect also has to structure the interaction within the project and understand the project's budget.*
>
> **— René Görgens**
> **Senior architect and consultant**

An architect needs to ensure appropriate integration patterns are used, solutions will scale and handle large data volumes, and security and per-formance requirements are met. The architect is also responsible for mak-ing sure data storage will meet regulatory requirements.

Architects are masters at the whiteboard, diagramming solutions, ensuring the customer and project teams understand the solution, and document-ing architecture landscape diagrams and decisions in design documents.

An architect not only deals with the design but also oversees implemen-tations, determines environmental and release strategies, ensures best practices are followed, and acts as advisors to project teams when they have issues and unexpected obstacles.

The following diagram highlights example areas that need to be consid-ered when designing and implementing a well-architectured solution that best leverages the Salesforce platform.

DESIGNING AND IMPLEMENTING A WELL-ARCHITECTURED SOLUTION IN SALESFORCE

Governance[1]
- Design Patterns
- Best Practices
- Data Governance

Deployment[2]
- Deployment Models
- Environmental Strategy
- Release Management

Salesforce Products[3]
- Core Salesforce Products:
  - > Sales Cloud
  - > Service Cloud
  - > Community Cloud
  - > Marketing Cloud
  - > Einstein Analytics
- Niche Products:
  - > CPQ
  - > Field Service Lightning
  - > Commerce Cloud
- Integration and Platform Products:
  - > Mulesoft
  - > Heroku

Salesforce Technologies[4]
- Apex
- Visualforce
- Lightning Components
- Platform Events
- Shield
- Salesforce Connect
- Einstein
- Single Sign On
- oAuth Authorization Flows
- IoT

Solution Considerations[5]

Authentication	Data Migration	Data Volumes	Licenses
Integration	Performance	Security	Platforms Limits

Governance[1]

The Salesforce architect needs to ensure that standards, frameworks, and best practices are followed when designing and implementing the solution.

Some of these include:

- Ensuring that appropriate design patterns are used
- Ensuring design standards are followed
- Ensuring best practices are followed
- Ensuring appropriate data governance

Deployment[2]

Salesforce updates the platform automatically three times a year. However, every customer defines how they will release custom functionality as part of a project implementation and after a project goes live. There will typically be a number of environments that new development, enhancements, and bug fixes progress through before reaching production. These include development sandboxes, integration, user acceptance testing (UAT), and staging environments.

An architect will advise on the:

- Deployment models
- Appropriate environments for the project
- How releases will be managed

Salesforce Products[3]

A Salesforce architect needs to be familiar with the breadth and capabilities of Salesforce products and understand how they will fit into an overall solution, together with custom development, AppExchange solutions, and external systems integrations.

Some of the products that an architect needs to be familiar with include:

- Core Salesforce Products:
  - > Sales Cloud
  - > Service Cloud
  - > Community Cloud
  - > Marketing Cloud
  - > Einstein Analytics
- Niche Products:
  - > CPQ
  - > Field Service Lightning
  - > Commerce Cloud
- Integration and Platform Products:
  - > Mulesoft
  - > Heroku

Salesforce Technologies[4]

A Salesforce architect needs to be familiar with the breadth of Salesforce technologies and decide when it is appropriate to use each one and how they will work as part of the overall solution.

These include but are not limited to:

- Apex
- Visualforce
- Lightning Components
- Platform Events
- Shield
- Salesforce Connect
- Einstein

- Single Sign On
- oAuth Authorization Flows
- IoT

Solution Considerations[5]

An architect needs to consider many factors when designing a solution. Some of these include:

- Authentication
- Integration
- Data Migration
- Performance
- Data Volumes
- Security
- Licenses
- Platform Limitations

Some of the questions that need to be answered include:

- What authentication methods will be used for internal and external users?
- How will Salesforce integrate with external systems?
- What is the data migration strategy?
- Is the solution appropriate for current and project data volumes?
- How will sensitive data be secured?
- What are the appropriate licenses for internal and external users?
- Is the solution designed with platform limitations in mind?

An architect does not need to be an expert in every product and technology. That said, an architect must be curious enough and able to understand how the different components and technologies work together to provide a coherent end-to-end solution that meets not only functional requirements but also non-functional requirements, such as performance, scalability, security, and availability.

In the real world, a Salesforce architect's job title will often be *solutions* architect or *technical* architect. Although both are focused on translating problems into solutions leveraging the Salesforce platform, a technical architect will have deeper technical knowledge than a solutions architect and often comes from a development background. A technical architect will often be hands-on and involved in the implementation activities and even lead the development team. In some organizations, one architect may take on the role of both solution and technical architect, whereas in larger projects, a dedicated solutions architect might work alongside a technical architect or technical team lead. A solution architect often comes from a business analyst or functional team lead background and is more involved in the end-to-end solution delivery and interfacing with stakeholders.

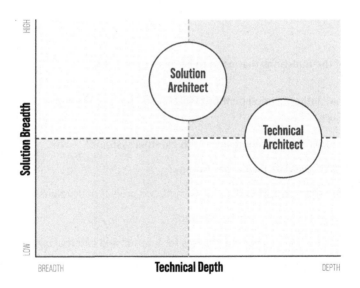

A solution architect will typically have a greater focus on the solution as a whole whereas a technical architect will be more involved in the technical aspects of the solution.

JOB DESCRIPTION

The role of a Salesforce architect will vary from company to company. In smaller organizations, the role may be more hands on, with an architect also acting as a technical lead and even coding. In larger organizations, it is usually focused on design. Note also that the responsibilities of an architect working in a consulting organization will be more client- and project-based, including pre-sales activities. An architect working in an end-user organization will be involved in strategy and solution evaluation, as well as work on projects.

A Salesforce architect role typically involves:

- Defining strategy and evaluating solutions
- Defining and designing solutions
- Documenting and presenting solutions
- Supporting and advising project teams

Defining Strategy and Evaluating Solutions

An architect is responsible for developing a CRM and technology strategy, roadmap, and target architecture. The architect also leads technology and solution selection, including working on proof-of-concepts, and often coordinates multiple vendors when Salesforce is one part of the solution with other vendors (e.g., AppExchange solution providers or other cloud-based platforms). The architect also provides upfront estimates of effort for projects.

Defining and Designing Solutions

Part of an architect's job description includes leading or participating in requirement-gathering and process or system analysis, including the technical aspects of business requirements. The architect leads technical design sessions and translates requirements into well-architected technical solutions that best leverage the Salesforce platform.

Documenting and Presenting Solutions

The architect documents the solution in various formats, including solution architecture documents, architectural and infrastructure diagrams, and solution design documents. An architect also validates and presents the solution architecture to project teams, stakeholders, and senior leadership.

Supporting and Advising Project Teams

The architect provides oversight and guidance to project teams during solution delivery, including recommendations and validating technical design decisions. The architect also provides advice and assistance to developers for technical issues and ensures a quality solution is delivered. Architects are responsible for making sure that Salesforce best practices are followed, and for conducting technical design reviews for projects. Architects manage the technical scope and client or stakeholders' expectation. Most often, architects support multiple projects at the same time through all stages of the project lifecycle from requirements to implementation.

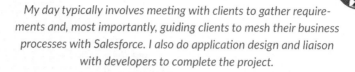

My day typically involves meeting with clients to gather requirements and, most importantly, guiding clients to mesh their business processes with Salesforce. I also do application design and liaison with developers to complete the project.

— Frank Mamone
Application architect

TECHNOLOGY-RELATED JOB REQUIREMENTS

Both solutions and technical architects are some of the most skilled workers in the Salesforce ecosystem because they have knowledge that extends across multiple development platforms. The required technical skills and experience will differ from employer to employer but may include some or all of the following:

- Extensive experience creating the solution design and architecture for complex Salesforce implementations.

- Experience across the full life cycle for a number of large and complex Salesforce projects that included several clouds (e.g. Sales Cloud, Service Cloud, Communities Cloud) and integrations with external systems and other cloud platforms, such as AWS, Google Cloud, and Azure.

- Experience and knowledge of enterprise and Salesforce integration patterns, including SOAP/REST web services, APIs, batch processes, connectors, middleware, etc., and when to use each one.

- Knowledge and experience in APEX, Lightning Web Components, VisualForce, ANT, and Visual Studio Code tools.

- Knowledge and understanding of the Salesforce development platform and best practices.

- Knowledge and understanding of current architectural design patterns, standards, technologies, and techniques.

- Project management experience using the Agile delivery methodology.

- Bachelor's degree in a related field, which could be engineering, computer science (for a technical architect), or business (for a solutions architect).

- Salesforce certifications, including Application Architect and System Architect.

> *The Certified Technical Architect (CTA) credential is perhaps the holy grail of all Salesforce certifications.*

You might assume that only the most advanced developers become architects, but this is untrue: Despite the nine certifications and review-board approval required to receive the covered Certified Technical Architect designation, which only a small number of people in the world have, you do not need to be a fantastic coder to be a solutions architect, a technical architect, or even a CTA. You do need to read and understand code, and you need to understand best practices and code patterns.

GENERAL BUSINESS AND SOFT SKILLS

Salesforce architects are the IT professionals responsible for designing solutions that solve business challenges and allow businesses to become more efficient. As a result, the general business and soft skills necessary of this key team member include:

Big-picture thinking

Architects solve immediate challenges but must keep the solution in perspective in terms of an existing IT landscape, longer-term technology trends, and the strategic goals of an organization. That said, in addition to being big-picture thinkers, architects must also have enough attention to detail to rapidly learn and take advantage of new concepts, business models, and technologies.

Strong relationship-management skills

Architects are both internal and external facing, meaning they manage projects and the team members working on those projects, as well as serve the end-user. To best do this, architects need rapport with both the internal team and the end-users who are using the platforms that architects are developing.

Excellent communicators

Architects need to develop strong interpersonal relationships with technical audiences, non-technical audiences, and senior management. They also work with people in a variety of positions, including technical leads, junior developers, executives, and end-users—and they need to change their language accordingly. The necessary skills include strong stakeholder management and communication skills, excellent presentation skills, and excellent written and oral communication skills.

Being a team player

Architects solve problems for the team, and they take on leadership positions when necessary. As a result, they need to be able to both take the initiative to solve problems and work with team leads, developers, business analysts, and administrators. To best balance these skills, they need to show up as helpful, collaborative, and working toward a common goal.

> *The most important soft skill in my job is perseverance, whether that means not giving up in your pursuit of your next career step or finding the best way to solve a business problem or achieve a business goal with Salesforce.*
>
> **— Bob Sheridan**
> Solution architect

TIPS FOR JOB-SEEKERS

If you are interested in pursuing a career as a Salesforce architect, consider the following tips:

1. First and foremost, clarify whether your experience and interests are better suited to a *solution* or *technical* architect role.

Keep in mind that architects can come from different backgrounds. You can have a background as an administrator, business analyst, or developer. Regardless, if you have a passion for considering the bigger picture and translating business problems into solutions involving the Salesforce platform, there is a path to follow. That said, be sure you know and understand the different paths, as well as the differences in expectations between a solution architect and technical architect so that you can communicate how your background and interests align with the role for which you are applying.

2. Remember that becoming an architect requires knowledge and experience.

You do not need twenty years of IT experience, but you do need to gain experience in a variety of scenarios and technologies, and this experience can come from the environment that you are in. For example a Salesforce consultant or someone working in a large organization using multiple Salesforce products will be exposed to more projects than someone working in a small or medium-sized organization.

3. Set a goal and plan how you will study and obtain experience in the domain knowledge areas that Salesforce has defined.

Salesforce has defined a path to becoming recognized as a certified technical architect. Follow the steps, build up your knowledge, and work your way toward your goal. Complete the designer certifications and earn the application and system architect credentials as milestones.

4. Volunteer.

If you are not in an architectural role currently, volunteer to work on projects that need architectural input and contribute where you can to gain experience.

5. Practice.

A Salesforce architect is expected to be able to present a solution using some key artifacts, including a system landscape diagram, data model, and role hierarchy. Practice and improve your skills in developing these.

6. Get involved.

Attend Salesforce events, like World Tour and Dreamin. Get involved in the online Trailblazer community and join online collaboration groups. Complete superbadges. Go to user group meetings. You could meet someone who knows of an opportunity that could help you.

7. Look for opportunities in your current company and role to apply architectural domain knowledge.

You do not need twenty years of IT experience, but you do need to gain experience in a variety of scenarios and technologies, and this experience can come from the environment that you are in. For example a Salesforce consultant or someone working in a large organization using multiple Salesforce products will be exposed to more projects than someone working in a small or medium-sized organization.

8. Develop an architect's mindset.

Check out what Amit Malik, a global master instructor with Salesforce, says about developing an architect's mindset.

SEVEN HABITS FOR DEVELOPING AN ARCHITECT MINDSET

Amit Malik, a global master instructor with Salesforce, suggests seven habits that will help train a person to think like an architect. These are:

1. Learn when to use clicks vs. code.

2. Engage meaningfully with the Salesforce community for at least ten minutes a day.

3. Understand the customer and their world. Have an understanding of the customers' industry, their challenges, and where they are headed in the future. Malik suggests reading Requests for Proposals (RFPs) to gain this insight.

4. Address a client's full range of business needs by thinking about the big picture and designing cross-cloud, for example including Marketing, Sales, Service, and Einstein Analytics.

5. Practice the fundamentals and fully understand concepts before applying to business problems. Think quickly and be able to come to correct conclusions on your feet.

6. Practice your communication and presentation skills, and include system landscapes, data models, charts, and architectural and swim lane diagrams in your solutions presentations.

7. Give back to the community by mentoring, speaking at lunch-and-learns, blogging, or presenting at user groups.

Day in the life:
CHRISTINA INGERSOLL

Chris Ingersoll is a Salesforce architect with sixteen Salesforce certifications, including System Architect and Application Architect. Christina manages overall functionality, operational efficiency, and data integration of Salesforce. She works from her home in northern Colorado for NEPCon, a global NGO based in Denmark that manages the logistics of sustainability audits. Chris holds a degree in biology from Carleton and an MBA from MIT and has been working (off and on) with Salesforce since 2006.

6:00 a.m.

Chris's days often start early, as you would expect for someone working Mountain Time in the United States for an organization based in Denmark.

Her first meeting is with the technical team. Since NEPCon is primarily remote and completely global (with staff and activities on six continents), the technical team includes three Salesforce specialists, plus other staff who manage NEPCon's web presence, email and file sharing systems, and digital marketing. The technical team has two Americans, a Mexican, two Estonians, two Vietnamese, a Dane, and a Latvian. The team has a shared set of projects and priorities and meets every month to discuss progress and areas of collaboration.

7:30 a.m.

Chris has a brief pause, which means she can drink a cup of coffee and more fully wake up.

8:00 a.m.

Quick check-in with Roger, the other main Salesforce specialist on her team. Although it's a small team, Chris sees a lot of benefit in having another Salesforce expert to share the work, and, more importantly, to share technical ideas, tips, favorite apps, and to catch each other up on new Salesforce features.

The Salesforce team is currently working on a game-changing development that will allow audit data to be entered and processed much more rapidly than the status quo. This project has major implications for the entire organization, so it requires both technical and project management skills. The technical architecture and processes have been mostly worked out, but as with all projects of that scale, the harder part is ensuring that the team has input and commitment to testing and content development from other senior staff members.

8:30 a.m.

After the one-on-one strategy meeting, Chris gets to check emails for the first time in the day. Some of the emails are ticket submissions for technical questions or support. Most of these tickets are resolved by a Salesforce assistant, but everyone on the Salesforce team pitches in to help make sure that the global staff of over 200 has issues resolved as quickly as possible.

Resolving issues and responding to email discussions about the mix of projects-in-process takes a couple of hours. Today, Chris is responding to a request to create a new conflict-of-interest form available without authentication but from a custom link that is written in twenty different languages, all of which populate the same data fields in Salesforce when the user completes the form. The form will alert the internal manager should anyone answer that they do need to disclose a conflict or potential conflict of interest.

11:00 a.m.

11:00AM

Chris takes a break for lunch and to fulfill orders for her side hobby. One great benefit of working from home is that she is able to maintain a hobby of raising and selling rare and unusual houseplants and edible landscaping varieties. It's a small hobby, so in about an hour, all the orders are packed up carefully and taken to the post office for shipping out worldwide. Those mid-day Mountain-Time hours are quiet for NEPCon, since most Europeans are done for the day and most of the Asian staff has not started work yet.

Noon

The afternoon is time to work on development and testing, which is one of Chris's very favorite things. It's great to have several open, quiet hours without a lot of meetings to make progress on detailed and intricate process automation. Today, Chris is working on a series of user-interactive and auto-launched flows that will help the team's auditors create customized checklists (in the right language) and allow them to easily input findings from their audits. When the findings are complete, the user will be able to press a button to have the original requirements and the corresponding findings appear in a Word document table.

3:30 p.m.

Chris spends time with her kids and spouse and tends to the plants.

Though it's an on-again, off-again work schedule over the course of the day, Chris finds that the time for meetings, time for "home life," time for focused development, and time for documentation is a great mix, even if it seems unconventional.

6:00 p.m.

Chris has one more meeting with a technical assistant, Andreas, who is based in Bali. Since there's a 15-hour time zone difference, his morning is not too late in the day for a call with Chris. Andreas is helping to support a big translation effort. Since NEPCon's clients (and staff) work in over twenty languages, many external-facing elements need to be carefully translated. Luckily, lots of talented staff members are available to help!

7:00 p.m.

The meeting with Andreas goes well, and it's satisfying to wrap up a day knowing that the work continues (around the clock!) with colleagues in Bali, Russia, Eastern Europe, Western Europe, and the East Coast all contributing and weighing in before Chris is awake the next day. Chris has dinner with her family, puts her kids to bed, and then relaxes with a book.

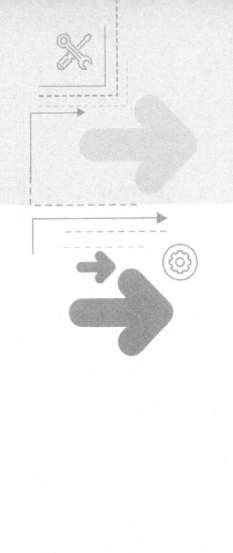

PART TWO

CAREER PATHS

To a certain degree, choosing a career path is based on guesswork. You cannot know for sure whether a job is a good fit until you are walking down the path and experiencing the day-to-day tasks associated with that particular career.

That said, the more information you collect about a career path, the more educated your choice will be. Choosing your career path is as much an inward-facing discovery process as it is an external, experiential one. To make the best decisions that guide you forward, you can look inward at your own unique constellation of preferences, strengths, and personality traits, as well as outward to collect details from other people who have information about the career path or paths you are considering.

- **In Chapter Six,** you will consider the different factors you can use in your internal discovery process.

- **Chapters Seven through Eleven** will provide detailed information about the differing career paths, including case studies from people who are working in functional, technical, consulting, and entrepreneurial careers.

- **In Chapter Twelve,** you will review the tips for entering the Salesforce ecosystem.

It bears noting that every career is different, so any book about career paths requires a giant disclaimer.

GIANT DISCLAIMER

A variety of paths will always exist for taking a person from Point A to Point B. One of my recent customers is a hairdresser who heard about Salesforce from a client and was instantly excited about the possibilities of helping small businesses move to the cloud and improve their sales and marketing processes. She started her career in Salesforce as a part-time consultant while still working as a hairdresser with hopes of transitioning to becoming a full-time consultant. Others follow the more traditional route: They graduate with bachelor's degrees and begin their careers in companies that use Salesforce, from which point they learn and grow their skills and experience.

The point here is this: This book provides an overview of the general pathways, but your particular career will likely meander off-path and present a variety of different opportunities based on your network, your capabilities, your environment, and your goals.

CHAPTER SIX:
The Internal Discovery Process

Every person has a unique constellation of personality traits, strengths and weaknesses, and preferences that will determine whether a job is a good fit or a lousy fit. Therefore, having the self-awareness to look inward will help you identify the environments in which you are most likely to thrive and avoid the environments that will stifle you.

For instance, if you work for a smaller company, you will face less bureaucracy, but there will also be less organization and consistency. Are you someone who will flourish in this environment, or will it feel too chaotic? Knowing the answer to this question upfront can help you choose a career path that is more likely to position you for success and happiness.

In this chapter, we consider six factors that can impact the direction you choose:

1. **Small firm versus large firm**
2. **Travel preferences**
3. **Variety versus predictability**
4. **Are you a people-person?**
5. **Industry preferences**
6. **Entrepreneurship and "freedom"**

To have a successful Salesforce career, you should really have a passion to solve a business's problem. If you have that passion, jump in because whether you are a developer, consultant, business analyst, or administrator, you will be successful.

Later in my career, I realized that if you enjoy what you do, you are always good at it.

–Jayant Umrani
Founder & CEO of Bolt.today, a consulting firm

As you read through this chapter, remember that there are no right or wrong answers: There are only true and false answers. You might *want* to be someone who is spontaneous and agile, but the truth is that you much prefer consistency, repetition, and structure. To get the best results from this discovery process, set aside all notions of who you *should be* or who you *want to be*. Being honest and upfront about your true personality traits, preferences, and capabilities will save you a world of hurt down the line. If you can start off down the right path, you won't waste years of your life struggling to find peace in your career, nor will you have to backtrack, rewind, or reinvent yourself.

Being honest about *who you actually are* instead of *who you think you should be* will save you a world of hurt down the line and more likely steer you in the direction of a career path you love.

CONSIDERATION #1:

Small Firm v. Large Firm

Are you better off working for a small firm or a large firm? To answer this question, you need to understand yourself, as well as the pros and cons of both large firms and small firms.

> *The beauty of working for a small company, especially if you are the only admin, is that you get to be autonomous. You get to make a decision and that decision is your responsibility, so you can feel that you are directly contributing to the success of the organization you are working for. But on the other side of the coin: You are the only person, so that comes with inherent stress because there is no one else.*
>
> **—David Scullion**
> **Senior administrator**

In this section, we take a look at the personality traits, preferences, and capabilities that align with large companies versus those that align with smaller firms.

LARGE FIRMS

Let us start with the hiring process. It is not unusual to spend months competing for a job at a large firm. Because these firms have multiple employees doing the same job, they can spend more time looking for the perfect candidate. To land a job at a large firm, you will likely need patience, as well as some backup income that can support you as you navigate through the hiring process.

Once you have been hired, you will find that large firms generally have more bureaucracy, a more rigid set of rules, and better organization than their smaller counterparts. They have had time to refine their processes and the resources to consult with attorneys, so they have step-by-step procedures that employees follow. This can be nice—you will know what is expected of you—but it also comes with its fair share of red tape.

Can you survive red tape, corporate meetings and picnics, and complex hierarchies? Only you can answer that question.

Keep this in mind, too:

Large companies tend to be significantly more formal and impersonal than smaller companies, though this is not always true.

Despite its large size, Salesforce, for instance, is known for its strong corporate culture and tight community. Regardless, an impersonal culture is not necessarily a bad thing. Some people prefer to keep their personal lives separate from their professional lives, which is much easier to do in a company of 20,000 employees than it is in a company of 20 employees.

If you are, however, looking for a large firm with a tight-knit group of colleagues who become your friends, a quick web search will tell you what the corporate culture of most large firms is like. Big firms have a large online presence, so you will likely be able to read reviews from former and current employees.

Despite the tendency to be impersonal and formal, large firms tend to have more opportunities to find mentors, if you are willing to look. Because you will be working within a network of many people, you can likely find someone who understands you and who is willing to help you move forward.

Speaking of moving forward, larger firms offer a more direct line of upward mobility. It is much harder to climb the corporate ladder at a boutique firm of twenty employees.

One last note about large firms: If you are looking to specialize, one of the great perks of working for a large firm is that you will likely have a job that is much more focused than you will at a small firm, whereby employees are expected to wear many hats. Your job will be defined, and you likely will not step too far out of the boundary of your job description without a promotion and a raise.

I wore more hats when I worked for a smaller company. I was their administrator, their developer, and their business analyst. I was doing reporting, managing all their processes, managing admin stuff (including their profiles), as well as building applications and doing development work for the operations team. I was gamifying the sales team processes, so I was involved in sales as well.

I was wearing all the hats, as opposed to where I am now, which is: I have one job, and it is to make sure development is pushed forward. I work on building applications all day, which is nice because it means I can focus on doing my one job really well.

—Dominick DeFazio
Developer (at the time of interview)

SMALL FIRMS

The beauty of small firms is that they are still being defined. When you work for a small firm, either as a Salesforce consultant or as a Salesforce end-user, you have a bigger influence on the direction of the company, the corporate culture, and the decisions made within that company.

Of course, the great big downside of this is that if the corporate culture is not a fit, you may feel largely out of place. With a large firm, you might be able to transfer departments or, at least, meet colleagues in other departments who are kindred souls, but smaller firms offer nowhere to go. If you do not have a great working relationship with your boss, you probably cannot transfer divisions to escape.

You will likely find more flexibility in working for a small firm. Because these employers do not have to accommodate hundreds or thousands of different scheduling requests, they are more likely to grant your request to work from home on Fridays or to change your work hours to accommodate your child's school schedule, assuming they are in a position to do so.

You will also have the opportunity to wear many hats at a small firm. Because these firms are oftentimes tackling problems as they arise, agile people make for better employees at small firms. If your feathers get ruffled upon being asked to troubleshoot a problem that exists beyond the scope of your job description, you will likely feel annoyed at a small firm. If you love the challenge of ever-changing requests, you might thrive with a small firm.

> In the smaller startup environment, you are so much more of a core part of the team. That's true to an extent at a bigger company, but it is not so obvious. At the smaller startup, I sat in on all the executive team meetings because my data and reporting drove the meetings. I was sitting with the CEO and COO, and I was just 22-year-old Dominick fresh out of college providing the data for their meetings.
>
> This is also what made it so hard to leave because I felt like the work I had done for that company drove most of their business processes. By the time I left, I had rewritten all of their triggers and coding, so I was saying goodbye to my baby.
>
> **—Dominick DeFazio**
> **Developer and chief technology officer**

Smaller firms, though, are generally considered less stable. They often do not have the resources and deep roots of their larger counterparts. Some mom and pop firms struggle to make payroll, so be aware that smaller firms might be more likely to experience downsizing (or complete closure) than larger firms.

On the other hand, you could benefit greatly from sticking with a small firm through the ups and downs. Small firms can become larger firms, and trusted employees are often given large promotions when this happens.

Large Firms	Small Firms
More structure, clearer rules, better organization, better benefits.	Less bureaucracy, fewer benefits, and more flexibility in rules, hours, and working preferences.
Harder to have your voice heard and to drive change.	Easier to drive change.
Tendency toward impersonal, formal corporate culture.	Tendency toward personal corporate culture.
More opportunity for mentorship.	Closer personal relationships.
More defined job roles/opportunity to specialize.	More variety/opportunity to wear many hats.
More stability.	Greater risk.
Defined upward mobility.	Fewer opportunities to climb the corporate ladder. That said, small firms can become large firms. If you work for the firm from the ground up, you might benefit more than working for an already established firm.

CONSIDERATION #2:

Travel Preferences

How do you feel about traveling—locally, nationally, or internationally? Though exceptions certainly exist, if you work for an end-user, travel will probably be limited. If you become a consultant, though, some amount of travel is probably in your future.

This travel might be contained to local neighborhoods, and the travel might occur during work hours, meaning you will still be home for dinner. That said, some consultants travel across the country or even across the globe.

Let me be real about what this means. Traveling sounds glamorous, and it can certainly be exciting, but it can also be tedious. If you are a consultant who travels to visit clients and potential clients in the same city, you will spend a lot of time in the car, train, or bus. You can listen to podcasts or make client calls to pass the time, but a considerable amount of time will be spent commuting. If you live in a large city, such as New York, London, or Sydney, dealing with traffic jams and long commutes might annoy you. Likewise, you might simply find it stressful or unpleasant to find yourself driving to and from meetings and networking events all week long. Some people feel unproductive. They get jittery and anxious when they are not performing tasks directly associated with their jobs. Others enjoy the breaks in the day, and they particularly love meeting with new people across a variety of industries.

The majority of consultant positions are remote and fast-paced. A consultant has to be willing to work at non-traditional times and days, and often, a consultant has to be willing to spend a considerable amount of time traveling. If you cannot self-motivate, you won't be successful in this kind of environment. And, by the way, there is no shame in admitting that you need more external direction and motivation. Know who you are so that you can set yourself up for success.

—Marc Lester

Senior Salesforce consultant and a planning team member for the Florida Dreamin' conference

Of course, traveling to different cities and countries is an entirely different story. Some consultants spend more time traveling than they do at home, leaving Sunday night and returning Thursday or Friday night. This might sound exciting, but take a look at what it actually entails before you decide that traveling is for you:

- If you have a family, you will miss important events, like your kids' games, your anniversary, and even holidays.

- You, too, will spend a considerable amount of time commuting, either by plane, by car, or both.

- You might not have anything to do in the evenings. What are your plans after work? If you adapt to new environments easily, this might not bother you, but knowing ahead of time what your plans are when you are not working during evenings and weekends will help you decide whether travel seems preferable or otherwise.

- All of your routines and rituals—like your 6 a.m. boxing class—will be interrupted. Any personal hobbies or fitness routines will need to be adapted or placed on hold. On the other hand, if you love early morning runs through new cities and exploring hiking paths, this might be the life for you!

One way or another, some amount of travel will probably be required if you are a consultant. Consultants at large firms might even be sent to work on longer-term projects at an end-user's office as temporary staff members during a Salesforce project.

If you prefer staying in a fixed place, consider working at an end-user firm. Or, search for a consulting firm that requires little to no travel and allows employees to work remotely. They do exist! In fact, Yelena Slobard, a business analyst for a medium-sized consulting company, had this to say, "I work from home 90 percent of the time. I spend about 50 to 70 percent of my time in phone or video meetings with clients, 20 percent of my time in phone or video meetings with colleagues, and the rest of my time working from home on projects. Very rarely am I required to travel."

The Life of a Traveling Consultant

Upon graduating from Syracuse University in 2015, Jordan Elkin knew he wanted to use technology as a force for good. He entered the world of tech consulting, and quickly landed his first client in fine arts in New York City. Jordan learned Salesforce and decided he wanted to pursue it full time instead of being a technology generalist.

To gain further experience, Jordan left his first role and joined a consulting firm where he worked in print, radio, and digital media. By 2017, he was working for EY, which is one of the largest consulting firms in the world.

For eighteen months, Jordan traveled the country helping clients with enterprise implementations, trainings, and integrations. By 2018, he had worked on projects in approximately ten cities, and he wanted to come home. He was born and went to school in New York, and he wanted to find an in-house role. Jordan left the consulting world to accept an internal position running the Salesforce program at a private equity firm.

The Life of a Traveling Consultant (...continued)

Jordan generously shared his experience with the pros and the cons of being a traveling consultant.

"The cool part about being a consultant is that you get your feet wet in almost every area of a Salesforce cycle. You spend time in design sessions, and you get to know high-level executives and key stakeholders, so you can build relationships and become a trusted advisor to people who can influence your career," he said.

Jordan also enjoyed the tight bonds he formed with his teammates. After all, they traveled to new cities and worked long hours on projects. Since part of his team worked in other countries, he developed global connections.

But in the end, for Jordan, the pros did not outweigh the cons.

"I wanted to find a balance in life," said Jordan. "I didn't want to get on a plane at 4:45 every Monday morning and come home late Friday night, having no time for friends or family," he said. "I was born and raised in New York. This is my home. When I was in a different city, I was always wondering what my friends and family were doing back home."

This is not to say that Jordan would discourage others from pursuing a career as a consultant.

"This is a lifestyle that some people love. When you work for a big firm, you get to go to places you have never considered going," he said. "I think it's a wonderful experience. You get to explore the world, meet new people, and really understand how life works outside of your own bubble."

"But whether it aligns with your long-term goals is another story. That depends on whether you want to be home with your family and friends. If you do, a long-term career as a consultant is probably not the path for you."

Consultants who travel extensively can expect to live from hotels. After enjoying the many benefits of this, Jordan found that he needed to be particularly focused to remain healthy.

"It's all about planning your day so that you can start your day right by going for a run or heading down to the hotel's gym because you will be onsite with your client past sundown," he said.

In 2018, Jordan left the world of consulting to take an internal Salesforce role at a private equity firm.

"It has been an adjustment," he said, "but I couldn't be happier here. I have to say that being a Salesforce customer instead of an implementation partner has been a wonderful change."

CONSIDERATION #3:

Agility v. Predictability

Are you happier when you understand exactly what is expected of you, and you are able to repeat and predict the routines you need to go through each day? If you are, you might be better off pursuing a career as an end-user.

What about personality types? If you can handle a variety of personality types, consider the number of people you would work with as a consultant, including different clients, as well as your non-technical and technical colleagues. If you prefer working with one or two people you understand and whose behavior you can predict, you might be better off pursuing a career as an end-user.

You need to know how much context-switching you can take on. If you are looking for a predictable work environment where you like to know in advance what is going to happen, the consulting world might not be for you. Successful consultants embrace change, and the challenges that come with it.

One morning you might improve the sales process of a manufacturing company doing $15 million a year, and in the afternoon you may roll out an omnichannel customer service solution for a call center of 500 agents at a publicly-traded company. If you want to be a consultant, you need to enjoy diversity and be ready for it.

—Aymeric Zito
CEO of ProQuest Consulting

After all, a consultant's job, by definition, is to adapt Salesforce to the clients' needs, and these clients come in a variety of shapes and sizes. Some are kind. Some are hot-headed. Some are articulate and straightforward. Others speak in riddles.

Sometimes a consultant knows exactly how to solve a client's problem. Sometimes, the consultant needs to put a giant puzzle together.

Agility, then, is necessary to the role of a consultant. If you can take what is thrown at you with grace, and you enjoy spontaneity and the unknown, you will likely thrive as a consultant. If you enjoy the structure and predictability of routines, and you expect professionals to act, well, professionally, then consider working as an end-user.

> *Typical day? Never heard of this in the Salesforce ecosystem!*
>
> **—Lorenzo Alali**
> **Salesforce administrator and business systems analyst**

CONSIDERATION #4:

Are you a people-person?

My earlier advice bears repeating here: Be honest about *who you actually are* instead of *who you think you should be.*

You might have a large group of friends. You might be gregarious, demonstrative, and social. All of this might be true, and it might also be true that you are not a people-person.

> My experience with personality types is this: People do business with people they trust and like, so to be a people-person, you have to have the soft skills that make you trustworthy and likable. You also need to be willing to uncover what it takes to make someone else successful. A lot of people go into business asking: "What do I need to be successful?" A true people-person will ask: "What do I need to do so that you can be successful?"
>
> **—Richard Clarke**
> **National Salesforce practice director and principal technical architect at PS+C Artisan**

A world of difference exists between being a people-person and being an outgoing person with a ton of friends. A people-person has tremendous interpersonal instincts, can empathize with differing perspectives, is able to see both sides of an argument, can diffuse emotions, and does this without getting his or her own feathers ruffled.

Ask anyone who has worked as a consultant: People can be difficult. When they are your clients, or the clients of the consulting firm for which you work, you have to figure out how to work with them nonetheless. The obvious examples, of course, are the people who are rude, dismissive, hotheaded, unfair, judgmental, and demanding. Add to this list the clients who suck your time, who do not pay on time, who are thin-skinned, and who have flat-out annoying personality traits.

If you are a people-person, you can look behind all of this negatively and still find someone you like, or at least, someone you can act like you like.

Ask yourself these questions:

- "Am I someone who routinely sees both perspectives in an argument?"

- "When someone is angry with me, am I able to remain calm and de-escalate the tension rather than escalate it?"

- "Do I find things in common with most people, even the people who are generally disliked by others?"

- "When working with other people, am I able to maintain firm but pleasant boundaries so that my relationships remain professional and strong, but without me feeling taken advantage of?"

- "Do I enjoy meeting new people?"

- "When I meet people with difficult personalities, can I usually find a way to have a pleasant working relationship with them?"

- "Am I able to read between the lines to determine why a person is acting the way they are acting?"

- "Do I believe that most people are good people who are behaving within the context of the paradigms that make sense to them, even if they don't make sense to the rest of the world?"

If the answers to these questions are truly and authentically yes, you might thrive as a consultant. If almost all of them are a no, consider working at an end-user firm.

> *I don't see this as a technical career. I see it as a career in enablement. Your goal at the end of the day is to make sure that your client and their end-users succeed.*
>
> **—Jordan Elkin**
> **CRM program manager**

CONSIDERATION #5:

Industry Preferences

Salesforce has a presence in almost every industry. Topping the list are financial services, healthcare, life sciences, communications and media, retail, public sector, and automotive and manufacturing, but this list is far from complete.

If you have a specific area of interest and want to grow your knowledge of a specific vertical, consider working at an end-user firm where you can apply your Salesforce expertise while building your knowledge of this industry.

Salesforce is a mature ecosystem, now. It's not like it was ten or fifteen years ago. There are heaps of opportunities, but this also means there are heaps of talents. You cannot be an expert in every area, so identify where you can add value. If you have a customer service background, specialize in Service Cloud. If you have a sales background, specialize in Sales Cloud. Putting your strengths together with your industry background is a way to stand out.

—Vamsi Krishna Gosu
**Founder and director of Techforce Services,
an Australian consulting firm**

On the other hand, one of the upsides of being a consultant is that you can learn about many different industries from a wide variety of business people. Most consultants say that much of their professional and personal growth comes from the exposure to different ideas they pick up from the hodgepodge of industries in which they have clients.

I usually have clients in customer service because I have experience in customer service myself. I used to work as an agent and supervisor of a big call center. Part of my personality as a supervisor was taking care of my agents, explaining to higher management what the agents needed. I now do exactly the same as a consultant. I think from the agent perspective, and therefore I advise from the agent's perspective.

—Natasja Daams
Salesforce consultant

CONSIDERATION #6:

Entrepreneurship and "Freedom"

Are you considering a career as a freelance Salesforce consultant, or as a consultant who opens your own shop and hires employees? If so, this section is for you!

One of the big myths of entrepreneurship is that it accompanies a tremendous amount of freedom. Sick of their nine-to-five jobs, employees have daydreams of venturing out on their own and working for themselves. They imagine sitting on the beach and drinking mai tais while casually answering emails from their laptops. They dream of winters spent skiing and summers spent traveling. They can take mid-morning boxing classes and meet their significant others for happy hour. Yoga on a Wednesday afternoon? Consider it done!

Or so they think.

Those of us who are entrepreneurs know the truth. Sure, entrepreneurs set their own hours. Those of us who have children can carve time in our schedules to attend our children's school performances. Those of us who do not have children can wake up at 8 o'clock instead of 6 o'clock—at least, we can when our clients are in the same time zone. We do not have to punch time cards, nor do we need to cross our fingers and hope our bosses approve our vacation requests.

But entrepreneurs never clock out. If a client calls on a Friday at 5:30 in the evening, the entrepreneur is ultimately responsible for making sure that the client is taken care of. I have hired contractors in the United States who meet with me via video conference at 7:30 at night to accommodate the fact that I am in Australia.

This is the life of a consultant in any industry. If you become a freelance consultant, you will not have a boss, but you will have multiple clients who spread the word about you and build (or destroy) your reputation. Your ability to attract new clients is based, at least in part, on your ability to have existing clients who happily refer business to you.

Mai tais on the beach? Maybe, but never drink more than one. Most likely, a client will call needing your assistance. Winters skiing? Sure, but expect to spend a good portion of that time in the lodge. Summers traveling? Plan to be tethered to your laptop on planes, on trains, and in automobiles.

I can go on vacation, but that doesn't mean I'm not working. I was on vacation in Hawaii for my twenty-fifth anniversary, and I was writing code while the rest of my family enjoyed Hawaii.

—Pat McClellan
AppExchange vendor

You get the point:

Entrepreneurs are essentially on-call around-the-clock—at least in the first years of operation. Yes, you might build a business such that you have employees who do the work for you, but this will take years of hard work. In the beginning, you will wear all the hats: You will not only work in your Salesforce role as a consultant, but you will also spend time writing proposals, meeting with potential clients, invoicing existing clients, collecting on those invoices, building your website, and on and on—much of which you will be unable to bill for.

As you build your business and hire people to work for you, you can add to the list such things as managing schedules, hiring and training, and payroll. Speaking of payroll, if your business slows down, you will still be responsible for finding money to make payroll. If it slows down drastically, you will be the one who tells your employees that they have to take a pay cut or, worse yet, face a layoff.

Don't get me wrong: Being an entrepreneur has its upsides. For many of us, having control of a business and decisions related to that business outweighs any of the downsides. When you are in charge of your own operation, no one else tells you what to wear, how to behave, or whom to do business with. You control your own work relationships. You can decide whether to work alone and in silence, at a coffee shop, at a shared work-space, on a beach, or in a ski lodge. You establish your own brand, your own culture, and your own rules of operation. You can decide to take on a light client load and work just a few hours a day, or you can decide to take on as many clients as possible and grow your operation quickly.

But to be clear, the stress does not dissipate when you become an entre-preneur. Most freelancers and business owners, small and large, say that the anxiety and stress increase as their business grows. Beyond that, en-trepreneurial "freedom" is a myth. Rather than clocking out at 5 p.m., you will feel responsible for taking care of your clients and your employees, whether they call you at 8 p.m. or 5 a.m.

If you work for yourself and you work from home, you only have to work half a day. Just figure out which twelve hours that is.

—Pat McClellan
AppExchange vendor

The final question you should consider about being an entrepreneur is this:

How much risk tolerance do you have?

To succeed as an entrepreneur, you are going to have to take some risks. The financial risk is obvious—you might not secure enough business to cover your expenses—but there are other risks as well. You will have to walk into networking meetings, without knowing a single soul, and risk making a fool of yourself. You will put your reputation at risk; if something goes wrong, the buck stops with you. You will risk economies that collapse. And you will risk that the Salesforce industry itself is disrupted, replaced by some greater technology that puts your consulting firm out of business. This is a risk that is unlikely to come to fruition, of course, but I suspect that if you were to rewind by twenty years, the taxicab industry would not have expected to be nearly extinct by 2020!

For a free analysis of your current career opportunities, head over to
https://cloudtalent360.com/career-assessment-book-offer/

Day in the life:
PAT MCCLELLAN

Pat McClellan is the developer and entrepreneur behind Proton Text, an app available on the AppExchange. He works from home—and he works a lot of hours. "I work a lot of hours because I like to," he said. "Some people would say I am goal oriented. A therapist might say my self-esteem is tied to approval. Either way, I love my life. I work at least six days a week, and I work long days, but when I wake up, I am excited to get to work."

6:00 a.m.

Three days a week Pat swims for an hour, which is when his workday begins. During his morning swim, Pat is either thinking through code, or he is considering new features that his customers have asked him to implement into his app.

7:30 a.m.

Pat eats breakfast at his computer. Once or twice a week, he receives an email or a call from a customer who has a question about how his app works, or who is receiving an error message. When customers call asking for help, Pat makes this the number-one priority of his day, pushing all meetings until later that day or week.

"I have to focus on customer service to differentiate myself from the big guys who have a technical team of hundreds," he said. *"But when customers call those companies, they don't answer. When my customers call, I answer. I know all of them, and they know me."*

9:00 a.m.

Pat spends a large chunk of the day coding. He says that his nephew, a developer for a large company, gets to code about three hours out of the week because he is in meetings the rest of the time. Pat, on the other hand, gets to code all day long.

Noon

A quick lunch break, and then Pat returns to coding. **12:00PM**

2:00 p.m.

Pat pushes a patch to his customers. Because he works for himself, he has agility. If a customer calls to report a bug, Pat can go usually push out the fix within the day.

2:30 p.m.

Often, Pat's customers give him ideas for new features, so he is usually aware of the next thing he wants to add to Proton Text. For instance, one day, he worked on a feature for a color-blind client—replacing a color-coded light with icons.

5:00 p.m. Dinner Break!

7:00 p.m.

Back to coding. Pat normally codes for an hour or so after dinner.

8:00 p.m.

Pat plans for the following day, which is a "marketing day." On marketing days, Pat networks with user groups and admins. He also writes short articles for content marketing on LinkedIn, and he posts weekly to his lightning blog (blog.proton7group.com).

"It's all focused on building my personal brand and professional brand because I know I am going up against four other major competitors who have hundreds of customers who are very entrenched," Pat said of his marketing days.

CHAPTER SEVEN:
The End-User Functional Pathway

As I mentioned earlier, rarely is there a set-in-stone path that every person will follow, and certainly that is true within the Salesforce ecosystem. That said, in any career, there are always logical next steps. In this chapter, we will look at the functional roles that may begin as an end-user administrator, business analyst, or even project manager. In these functional roles, you would work for a company that uses Salesforce to run its business. This company can be large or small, and it can be in a range of industries, such as financial services, healthcare, communications and media, or retail.

In this context, the word "functional" means that you would be working closely with the business to understand, define, and implement solutions. In Salesforce, the term functional is used opposite "technical," which, rather than focusing on business interactions, focuses on building solutions using a deep technical understanding of Salesforce.

END USER FUNCTIONAL CAREER ROLES

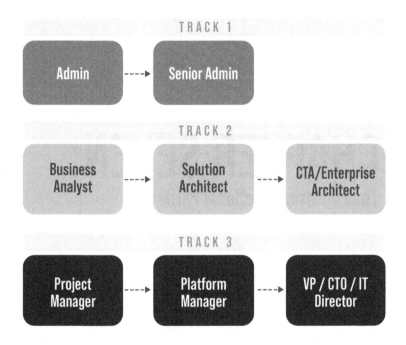

This End User Functional Career Roles diagram depicts three tracks for functional Salesforce roles. The first track is where many people start and where they find their home working with businesses, and configuring and administering Salesforce. Larger organizations will have a number of administrators and will offer the possibility of advancing to senior administrator, which is a role managing other administrators. This is a popular track, one that often offers a mix of day-to-day operational and project work.

The second functional track is the solution-level track and is usually project-focused. These roles are focused on understanding requirements, defining solutions, and implementing projects to meet business objectives.

The third track is for people who enjoy managing projects and people. Project managers, platform managers, and senior IT managers spend considerable amounts of time managing projects, stakeholders, and teams, as well as communicating and defining strategy and how Salesforce can best be used to support business objectives.

Keep in mind that this progression is not available at every firm. A large-scale end-user might have multiple jobs dedicated entirely to the Salesforce platform, meaning the employee can move from administrator to senior administrator to platform owner, whereas at small- and mid-sized firms, some roles simply might not exist. When horizontal movement is not possible within a company, Salesforce administrators who want to advance their careers switch firms.

As mentioned previously, much overlap can exist in roles, depending on the organization, and different organizations use different titles to describe their positions. These are the most common titles that might be assigned to a functional professional working in a Salesforce role, but keep in mind that actual roles may be a mixture of these descriptions.

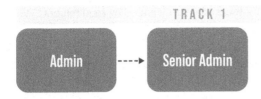

TRACK 1

Administrator

Administrators manage the day-to-day use of Salesforce and support the team members in their use of Salesforce. This is an operational, project, and administrative role. Administrators manage data; maintain the system; administer users profiles, roles, and permissions; respond to user requests; work on projects; and implement configuration changes.

At a small end-user firm, an administrator might be the only Salesforce-related staff member on board, meaning the administrator also acts as the senior administrator, the platform manager, the business analyst, the project manager, and the developer. Any of the company's needs beyond the administrator's competencies would be outsourced to a Salesforce consultant.

From the position of administrator, a person can move up to senior administrator within their own company if the company is large. If the company is small, the person moves to another company to become a senior administrator. An administrator or senior administrator may also move to a dedicated business analyst role.

Senior Administrator

This is a leadership role that involves collaboration with management to implement and improve Salesforce-related processes. The senior administrator works in a firm large enough to employ several administrators and is responsible for managing the administrator team and overseeing the adoption of new processes and applications within the Salesforce ecosystem.

TRACK 2

Business Analyst

A Salesforce business analyst works as a bridge between IT and the various departments of a company. The analyst is responsible for understanding not only the capabilities of Salesforce, but also the various business processes at play within an organization. The business analyst role is typically reserved for large end-user firms. (At a smaller firm, a developer or administrator would assume the analyst's job functions.) At these end-user firms, the business analyst is one of multiple Salesforce resources working on a team. Whereas the administrator on the team manages the day-to-day use of Salesforce, the business analyst is tasked with understanding the business, documenting needs, and overhauling processes.

Solution Architect

A solution architect takes customer requirements and business challenges and translates them into solutions leveraging the Salesforce platform. A solution architect role has overlap with a business analyst, though an architect is distinguished for being the person responsible for solution design and architecture, assisting the business analyst with gathering and documenting requirements. Going beyond technical design, an architect will consider aspects such as security, scalability, performance, licenses required and integration, and ensuring the solution meets project requirements and aligns with enterprise standards, technology roadmaps, and business objectives. A solution architect in an end-user organization will typically work on multiple projects, not all of them Salesforce related.

CTA (Certified Technical Architect)

A solution architect who would like to specialize in Salesforce architecture may aim to achieve the CTA certification credential. A CTA has knowledge, skills, and experience in all Salesforce domains. These architects typically work on complex enterprise-sized projects. They understand how Salesforce fits into and integrates in an overall IT landscape. As the most knowledgeable Salesforce person on a project, they often act as advisors. They require high-level communication and presentation skills and interact with all levels of an organization.

Enterprise Architect

A Salesforce architect may decide they are interested not only in Salesforce architecture but also in architecture at the enterprise level. An enterprise architect is not a specific Salesforce role, but rather uses Salesforce as part of an entire IT landscape. Enterprise architects, therefore, have a broad technology focus that includes but is not limited to Salesforce.

An enterprise architect aligns architecture with organization strategy and objectives. They focus on defining and delivering the target architecture and the technology roadmap.

TRACK 3

TRACK 3

Project Manager

When an organization is implementing Salesforce for the first time or has major initiatives to expand its use, it will need a dedicated Salesforce project manager. This is a typical project management role; however, project managers working in a Salesforce environment will be more successful if they understand the capabilities of the platform, which will allow them to manage stakeholders' expectations, resolve issues, and manage the project team.

Platform Manager/Owner

This job title is relatively new, having evolved over the past few years as Salesforce platforms have grown in scope. The Salesforce platform owner is a member of the IT team and serves as the champion and steward of the platform within an organization, managing development and delivery teams through the various phases of Salesforce configuration and development. This person understands each aspect of Salesforce as it is implemented and integrated within each department of a company and is responsible for all of the guidelines related to use of Salesforce.

Vice President, Chief Technology Officer, IT Director

Although IT management roles are not Salesforce-specific, professionals who aspire to reach this level can pursue it through Salesforce channels. These management roles are focused on ensuring all technologies are aligned to support business objectives, approving technology roadmaps, and overseeing larger projects.

Increasingly, cloud solutions, including Salesforce, are playing a large part in the future landscapes of IT management, so having a Salesforce and cloud background can be critical for managers steering an organization into the future.

Other Functional Roles

In some organizations, sales, service, or process improvement roles may not be Salesforce-specific but may nonetheless be heavily focused on determining how Salesforce can be used to improve business processes. For instance, a sales excellence manager might be described as a person who seeks to improve the processes that support the sales team and makes them more efficient and productive. These processes, though, might be largely dependent upon Salesforce. Depending on the organization, this type of role may be a combination of Salesforce administrator, reporting analyst, process improvement specialist, and project manager. Other titles that fall into this category include customer success manager, sales support manager, and process improvement manager.

Fortunately, the need for Salesforce professionals working in functional roles is high. Salesforce reports a 37 percent annual growth rate in administrator jobs alone. Of course, getting your first job is not always easy, so let us take a look at some case studies of people who are working in various functional roles. These case studies represent workers at both small and large firms.

> Visit **https://cloudtalent360.com/career-assessment-book-offer/** for a free career assessment, and to learn about the Salesforce Career Accelerator Program, which is an interactive, video-based and group coaching program that teaches smart, effective strategies to Salesforce professionals who want to maximize their career and earning potential.

CHRISTINE MARSHALL:
The Accidental, Solo, Global Administrator

Christine Marshall, Salesforce MVP, is an accidental administrator, a solo administrator, and a global administrator for an engineering company. She also leads the Bristol Salesforce Admin User Group.

Within the world of Salesforce, Christine Marshall says she is a walking stereotype. She is at once an accidental administrator, a solo administrator, and a global administrator, which means that she came by her Salesforce career quite by accident, that she works as the only administrator at her firm, and that she serves a group of end-users who work for a firm with a global presence.

At the time of our interview, Christine worked remotely from Bristol, England, for an engineering company with headquarters in France. Christine started her career with a degree in English literature. Unsure of her career path upon graduating, she held various roles, including sales support management. The company she worked for, a construction equipment dealership, was using an antiquated CRM that could no longer be updated.

Christine suggested an upgrade, and her supervisor agreed, charging her with the task of finding and implementing the new system. She did not need to look far to find that the main headquarters was already using a CRM that would be a major upgrade.

That CRM was, of course, Salesforce, which is how Christine became an accidental admin.

Christine implemented Salesforce and continued to use it in her role supporting the sales team. She later moved onto another job, this time as a project manager for a company that also happened to use Salesforce. In this role, Christine spent time reconfiguring the platform, and she realized that she liked the Salesforce aspect of her job most of all.

When a recruiter contacted her about a full-time Salesforce role, Christine jumped at the opportunity, and since 2016, she has been a fulltime Salesforce admin.

She currently works for a global engineering company headquartered in France with offices in the United States, Canada, India, and across Europe. As a solo administrator, Christine takes care of the entire user base of more than 300 sales employees, who use the platform to manage their pipeline of opportunities and leads. When Christine joined the team, they had not yet customized the Salesforce platform in-depth, which meant she started with a blank canvas.

Christine spends much of her time supporting users, answering their day-to-day questions about the platform, troubleshooting, and training users on the features of the platform. She has a super-user group, which she meets with every other week to discuss the most important customizations and needs from a user perspective. These super-users also help her respond to user needs in other parts of the company. Because the company has users in Germany, France, India, and other non-English-speaking countries, these super-users are invaluable in helping train employees in their native language. As well, Christine formed a steering committee, which she meets with every eight weeks, to define her high-level priorities as they relate to the business's overall objectives.

While Christine fell into her career as a Salesforce administrator, she has some advice for people getting started:

- **First,** leverage any background that you might have in sales support, marketing, reporting, analysis, or project management, as these are translatable skills.

- **Second,** be proactive in personal development, getting badges through Trailhead, Salesforce's robust online website dedicated to teaching Salesforce skills. Then, apply that knowledge to gain Salesforce certifications. She admits that nothing matches real-world experience, but attaining badges and certifications shows interest, passion, and motivation. Finally, involve yourself in the Salesforce community as early as possible. Attend local user groups and connect with people already in the Salesforce ecosystem who can put you in touch with recruiters and people who are hiring.

The good news, said Christine, is this:

There are a lot more jobs than people who can do them.

Once you have a bit of experience, you should have no trouble finding a job as a Salesforce administrator.

CASE STUDY

DAVID SCULLION:
Senior Salesforce Administrator
for News Corp

David Scullion is a senior administrator for News Corp Australia, where he has three desks: one at his home, one at a local office, and one at a major state news station.

David Scullion is the senior Salesforce administrator for News Corp Australia, which has several Salesforce instances and more than 1,500 users. He has a home office, a desk at the local newspaper office about ten minutes away, and a desk in Brisbane at the company's state office.

David is a great example of moving up, one step at a time. His career path is a direct result of his ability to continue to learn and grow.

David's career in Salesforce started eleven years ago. He was working for an accounting software company that purchased Salesforce, and David's boss, the director of information technology, assigned David as the administrator. Though David started working with mainframes straight out of high school, he didn't have any experience with Salesforce.

He took four hours of training and jumped into the deep end.

And David quickly realized how helpful Salesforce would be. The company did not have any helpdesk software, and its case-logging system was archaic. Salesforce solved that problem.

"I just started building from there," said David. *"I taught myself. At the time, the support community wasn't what it is now, so I went to Google and searched for help when I needed it. After some time, the company saw how valuable it was, so they paid for me to get my Administrator certification."*

Studying for certification helped fill in the gaps of knowledge. At the same time, the fact that he was working within Salesforce helped him pass the initial certification.

"I would say that it's a lot harder to get through a certification if you are not actually working in a job that requires those skills," he said.

The next big project for David was to roll out a community for its channel partners. David used Salesforce to implement proper record security and software renewals. Following that successful project, he integrated Salesforce with the legacy systems and the company's own accounting software—a process that took a few years.

And then it was time for a change. David moved to an education company that ran seminars that helped people build their portfolios by buying and selling properties. The company had twice the users as his previous job and had a more sophisticated Salesforce instance. He worked on day-to-day aspects (credit reports, answering questions, and fixing data) and built a customer community for the company's partnership with a real estate company. This required several complicated levels of security and record ownership.

David had help from developers and was not expected to write code. At this point, he had not earned any additional certifications, but he was starting to join user groups and online communities as they began to grow in popularity.

When the News Corp job came up three years ago, David jumped at the opportunity.

And it was a big change.

"At the smaller companies, you can sort of do what you want and move along with your ideas. News Corp was the first structured environment I worked in. I was part of a team expected to follow structures. There is a release cycle. Everything is done for a reason. We deal with compliance and can't produce without a ticketed approval."

News Corp runs a monthly release cycle, so every month, David attends a prioritization forum with stakeholders who decide what they want released. The Salesforce team devotes half of its time—ten days—to the new release. Early in the month, David and the tech lead size up the tasks and begin developing (or assign developers to more complex tasks) so they can stay on schedule.

For instance, David is currently releasing ten new features this month and an additional seven the following month.

The other half of David's time is spent:

- Problem-solving. David helps the two junior administrators who do triage for service desk tickets.

- Tending to internal maintenance. David is charged with environmental management, such as refreshing sandboxes, which can take three or four hours for each sandbox as they need to be populated with data and legacy systems.

- Managing News Corps print and digital catalog, which includes updating prices and automating related processes.

- Responding to auditors.

- Connecting with the sales team and getting feedback on their experience with Salesforce.

- Attending weekly deployment team meetings to manage and plan for deployments.

- Attending weekly ad sales meetings.

- Working with global consulting partners, who are hired to work on specialized projects.

It's a lot, and David says that at times it can even be scary. When he first started at News Corp, he experienced growing pains.

"I couldn't just go change a field because I didn't know what I would break," he said. Salesforce is used to track every customer who advertises with every News Corp paper in Australia, which is a lot. *"And if I broke the environment, there would be serious implications to the business."*

Fortunately, thanks to hard work, David has been successful in his role, and News Corp rewarded him by sending him to TrailheaDX in San Francisco.

"It was a big reward, and I started to fall back in love with Salesforce. I wanted to better myself, and DX reminded me of all the other things I could do."

Beyond that, he was able to test for Advanced Administrator while at DX. This was the hardest test David had ever taken, but he passed.

"I came back with a renewed passion to learn Salesforce," he said.

Right in time! His company announced a competition: Road to Dreamforce. The rules were: Complete two certification tests in six months and receive 100 trail badges. The person who receives this first goes to Dreamforce.

David decided to take tests for Sales Cloud Consultant, Service Cloud Consultant, and Community Cloud Consultant. He passed all of them on the first try. He also earned 190 trail badges.

(You know where this story is going.)

(But you're wrong!)

"Funnily enough, my boss won," David said. *"It did put me back into learning mode."* I thought: *"What am I going to do next? How am I going to get better?"*

David started studying for the Platform Developer 1 certification.

"I thought I was prepared to take the exam, but it was an epic failure," he said.

With his ego slightly deflated, David took a step back.

And then, at Down Under Dreamin', a Salesforce event in Brisbane, he shared a beer with the keynote speaker, an architect for Google.

"His message to me was, 'Don't give up.' He failed his CTA twice, but he wasn't giving up, so that's when I decided that my path forward is to head up the architect pyramid."

His advice to people building their Salesforce careers is to take it one step at a time, and to commit to becoming better versions of themselves.

"I believe to be a good Salesforce person, you need to understand the technology platform, but you also need to be able to relate to the business. Even if you're a developer, you still need to be able to talk to business. You can do all the thinking and have big eyes, but if you don't know what the business is like, you can't interpret what the business really needs."

VERONIKA PEYCHEVA:
CRM Change Analyst for Experian

Veronika Peycheva is the CRM change analyst for Experian, the credit-reporting company. She lives in Bulgaria and works from her home office.

Veronika Peycheva has spent the past two decades in sales and marketing, so she witnessed the industry transition to digital.

She began her career as a salesperson for a travel agency before joining the communications team at Petrol Holding, a Bulgarian investment company specializing in oil and energy, real estate, business aviation, leisure and hospitality, and financial services. At Petrol, Veronika worked in the PR department, but she quickly returned to the travel agency, where she was responsible for transitioning and maintaining the company's digital presence, as well as automating business processes.

From there, Veronika had several career changes, all in marketing and sales: She managed marketing projects for an information security firm, managed web and marketing activities for a software company, and automated marketing and CRM systems for an IT company.

When she got hands-on experience with Salesforce, the first thing she noticed was how easy it was to measure the link between sales and ROI. Beyond that, she found that the ability to gain skills in Salesforce was astounding.

"The information available for progressing in Salesforce was unbelievable," she said. *"Add to that the community, and I was able to learn very quickly."*

Veronika sat for (and passed) three certifications: Administrator, Advanced Administrator, and Platform App Builder.

In 2016, she joined the credit-reporting company Experian, where she currently serves as a CRM Change Analyst.

"At the time there were very few people working with Salesforce in Bulgaria, so there was definitely a demand for Salesforce practitioners. In the last years more local and international companies started looking for Salesforce professionals and the market has opened up a bit. The number of people who work with Salesforce have grown, and we now have local Salesforce communities where we share knowledge and experience and help each other progress in the area."

Veronika works primarily from her home office, where she handles streamlined work requests alongside training teams, business analysts, and developers. Part of the work of a change analyst is onboarding new teams and processes and, at the same time, making sure to sustain a simple and streamlined user experience for everyone in Salesforce.

This is her first time working for a large company (Experian has more than 16,000 employees), and she has noticed a definite shift in culture.

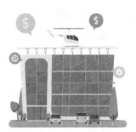

"I have always worked in small subsidiaries where I know the people, I know the process, and I have ownership of what to do next. I miss being able to customize Salesforce all at once without having to run everything by a number of stakeholders and the various users, but I do enjoy the challenge of keeping it simple while still serving the needs of a number of different business scenarios. Regardless of whether you are working in a large or a small company, the feeling is the same when people are happy that you've just helped them be more productive, do their job more easily, and get their everyday processes more streamlined."

Despite the limited demand for Salesforce professionals in Bulgaria, Veronika is optimistic about her future, and she encourages other people to dip their toe into the industry.

"I think it's a great place to start. I know there is a lot of buzz in other parts of the world about the high demand and the high-paying job market, but even in Bulgaria, it's exciting to be part of this community and work with a product that is constantly evolving."

Because of her marketing background, Veronika has paid close attention to Salesforce's positioning with respect to global marketing.

"Salesforce is rethinking customer experience. One of the reasons I stepped out of digital marketing and advertising at the time was because it felt intrusive. Although there were good signs, we still had the challenges of a lot of irrelevant content. Salesforce has taken things to a whole new level by making the customer part of the product and part of the community. It feels relevant."

"I'm part of something exciting."

LORNA O'CALLAGHAN:
First-Time Platform Manager

Lorna O'Callaghan holds a masters degree in medieval history and is a first-time platform manager for a finance, insurance, and banking corporation based in Sydney in Australia. She also co-leads the local Women in Tech community group.

Lorna O'Callaghan is a systems/platform manager who oversees a team of four Salesforce specialists who work for a finance, insurance, and banking corporation and is based in Sydney, Australia. Lorna's team includes a developer, two administrators, and a business analyst.

The role of platform manager is a relatively new one, having evolved in the past few years when companies began to realize that they needed one person to coordinate and be in charge of all Salesforce-related activity within a company. After all, the use of Salesforce can start off small in one business unit, but quickly grow to support sales, service, and marketing processes.

The platform manager is the go-to person for Salesforce related projects and initiatives. They have the big-picture overview of how Salesforce is currently used in an organization, and they formulate the plans, initiatives, and recommendations on where to invest for the future. They deal with a range of stakeholders including Salesforce representatives (account managers, customer success managers), internal executives, end-users, and the Salesforce project teams and support teams. It is a role that the Salesforce ecosystem should expect to see grow over the years as Salesforce becomes more central to the systems landscape and is integrated across the enterprise to other systems.

Unlike many of the career paths that Salesforce lays out in Trailhead, platform manager does not fit into a cookie-cutter model. Take Lorna, for instance.

"I have grown into a team leader, slash platform manager. My role is quite multi-hatted, and I feel there is still a gap in material for people like me."

Lorna's journey did not start off in IT. Her undergraduate degrees from Ireland's University Cork College were in English and history, and she received a master's degree in medieval history. But by the time she received her degree, she had already started to deviate from this career path. A friend had asked Lorna to join her on the student IT helpdesk to troubleshoot inquiries. Much to Lorna's surprise, she loved it, in part because of the people she worked with, who had all sorts of diverse interests.

Lorna felt like she belonged, and she quickly discovered it was easier to find jobs in IT than medieval history. When she was offered a position as a trainer in the university's IT department, Lorna took the job.

Her journey in the Salesforce ecosystem began in 2012 when she received a call from the IT director of Ireland's largest recruitment company and was hired as a software systems engineer, a title that even Lorna found strange given that she had never done any coding.

Eventually, Lorna realized that a different title suited her role better: She was a Salesforce administrator for the recruiting team. Prior to this job, Lorna had managed an Access database, but Salesforce was brand new, and she was thrown into the deep end. To find her way around the platform, Lorna became involved in the community, joining online groups to ask questions. Her manager also acted as a mentor.

A few years later, Lorna decided to leave Ireland and relocate to Australia. She knew she wanted to pursue a career in the Salesforce ecosystem, so she worked a series of temp roles and for a couple of nonprofits as a Salesforce administrator.

Eventually, she took a temporary position for a software company that needed help with a three-week data migration project. Lorna stayed for two and one-half years, first to complete the data migration, then as the Salesforce lead for one of the company's divisions. In this role, she was responsible for design, configuration, deployment, and support of system and business processes across opportunity management, contract management, account management, and lead management, as well as the governance of all processes across her division on the platform, analysis of platform usage, and providing insights for strategic planning, customer and customer segmentation insights, training of all end-users and management reporting. Although Lorna had support from a Salesforce team, other admins based in the company's UK HQ, she was essentially a solo admin and business analyst.

Eventually, she joined the Salesforce team officially and became the lead for the project management office, acting as the regional partner across all divisions for larger initiatives, frameworks and overall process governance. Lorna says she was the "solo administrator within an informal framework."

For the past year, she has been the platform manager at her current position, which has hundreds of internal users as well as external users. Lorna's team of five manages the entire platform where the work is split across BAU queries and minor enhancement requests as well as larger initiatives and projects, so her days are busy.

It is hard for Lorna to describe her role: She is part scrum master, part project manager, part team lead, and part strategic advisor.

What they don't tell you when you become a manager is that 80, 90, sometimes 95 percent of your time is spent in meetings. That was a big shocker. You are far less hands-on with the platform when you start leading teams.

In my role, I rely on my team every single day. They are the ones I trust to help me make the best decisions for our platform. Because I don't have the opportunity to be hands-on with the platform anymore, having a team of experts around you is critical to its overall success in your organization.

—Lorna O'Callaghan
Platform manager

"A lot of my time revolves around the sprint. We run fortnightly sprints where the first few days are ensuring everything is on track, working through any blockers which arise, and managing any outliers which might come our way. Then half way through the sprint, the functional consultant and I start looking toward the next sprint and working through prioritization with our business unit champions." she said. Another part of her day is checking in with other team leads in the company who manage processes that might impact the Salesforce instance. Lorna also manages the contracts and engagement with Salesforce itself.

One of the challenges Lorna has experienced is this: Though Lorna manages developers, she does not code.

"I don't have that level of technical knowledge of the platform, so when I took on this job, I had to consider what my role would look like," she said. "How was I going to lead a group of people who have more technical knowledge than I have?"

Beyond that, Lorna had never been in a managerial role. Though Trailhead is a great resource for learning new Salesforce-related skills, Lorna also needed leadership skills.

"In some ways, I was lucky because there was a three-month gap between the time I was interviewed and the time I was officially hired because my visa took some time to process. It gave me an opportunity to look at what the role was going to require and decide how I was going to go about managing people."

A great resource for Lorna was *The Manager's Path: A Guide for Tech Leaders Navigating Growth and Change* by Camille Fournier. She is also pursuing additional certifications to close the gap between what she knows and what her technical team members know.

"I am definitely finding that I need to have a bit more hands-on technical knowledge, and I would wager a lot of platform managers are in a similar multifaceted role where they need to expand their technical skills," she said.

And what about soft skills and general business skills?

"I need to have expertise on the business and in the industry to be a super-strategist. I need to know the direction of the platform, understand industry trends, and use that knowledge to produce a roadmap and program of work that aligns to the direction of the company. Of course, this means I need to carve out time for reading multiple blogs as well as internal whitepapers and industry publications."

One last bit of advice from Lorna is this: Carve out space to think and innovate.

"If you spend 90 percent of your time in meetings, it is easy to forget this, but you need to create space for your own thoughts. We have a quiet room in our building, and I have recently started taking time to write everything down on the white boards in the room, and then just sit back and figure out how it is all connected. If I don't consciously make time to do this, it has an impact on what I am trying to do here because so much happens so fast."

"Another important thing for me from a leadership perspective is that it's really important for a team to have space to think and innovate, too. As a team we try to have regular innovation days where the team can build anything they want together, just for fun. Getting those creative juices flowing is vitally important to nurturing your team, and ultimately strengthens them and the platform in adding significant value to the business."

Day in the life:
MEET LORNA O'CALLAGHAN

Lorna O'Callaghan is a platform manager who works for an Australian finance, insurance, and banking corporation based in Australia. Lorna manages a Salesforce team that includes a developer, business analyst and two administrators. The platform manager role is relatively new, having arisen in the past few years as companies began to realize they needed a person to manage the entirety of a company's Salesforce instances.

Lorna was kind enough to share a day in her life, a Friday, which is the day after deployment of a major initiative. Lorna's team has another initiative kicking off the following Monday, and on this Friday, the company is renewing the licenses for both of the orgs that Lorna manages.

6:45 a.m.
Beep beep! Lorna's alarm sounds. Normally, she rises before the alarm so as to not awaken her partner, but today is Friday, the end of a long week, and Lorna needs a few extra minutes of sleep. Lorna checks her Whatsapp messages from family and friends who live on other continents, and she reads the news headlines. Lorna turns on the kettle to make coffee, brushes her teeth, and hops in the shower. When she's finished, she dresses and then enjoys a morning coffee with her partner, a ritual that she loves as it enables her to slow down and become present for the day.

7:30 a.m.

Lorna leaves to catch the train. Her commute is another time she uses to relax and keep herself present in the day. She used to listen to the news or a podcast, but now she listens only to classical music while on the train, which allows her to arrive at work relaxed and happy. She tries not to check her phone during the day's commute, though if she is feeling particularly energized, she might complete a badge or two on Trailhead. Today, though, she listens only to music.

8:00 a.m.

Lorna arrives at work and gets situated by filling up her water bottle and turning on her laptop to check her emails and read through the case queue.

8:30 a.m.

Lorna's team arrives, and they head out to their favorite cafe nearby for a daily coffee before the workday begins.

9:00 a.m.

Emails and planning time for Lorna while the team focuses on testing post deployment. This includes doing PVT (production verification/validation testing), which is testing with the end-users in the live environment to ensure everything works. During this time, Lorna reads the company briefs her manager has sent, which includes regulatory notices and performance briefs. Lorna also reads weekly updates from senior leaders and checks the company's social pages, particularly with respect to the equality, diversity and inclusion groups. Lorna is on the People Forum for her business unit where she champions diversity, inclusion, and wellbeing initiatives.

10:00 a.m.

The team has fortnightly sprints, deploying on the second Thursday night. Today is the Friday post-deployment, which is the only day when the team does not have a stand-up.

Instead, Lorna and the business analyst have pre-sprint planning. Having met last Thursday with the product owners for prioritization within their business units, Lorna and the business analyst decide what they will take into the sprint the following Monday and plan out the forthcoming sprint.

Typically, for this team of five, whereby 50 percent of the team's capacity is spent on business as usual and 50 percent is spent on project initiatives, a fortnightly sprint averages around 60 to 70 story points. (Think of "story points" as the individual pieces of a new initiative that, when put together, create the entire story.)

Lorna's team usually has one big initiative on the go, such as a new lead and opportunity management solution. The team also incorporates lots of smaller change requests into the sprint, such as new picklist values, page-layout updates, or new reports.

During their pre-sprint planning meeting, Lorna and her business analyst separate out all the story tasks so that on Monday, the team can size the prioritized items for inclusion. If the team has too many items for a sprint, Lorna will make the final decision on what will and what will not be included, and she will communicate this information to the product owners.

11:00 a.m.

Trailhead time! Each Friday, the team spends an hour on Trailhead working on anything they like. Lorna is studying for Platform App Builder. Others on her team are studying for PD1, Sharing & Visibility, and Pardot. The team celebrates whenever someone completes a badge and gets the on-screen confetti.

NEWS

Noon   12:00PM

During the week, Lorna is so busy that she usually has fifteen or thirty minutes for lunch. Fridays are a bit quieter, so she can take a little longer. Today, she eats lunch while taking a walk alone outside along the wharf. This is the time when Lorna listens to a podcast or the news to catch up on what's happening in the world.

1:00 p.m.

It's license renewal time for the company's Salesforce orgs, so she spends time looking through the quote from Salesforce and speaking with some of the product owners about licenses for their area. Managing a platform with multiple business units can be tricky, so Lorna also speaks with Salesforce and internal procurement employees.

1:30 p.m.

During the next sprint, the team will kick-off a new initiative, Lead & Opportunity Management, for a new team on the platform.

The company is excited and deciding whether to leverage the custom functionality that another business unit is using or to use the standard out-of-the-box functionality. The team has a complex platform, so the business analyst, developer, and Lorna are working through a series of recommendations to make to the team. Part of this includes poring over the process documents they have and shadowing some of the users to physically see what steps they take in their processes and learn about impacts on the other business units on the platform. This project will take a couple of months, so this is very early in discovery.

3:00 p.m.

The team has a "sprint retro" whereby they evaluate the highlights and lessons learned from the last sprint. Today, the team is reviewing a major deployment that happened last night—streamlining Activity Management processes across the entire user base. They previously all had different page layouts, fields, and reporting, so streamlining was complex, exciting, and immensely valuable to the users.

4:00 p.m.

Time to wind down and check emails. Because it's Friday afternoon, there's a bit of banter in the office, and the last hour of the day is nice and relaxed.

5:00 p.m.

Time to head home for the weekend.

CHAPTER EIGHT:
The End-User Technical Pathway

In this chapter, we will look at the technical pathway, which generally begins as a developer. As a reminder, technical pathways stand apart from functional pathways in that rather than focusing on business interactions, professionals who follow this pathway focus on building solutions using a deep understanding of Salesforce.

Professionals who follow the end-user technical pathways generally begin their careers as developers working for companies that use Salesforce to support their business processes. These companies can be large or small, and they can be in a range of industries, such as financial services, healthcare, communications and media, or retail.

END USER TECHNICAL CAREER ROLES

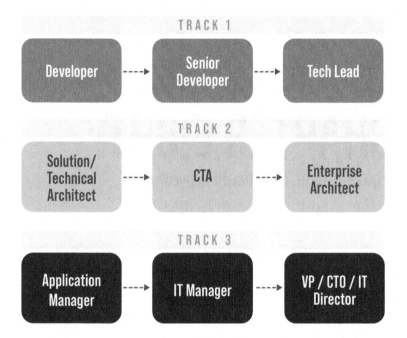

The End User Technical Career Roles diagram depicts three tracks for technical Salesforce roles. The first track is where many people start, and it is where many love to stay—coding and developing solutions on the Salesforce platform. Larger organizations will have a team of developers and offer the possibility of moving to a senior developer role and then technical lead.

The second track is the architect level track and is usually project focused. Professionals in these roles are focused on translating requirements into appropriate technical solutions using the Salesforce platform and other integrated components.

The third track is for people who enjoy managing applications, projects, and people. Application managers, IT managers, and senior IT managers spend their time managing systems, projects, and stakeholders, and communicating with the people impacted by the project. In addition, managers define strategy and how Salesforce can best be used to support business objectives.

Following are brief descriptions of the various roles that might be included in a technical pathway. Remember that overlap exists, and that companies have various titles that might describe similar positions.

TRACK 1

Developer

As their name suggests, developers develop the various features of the Salesforce platform. Their job duties include coding, configuration, maintenance, installation, testing, and debugging, as well as managing timelines and producing technical documentation.

At a small end-user firm, a developer might work as a solo developer alongside an administrator (or the developer might be the administrator). In a larger firm, the developer has room for growth, moving on and becoming senior developer, technical team lead, and perhaps IT manager, if capabilities, interests and opportunity align.

Senior Developer

A senior developer has much of the same job responsibilities as a developer but has generally worked a few years as a developer. The senior developer is responsible for assisting in technical design, helping other developers solve issues, and working on multiple projects and deadlines delegated to the development team.

Technical Team Lead

This position represents someone who has advanced in their career. A technical team lead generally has solution design and architecting skills and has delivered complex business solutions within the Salesforce ecosystem. The technical lead serves as the lead member of the company's development team and does limited coding.

From here, a person may be interested in becoming an architect or pursuing a managerial role.

TRACK 2

Solution/Technical Architect

A technical architect is similar to a solution architect. Both are focused on translating problems into solutions leveraging the Salesforce platform. However, a technical architect will have deeper technical knowledge than a solutions architect and often comes from a development background. A technical architect will often be hands-on and involved in the implementation activities and even lead the development team.

Some organizations may have just one architect that takes on the role of both solution and technical architect, whereas in larger projects, there may be a dedicated solutions architect who works with a technical architect or technical team lead.

CTA (Certified Technical Architect)

A Salesforce architect who wants to specialize in Salesforce may aim to achieve the CTA certification credential. A CTA has knowledge, skills, and experience in all Salesforce domains. Certified technical architects typically work on complex enterprise-sized projects. They understand how Salesforce fits into and integrates in an overall IT landscape. As the most knowledgeable Salesforce people on a project, they often act as advisors and require high-level communication and presentation skills and interact with all levels of an organization.

Enterprise Technical Architect

A Salesforce architect or CTA may decide they are interested not only in Salesforce architecture but also in architecture at the enterprise level. An enterprise architect aligns architecture with organization strategy and objectives. They focus on defining and delivering the target architecture and the technology roadmap. They have a broad technology focus including Salesforce and have a blend of business and technology knowledge.

TRACK 3

Application Manager ----> IT Manager ----> VP / CTO / IT Director

TRACK 3

Application Manager

An application manager is similar to a platform manager. The application manager manages the implementation, enhancement, and maintenance of the Salesforce application and other related systems to deliver business services to end-users and partners. The application manager manages custom Salesforce development work as well as maintenance and day-to-day "business as usual" requests for changes and enhancements. An application manager works with business stakeholders to prioritize requests and projects.

IT Manager

Professionals aspiring to specialize in IT management may progress from application manager role to IT manager. An IT manager leads the IT department and manages the IT resources, including but not limited to the Salesforce team. They are responsible for delivering IT priorities, which often include the expanded use of Salesforce.

VP/CTO/IT Director

Those professionals seeking to reach the senior IT management level may achieve it via working in Salesforce and IT management roles.

These management roles are focused on ensuring all technologies are aligned to support business objectives, approve technology roadmaps, and oversee larger projects. These professionals will manage IT activity and priorities and lead and manage the IT team. Increasingly, cloud solutions, including Salesforce, are playing a large part in the future landscapes of IT management. When an organization has already started implementing Salesforce, senior management will champion the use of Salesforce and other cloud technologies.

How does a person move from developer to senior developer to technical lead to IT manager?

Let us start with the requisites for moving from developer to senior developer. To secure this job promotion, act like a senior developer (without stepping on the senior developer's toes, of course). Take extreme ownership of the project, meaning that you should go above and beyond what is asked of you. Complete work to the highest standard. Look for ways to improve both coding tasks and the development process. Help other developers in the team with issues to get tasks completed. Look for opportunities to learn and grow. Be seen as a problem solver and someone that people turn to for help and advice. For each project, go out of your way to ask end-users and stakeholders for feedback. Remind them that you want to meet their goals.

In other words, step up your game. Instead of reacting to requests, try to understand the end-user, as well as their pain points, goals, and needs. Pay attention to the whole process. Raise your hand and recommend improvements to the process, and try to make other people's jobs easier.

Finally, and perhaps most importantly, ask what you need to do to be promoted. Then, go out and do that.

Develop a reputation as a problem-solver

Improve coding and development processes

Raise your hand and help other team members

Start with a bachelor's degree in IT, computer science, information systems, or a related field.

Find opportunities to learn and grow

Getting Promoted in Your Technical Career

Continue to earn certifications

Gain experience leading and managing IT projects and rolling out IT infrastructure across various technologies

Develop your soft skills

Complete work to the highest standard

Of course, this assumes that you are working at a firm that has room for growth. Like working as an administrator, a developer's upward mobility depends upon the size of the end-user firm. Large-scale firms have more job opportunities than small firms, so developers working for small firms oftentimes need to change firms to advance their careers. If you have a year or two of experience as a developer working for a small firm and come with great references, you will likely find a job at a larger firm that offers more by way of mobility.

Once you have grown to senior developer, the next step is technical team lead. This is often a matter of time. Most firms will require a minimum of four or five years of experience in technology implementation, as well as two or three years directly in Salesforce. You will also need to have demonstrated leadership skills.

This is where your soft skills will really come into play. As described in Part Four of this book, you will need excellent communication skills, conflict resolution skills, and feedback skills. You will also need to know how to bring out the best in people, hold them accountable, and inspire them to meet goals.

Management is not for everyone, and there is no shame in admitting that this is a role in which you would not thrive. If you prefer to work in a silo, dislike group projects, and cannot stomach the thought of firing someone, consider that you can shine as a developer, senior developer, or technical lead.

But if you are interested in moving into management, IT manager comes next. Keep in mind that an IT manager is responsible for the entirety of the company's computer and information systems. This includes but is not limited to Salesforce. From the hardware and software of an organization to its network, IT managers are charged with installing, maintaining, and securing systems.

Therefore, to move into this position, you will need to take your technical knowledge beyond Salesforce. Generally, IT managers would have a bachelor's degree in information technology, computer science, information systems, or a related field, as well as a few years of experience working in IT operations. They also need to have a firm grasp on IT infrastructure and best practices, as well as experience leading and managing large IT projects and rolling out IT infrastructures across various technologies.

How do you get this experience? The advice is simple: Insert yourself, without stepping on toes. If you make it known that you are willing to lend a hand on projects that fall outside the scope of your job responsibilities, you will develop this experience.

Fortunately, the need for Salesforce professionals working in technical roles is high. The annual growth rate for developers is 21 percent. Of course, getting your first job is not always easy, so let us take a look at some case studies of people who are working in various technical roles.

> Your career will grow faster if you have the initiative to take stock of where you are today, plan where you would like to be in the future, and take action. For a free analysis of your current career opportunities, head over to
> https://cloudtalent360.com/career-assessment-book-offer/

DOMINICK DEFAZIO:
From Sales to CTO at the Age of 23

At the young age of 23, Dominick DeFazio is the chief technology officer for a nonprofit, teaches classes in development, and works a side job as a contract developer.

Dominick DeFazio began his Salesforce career somewhat unexpectedly. He was working as a sales rep at a New York startup company that sold hearing aids. The startup used Salesforce for managing the sales team, following leads, and logging activities of the sales team, but Dominick knew that the Salesforce org was not properly configured. For instance, the time it took to log a single phone call often lasted longer than the phone call itself.

Dominick took the initiative to learn about Salesforce so that he could better use the tools Salesforce offers to improve process efficiency and automation. He started with Process Builder and workflow rules, and then he learned about ready-made tools and apps available through the AppExchange.

Dominick was quickly promoted to developer at the startup, leaving his role as a salesperson to focus completely on developing functionality in Salesforce for his colleagues to use. It became more and more clear to Dominick that he was well suited for the role, and as the projects grew in complexity, so did his skills.

Dominick also knew this was a rare chance for someone who went to business school—who lacked a degree in computer science or a related field—to get experience with developing. His experience in sales provided him with the background in understanding what a salesperson would look for from a developer, so he thrived in this role.

However, his pay was not competitive, and he lived in New York City, one of the most expensive cities in the world. After a year, he decided to look for another job.

"It was really difficult for me to leave the hearing aid startup because of how pivotal I felt my role was at that company."

However, Dominick was so impressed with one recruiter that he left his job at the startup to accept a position as a lead developer.

"This recruiter who hired me was actually recruiting for an internal role at the recruitment company he worked for, and I was impressed by his recruiting. That bode well, so I took the position as soon as it was offered to me," he said. *"It was a difficult choice, and I wanted to be done with it as soon as possible."*

At the time of his first interview for this book, Dominick was working two jobs. His primary job was lead developer for the recruiting company, and he had a side contract for a small nonprofit company whereby he wore many hats. Dominick helped with email marketing, development, tech strategies, and database management.

At the recruiting company, his work involved making sure that everyone within the recruiting company, from the front office to the back office, could complete their work within Salesforce, which he believes provides the best solutions for recruiters. As the lead developer, Dominick managed several other developers, including his roommate, whom Dominick had trained as a developer in his off-hours.

Dominick's days were always different, but they usually began by determining his priorities. At the recruiting firm, about ten to twenty projects were running at any given time, so his first step each day was to determine what needs to be done immediately. After determining his day's priorities, Dominick delegated and managed the developers who worked for him. The rest of the day was usually spent coding.

In the evenings, Dominick worked for the nonprofit or taught classes from his apartment to friends who were learning how to code. The classes have been so successful that three of his friends have started their Salesforce careers thanks to his coaching. One of them is his roommate, who worked under him at the recruiting company.

"My advice to the people I teach is this: Find an environment in which you are going to be able to learn the skills required to be a developer but not feel the pressure of being a developer," said Dominick. *"That environment is probably really rare, but oftentimes those projects that are most vital for a company are also the easiest projects. Start with the easiest first and then gradually increase the difficulty of projects. It's very easy to get scared off by seeing very complicated code, but there's really no reason to fear. Worst-case scenario, if you do not have the skills to write out a custom solution, oftentimes you can do the same thing with process automation tools."*

Several months after his first interview for this book, the nonprofit company Dominick worked for on a contract basis approached him to offer him the role of chief technology officer.

"They knew I had a full-time job, so they told me to name my price," he said. *"I couldn't really refuse that, but I was in a bit of a predicament because I felt committed to my full-time job."*

Dominick came up with a solution: He would ask his boss at the recruiting company if he could work remotely and on his own schedule. This way, he could commit to the nonprofit as CTO and keep working as a developer for the recruiting company.

"I thought it was a reasonable solution because my job involved coding, which can be done remotely, and I had already proven that I could work remotely."

"But right off the bat, the CTO of the recruiting company refused my offer."

Long story short, Dominick and his boss began a standoff that would result in Dominick and his roommate, a junior developer at the recruiting company, being fired two weeks later.

"Looking back, I wish I had handled it differently," said Dominick.

But it all worked out. Ten days later, Dominick's roommate was hired as a developer for Casper Mattress, a public e-commerce company that sells sleep products. Dominick's roommate earns a higher salary and is able to work remotely.

"He learned how to code by taking a class taught by me in our apartment, then he worked as a junior developer for seven months," said Dominick. *"Now he has an amazing job working for a company that has $400 million in revenue."*

As for Dominick, the "scuffle" with his boss at the recruiting company meant that he was fully available to commit to the position as CTO of the nonprofit company. It also meant that he was down to one job, freeing up some of his time.

But the story doesn't end there.

"The CTO of the recruiting firm— the guy who fired me—reached out to me a few weeks later asking if I would do contract work for the recruiting company."

Today, Dominick is working full-time as the CTO of the nonprofit and has a side job doing contract work for his previous employer.

NATALYA MURPHY:
Part-Time Developer with Thirteen Certifications

Natalya Murphy is a developer who received thirteen Salesforce certifications in three years.

No one can call Natalya Murphy an underachiever. She wrote her first computer program in fifth grade. She received thirteen Salesforce certifications in three years. And when she owned a custom framing business, she planned to become a Certified Picture Framer because this designation would mark her as someone who knows her stuff.

"In whatever field I am in, I have always been the kind of person who sets her sights on the top of the certification track," she said. *"So of course, I wanted to go for CTA (Certified Technical Architect), the pinnacle of the Salesforce certifications."*

But that's not the way it turned out.

To understand Natalya's career in Salesforce, let's back up to college. Natalya graduated from Lawrence Technological University, located in Michigan in the United States, with a degree in electrical engineering. To earn her degree, she was required to take a programming class.

"I really liked it," she said. *"And I realized that if I had to do it over again, I would have gone to college for a degree in computer science instead."*

By the time she had this realization, though, she was married, had a young child, and was in her junior year.

"Changing degrees at that point would have meant adding a couple of years to my college experience, so I stuck with electrical engineering but focused on computer engineering as a concentration," she said.

Natalya took as many programming classes as she could, and when she graduated college, she went to work for Electronic Data Systems, an IT equipment and services company that was eventually acquired by Hewlett-Packard. She worked first as a system administrator and later as a system engineer writing software before transitioning to a role as lead software development engineer for Qwest Communications (now CenturyLink).

At some point, she had a *"stroke of insanity"* and decided to open a retail custom framing business in Omaha, the largest city in Nebraska, a state in the midwestern part of the United States. This was a huge departure from her role in technology. For a while, she maintained her job with Qwest and built her independent business. Eventually, though, she had to make a choice, and she chose to focus on her custom framing business, walking away from her career as a developer. She used her tech knowledge to create the website for the business and optimize it to drive search engine traffic to the site.

Almost six years into running the shop, she made a decision. The recession had caused a drop in business, so she and her husband no longer had employees to help with fulfilling client orders. The business was consuming every free hour she and her husband had, her children were growing older, and she wanted to homeschool them. Together, she and her husband decided it was time to close down the shop. For the next five years, Natalya didn't run a business or do any paid IT work. She did work a little in WordPress as part of a volunteer project, and she learned a small amount of php, but she wasn't deeply involved in programming on a daily basis.

When her children were a bit older and more independent, Natalya decided to get back into the workforce, and she knew she wanted to be a developer. The trouble was that she had been out of IT for a decade. Everything she knew was a decade old, and her experience was no longer relevant.

"I turned to good old Google," she said, explaining that she conducted a search for the most in-demand programming jobs. *"Salesforce kept coming up, so I decided to look into this thing called Salesforce."*

Natalya, whose husband is in the military, discovered that Salesforce had a program called VetForce, which has since been renamed Trailhead Military. VetForce allowed veterans and their spouses to get trained and take their certifications for free. Natalya joined the community and started working through Trailhead modules, which were a prerequisite before she could sign up for a free certification class or get an exam voucher. She earned her administrator certification in 2017.

"Many of us have to take required computer training every year for topics such as security awareness, and I was rushing through the trailheads that were required for me to take the tests, treating them like I would any dreaded mandatory training. I just saw them as a necessary evil instead of as a great source of information. But when I took the administrator exam, I came to understand that the trailheads were the meat of what I needed to know," she said. *"I also realized the Salesforce certifications were going to be a lot harder than I had imagined."*

Even though the experience humbled Natalya, and she vowed to study a little differently, she passed the exam. That same month, she took a pro bono job as a senior developer for a nonprofit. Natalya continued to tackle one certification after another, and as she developed more and more experience, she also took on several paid freelancing jobs.

"Every one of my clients had multiple clients of their own that I was working with, and it got to be too much," she said. To simplify her life, Natalya approached one client and asked if they would be willing to commit to a minimum number of contract hours a week. This would allow her to phase out of doing work for other clients. As fortune would have it, the client was staffing up its Salesforce practice, and the company hired Natalya as a part-time developer.

Natalya has been with the company ever since.

Along the way, she set her sights on earning the coveted CTA certification. Earning a CTA isn't as simple as taking one test. First you need to pass a series of exams to earn your application architect and system architect credentials, and then you need to pass the CTA board review exam.

"I knew that to be successful, I needed accountability, so I started a study group through Ladies Be Architects," she said. She relied on this study group to pass two certifications. And that's when Natalya went to a CTA prep class.

"It was eye opening," she said, bluntly. During the class, she was led through a mock CTA exam, which she called *"a shot of reality."* Natalya walked away from the class knowing that she was nowhere close to being ready to take the CTA board review exam.

"Passing the CTA exam is not like passing the other exams," said Natalya. *"Passing CTA requires that you know all of the information from every one of those exams deep in your bones—and not just the surface level necessary to take a written test. You have to know it well enough to condense all that information. You have to remember all your integration patterns. You have to remember your different identity patterns. You have to remember your sharing rules and synthesize that to put it into a presentation and deliver it in front of a board of people so that you can pass the CTA."*

At the same time, Natalya was working on a deep development project alongside a solution architect and a technical architect.

"The architects spent a lot of time in meetings. I don't want to spend my time in meetings," she said. *"I like being a head-down developer."*

"I realized that CTA was not something I wanted to do," she said. *"I do not want to be an architect. I want to be a developer. I want to do that heads-down development and geek out on writing code. I want to figure out how to solve the pattern because that's where I am happiest."*

And this is why a person's career path is deeply personal. Natalya found a home she loved with development, and, at least for now, that's where her journey is leading her.

CASE STUDY

JULIAN VIRGUEZ:
Title Unknown, but Best Described as an Architect and Tech Lead

Julian Virguez is not quite sure of his title. He is part technical lead, part architect, and part developer.

Julian Virguez is an architect/tech lead whose Salesforce journey began as a consultant working in Java and Apex for an Australian consulting firm. Prior to that, he studied IT in Colombia and worked in tech support in the UK.

Through his job as a consultant, Julian began working with the CMS-related aspects of the business, where he slowly gained knowledge of Salesforce.

"I was very excited about it because, to be honest, I wanted to find a new career path, and this was very exciting. It was the boom of cloud computing and software as a service. Now, we take the cloud and SaaS for granted, but this was in 2012 when everything was in transition."

Julian went on to say that the transition was easy. The company he worked for needed more people to work in Salesforce, and they were willing to let Julian learn it from scratch.

"So that's what I did. I started learning by myself and work colleagues," he said, noting the many different projects and challenges he was given due to the variety of consultant work.

"Once I started working within Salesforce, I realized the power and capabilities of the platform."

As for how he learned the platform, Julian had this to say: "I just had to google everything and keep working until I got to a solution," he said. Julian also used the AppExchange and developer forums to find solutions during his initial training.

Julian eventually earned his Admin, App Builder, Platform Developer I, Platform Developer II, and Sales Cloud certifications.

Today, he works for a company that provides salary-outsourcing solutions to other businesses.

Julian's role is not entirely defined, but it is part technical lead, part architect, part developer. He has been with the company for five years, and his role has evolved as the company has grown. The "business-as-usual" support items are managed by others while Julian helps with strategic initiatives, such as identity management, integrations and mobile-app development.

"It's an architectural-level role, but since I have so much knowledge of the history of the company, I still do a little bit of coding and a bit of designing," he said. *"Mine is a varied role that is not easy to define. I was heavily involved with the Lightning migration."*

His team is small, with much space to grow, and because the company has been experiencing upward growth, his role is always changing.

"The company is very mature in terms of how they use Salesforce," he said, noting that this minimizes the need for excessive focus on the troubleshooting and user-training that other developers might spend time on. Rather, Julian spends time focusing on how Salesforce integrates with the other tools and technologies at the company.

"Salesforce is not the only answer for a company," he says. *"Part of my job is seeing whether Salesforce is the right answer for that need."*

Beyond that, having technical skills are not the only requirement of his job.

"You need to be an organized person," he said. *"You need to be able to work and collaborate well with others. And you need to do the extra ten percent and really care about the company and the solution you are providing."*

Julian says that being a technical lead requires a whole different set of skills than being a senior developer.

"As a technical lead, you have to be able to challenge the other developers to get better and come up with solutions," he said. *"Sometimes I think I know the answer of how to do something, but I have to let go of my way of solving things and see if the other developers have a better way of doing things. In the beginning, it was hard for me to let go of telling people how I think it should be done, but I learned that giving ownership and empowering the team led to better solutions, and it helped the people on my team grow."*

Beyond that, being a technical lead requires giving feedback and setting expectations, which can feel uncomfortable for everyone.

"I review code, which can be frustrating for new developers because they are learning, and I have to send back parts of code that do not meet our standards. Eventually, though, they realize that it makes them better developers."

To that note, Julian encourages lead developers to ask their team members to review code as well.

"It helps to normalize feedback and reduce making mistakes," he said.

RENÉ GÖRGENS:
Senior Architect, Consultant, User Group Leader, and YeurDreamin' Team Member

René Görgens is a senior architect for a consulting firm in Luxembourg.

René Görgens is a senior architect for a consulting firm in Luxembourg. René lives just on the other side of the Luxembourg border in Trier, a German city in the Moselle wine region. René is the founder and leader of Trier's user group, as well as a team member for YeurDreamin', which is the number-one Salesforce community event for Benelux, which are the three neighboring countries of Belgium, the Netherlands, and Luxembourg.

René is a night owl, so he graciously met with me for a Zoom interview at midnight in Germany while I ate breakfast at 8 a.m. in Australia.

René started his career doing freelance IT management for small offices. At the same time, he was a student assistant in the University of Trier's department of philosophy.

In 2007, René began his career in Salesforce at an asset management company that had just adopted Salesforce as its CRM.

"My beginnings were humble," he said. He wore many hats: data cleansing agent, administrator, internal support agent, and client service assistant. Eventually, though, René began working up the ladder. He enhanced the CRM solution through declarative development, Apex, and Visualforce, and architected and implemented customer applications.

With hard work, he was able to assume a broader role as senior solution architect, business analyst, and project manager responsible for the technical side of challenging projects, while also supervising the operational side of the team.

In 2016, he moved into a full-time business analyst role at the same company, working within the newly established project management office. René performed functional analysis on current projects, including new website implementation and document management review, as well as maintenance of internal governance framework such as process flowcharts, business procedures, and role descriptions.

In 2018, René assumed his current role as a senior architect at a Luxembourg consulting firm. He was kind enough to talk about his work as a consultant, as a senior architect, and as an active member of the community.

Let's start with his role as a consultant.

"Consulting is not about technology, but it is fundamentally about trust and relationships," he told me. *"If you have a real curiosity for who is in front of you, how they have evolved, and what their career ambitions are, then you can respect them. Don't try to bend them to your will. That isn't consulting. Consulting is about functioning as a tool to help other people realize their ambitions, and that means that you take a step back, and you are respectful of what you are hearing, and you are a good listener."*

"It helps to think of consulting as a sales role," said René.

"The key is getting people to trust you," he said. *"How do you do that? You show up when they expect you to. You can make a good start to a conversation by being respectful and letting people engage and asking them questions. It's the small gestures that set the tone of the conversation. Then, you say things that make sense. You have a good attitude and make a good impression. You cater to their ambitions and highlight what is important to the client."*

René noted that consultants need sales skills because they are often required to say things that can be difficult to say—and even harder to hear.

"You have to be able to say to a board or an executive: You have overlooked something in your company for three years. You have an inefficient process because you are trying to save money by using a free application. You have no functional coverage on this very important function, and Salesforce can fix this for you."

René called consulting *"a bit of a kabuki dance."*

"Consultants need to watch and react to the interplay of various moments in a setting that can turn around very quickly," he said. *"It takes quite a bit of social intelligence to be a successful consultant. A client's behavior can be part of their role, so they might feel obliged to probe, which can make them seem a bit more critical or a bit more severe, and the next moment, they are laughing and relaxed. You have to know when you are in a humorous situation, and you also have to know when that situation no longer exists and it is time to enumerate strictly and go about business in a very disciplined way."*

Beyond that, René said that good consultants should plant seeds for future projects.

"Give them ideas of what is possible, and encourage your client to set their next ambitious milestone."

When we transitioned our conversation to the architect side of his work, René cautioned developers from pursuing a role as an architect unless they also understand the requirements-gathering side of the equation.

"You can know the technology and tools to an almost perfect extent, but that's not enough," he said. *"You need to have skills as a business analyst."*

"If you are a senior developer who has not reached out to the community, leveraged Trailhead, and built a network so that you can extend your horizons beyond the technical sphere, then I think you might have a very narrow mindset. You will have an incomplete view and will be unable to explain why your solution will address their business requirements."

"But if you are a halfway good business analyst, then you already have a good chance of becoming a relatively good architect," he said, noting that an architect will need a sound understanding of processes that are built into applications and that support business functions.

René recommended that anyone pursuing a role as an architect should be "infinitely curious."

"You're not supposed to think as an architect: No, I can't do that. It's not something I know. Instead, when you hear about something new, you should be curious. Start by reading the superficial articles and researching more details. Then read a white paper. Become proficient. Do a proof-of-concept or write a small app that you can exchange with others. Take an exam."

"But you are not allowed to shy away from things. You have to adopt a mindset of continuous learning. You have to think: Wouldn't it be cool if someone gives me a new methodology that has not yet been used in my toolkit?"

Before letting René off the call—it was close to 1 a.m. his time—I asked him to talk about his experience in the community.

"The moment I discovered the community in Luxembourg was a pivotal moment," he said, noting that the Salesforce community defied the normal competitive boundaries established in other industries. In the Salesforce community, René found suppliers, advisors, consultants, and end-users all working together.

"*My first YeurDreamin' event in Amsterdam was a real eye-opener,*" he said. René was prepared for the content, but he was not mentally prepared for the number of connections he would make—connections with people who are famous in the Salesforce ecosystem, sitting next to him, inviting him to lunch, and asking to follow him on Twitter.

"*These are people with such inspiring stories, and when you go to an event, you find out they are normal people like me and you—totally normal and modest, even shy. And they will all help in any way they can.*"

René called the YeurDreamin' events "*a whirlwind.*"

"*It's like being thrown into a washing machine,*" he said. "*You come out all the better with the confidence to be appreciated and to appreciate and support others.*"

Today, René is a local user group leader, and he manages the social accounts for YeurDreamin'.

"*I should have gotten involved years earlier.*"

Day in the life: - - - - - - - - - - - - - - - - - -
MEET RENÉ GÖRGENS

René Görgens is a senior architect who works for a consulting firm in Luxembourg, a small, prosperous, and beautiful country hosting many EU institutions and having a more diverse economy than first meets the eye. René generously shared the details of one day in his life as a senior architect working for a Salesforce Gold Partner consulting firm.

René, who has thirteen years of Salesforce experience and six certifications, is responsible for delivering architected enterprise applications on Salesforce, whether they be out-of-the-box functionalities, custom developments, or both. His experience includes project management, architecture, and hands-on development. On this day in his life, though, he is a coach.

"I think coaching is a key skill that you should have when you are in a senior position," he said. *"Remember that you are being called upon to inspire. There are quite a few days when I am in a coaching experience."*

6:00 a.m.
René is a night owl, usually working until midnight or 1 a.m., but today, he is up early. Today is the first of a three-day on-site workshop he is facilitating at a client's country office to help 15 employees prepare mentally and practically for the client's Salesforce rollout.

After showering, dressing, and eating breakfast, René takes one last look at the presentation he has prepared for the morning, which provides an overview of the various elements the team will be discussing over the next three days.

"I don't tend to be nervous nowadays, but most of my previous meetings with these employees were brief, so I did not know them well," he said. During a typical day, René routinely meets new people, and he says that his ability to quickly form relationships is critical to his success as a consultant.

9:00 a.m.

René arrives on-site, where he kicks off the day with an overview. *"Essentially, my mission was to create human relationships and enthusiasm,"* he said.

10:00 a.m.

René wants to learn more about the team members' anxieties with respect to the forthcoming rollout so that he can help boost their confidence. He charts the team's positive associations, as well as their negative associations, answering their questions and discussing the CRM functionalities and scale of the roll-out.

NOON

René eats lunch with the team, where he continues to address questions about Salesforce, though conversations turn to more personal matters, such as hobbies and families.

1:00 p.m.

René spends the afternoon in smaller group meetings with the various groups of employees, including leadership, project managers, marketing team, and sales team. Over the next two days, he will spend more time ironing out the specific details of the plan so that he has  a detailed design that addresses all concerns. Today, though, is about bringing harmony, unity, and enthusiasm to the group.

"When I run a workshop, I talk to people from different departments who have different priorities and perspectives," he said. *"Often, I identify conflicts, but I see these conflicts as a benefit. The truth is, their perspectives are usually complementary. They all want the same goal, but they might lack information about some other department. When I can identify the conflicts, I can facilitate an opportunity for everyone to talk through their different perspectives so that they all see a bigger picture. I let them talk to each, and then quite naturally, they come to some conclusion that everyone supports in terms of the overall mission. This allows me to weave the conversation into a larger context and refocus everyone on the shared goals."*

"We should not consider conflicts to be an interruption. Conflicts are productive elements when they identify elements we have not yet considered," he said, noting that his smaller group meetings often help him identify amended requirements or new requirements he had not previously considered.

4:00 p.m.

During his meetings, René has identified several changes that will need to be made to make the roll-out more efficient, and he has a long night of working ahead of him. The implementation is relatively straightforward and will take place on Sales Cloud, but nonetheless, he is eager to return home and get to work in preparation for Days 2 and 3 of the workshop. Nonetheless, he takes the time to bring the group together to recap and reflect on the day. Throughout the day, René has addressed many of the concerns that the team identified during the morning session, so he can feel the enthusiasm rising, which was his goal for the day as the "coach."

6:00 p.m.

René eats dinner and gets to work. Tomorrow will be another long day, so he tries to wrap up his design work by 11 p.m. so he can get a good night's sleep.

CHAPTER NINE:
The Consultant Pathway

Consultants come in many forms: You can start a career as a consultant by working for an existing firm, you can transition from being an administrator, a developer, or a business analyst at an end-user firm to working for a consultancy firm, or you can start your own firm or become a freelancer. We will discuss the last two—starting your own firm and becoming a freelancer—in Chapter Ten about entrepreneurs. In this chapter, we talk about the career pathway that starts by working as a junior consultant and ends with being a managing consultant, as seen in the Consulting Career Roles diagram.

CONSULTING CAREER ROLES

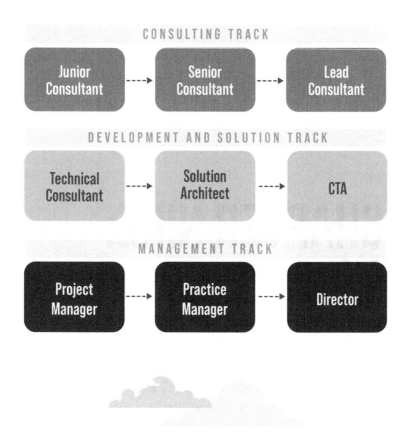

The roles, titles, and responsibilities in a consulting firm will vary and will depend on the company size. There will also be overlap between roles, particularly in smaller organizations, where the team will work according to the current demands of clients, projects, and opportunities presented. The following provides a general overview of typical roles found in Salesforce consulting companies.

CONSULTING TRACK

CONSULTING TRACK

Junior Consultant

A junior consultant is the novice member of a team of consultants delivering a solution to a customer. Junior consultants will have less client-facing interactions but rather execute tasks that have been delegated to them by senior or lead consultants. The larger consulting firms often hire people straight out of college into junior consultant roles. Alternatively, people who have Salesforce experience but are transitioning into a consulting role could start here.

Senior Consultant

Senior consultants are hands-on in helping the lead consultant determine the direction of a project. They are mid-level leaders who participate in the ownership of the project, work directly with clients, facilitate workshops, and develop and deliver key components. Senior consultants also onboard, train, and mentor junior consultants.

Lead Consultant

Lead consultants are the consultants who sit at the top of a project as owners. They are masters not only in Salesforce but also in business processes. As such, they innovate complex solutions, delegating much of the hands-on work to senior and junior consultants. This is where the buck stops: If a project encounters a problem, lead consultants are responsible for finding the solution and changing the direction when necessary. Like senior consultants, they also act as mentors and trainers to others on the team.

DEVELOPMENT AND SOLUTION TRACK

DEVELOPMENT AND SOLUTION TRACK

Technical Consultant

Consultants who are more technically oriented work on coding, configuration, maintenance, installation, testing, and debugging, as well as producing technical documentation.

As a technical consultant in a larger consulting firm gains experience, the consultant would move on to become a senior technical consultant. A senior technical consultant is responsible for assisting in technical design, helping other consultants solve issues, and working on multiple projects.

Solution/Technical Architect

After gaining experience in a number of projects and business scenarios implementing Salesforce, a technical consultant can move onto a Salesforce architect role. Architects use their knowledge and experience to recommend and design end-to-end solutions to complex customer problems. They ensure that solutions are designed appropriately and can scale for large numbers of users and data volumes. Salesforce will often be one component of a solution in an enterprise IT landscape, so an architect needs to be familiar not only with Salesforce, but also how Salesforce will integrate with the other systems in an organization. An architect requires high-level knowledge of the complete set of Salesforce clouds, products, and features, as well as other commonly used cloud and on-premise technologies and systems to design appropriate solutions.

CTA (Certified Technical Architect)

A CTA has knowledge, skills, and experience in all Salesforce domains. Certified technical architects typically work on complex enterprise-sized projects. They understand how Salesforce fits into and integrates in an overall IT landscape. As the most knowledgeable Salesforce person on a project and sometimes in the entire consulting organization, they often act as advisors and require high-level communication and presentation skills and interact with all levels of an organization. In a consulting organization, they are in very high demand and can be expected to work across multiple projects and help win new business.

MANAGEMENT TRACK

Project Manager

Project managers (sometimes called engagement managers) in a consulting firm will be responsible for managing one or more projects, based on the size of the projects. Some projects may only require part-time effort whereas large projects may require a full-time presence at the client site for the duration of the project or program of work. This is a typical project management role that juggles scope, resources, schedules, and budgets. However, project managers working in a Salesforce environment will be more successful if they understand the capabilities of the platform, which will allow them to manage stakeholders' expectations, resolve issues, and manage the resources in the project team.

Practice Managers

Practice managers manage the team in a consulting company. This includes the developers, business analysts, project managers, and architects). It is an operational role that consists primarily of oversight and management but can also include pre-sales, managing proposals and statements of work and even participating in the requirements-gathering workshops and solution design.

Director

A director has end-to-end accountability for a consulting practice, including strategy, sales, profitability, recruiting, delivery, consulting, and operational aspects. They lead business development activities and identify opportunities to ensure a strong pipeline of work to support growth plans.

Directors drive overall growth of practice for the long term and set the practice vision and strategy. They drive business development, alliance leadership, talent strategy, oversight of delivery work, and thought leadership. They participate in industry forums, events, and speaking engagements. Directors manage delivery on key accounts and projects to ensure a high level of customer satisfaction, and they are accountable for engagement performance, quality, risk, and customer and team satisfaction.

Directors help to grow and develop the consulting team through hands-on training and coaching. They support recruiting and onboarding of new employees and development of leaders. They develop and support high performing teams, individual growth, and career development for the practice.

Having someone to coach you will increase your chances of success in the Salesforce ecosystem. Head over to **https://cloudtalent360.com/career-assessment-book-offer/** for a free career assessment with professionals who can help you maximize your career and earning potential.

> *When you work as a consultant for a large firm, your career path is defined from day one. Spend two years as a staff consultant, then spend two or three years as a senior consultant, then move onto the next level. In my experience, performance reviews have focused on whether you are meeting the requirements that move you along that path. We referred to this as "up or out."*
>
> **—Jordan Elkin**
> **Former B4 consultant**

Being a consultant isn't for everyone. It requires certain soft skills and personality traits, such as being comfortable with discomfort and accepting a wide variety of personality types. This portion of the book is dedicated to case studies so that you can begin seeing the larger picture and answer questions such as:

- **"Could I be a consultant?"**
- **"What is it really like?"**
- **"How do soft skills come into play?"**

Before we consider case studies, though, let us take a moment to answer this question: How does a person gracefully transition from being an employee at an end-user company to being a consultant? Many administrators dream of moving from an end-user career to a career at a firm.

If you are completely new and wanting to break into a career as a consultant, my advice is that you become an in-house Salesforce admin and get used to helping one team. Deliver value. Make sure you are providing an ROI. As you build expertise, earn certifications, and really understand the business inside and out, then look at being an administrator for a consulting company, where you get used to juggling more projects. Then consider whether you have the skills and interest to transition from an admin to a consultant, where you will eventually lead projects, conduct business analysis, and work on high-level solutions.

If you already have experience and you are considering moving into a consulting role, take a step back and make sure you have enough in-house experience. Do you have experience in one org or in various orgs? If you have experience in only one org, then you will look at all solutions through the lens of that one org.

The nice thing about consulting is that you will see ten or twenty orgs in one year, which is great for learning new things. But make sure you have the chops: You need to know enough about Salesforce, have excellent time management and project management skills, and be able to communicate with the client.

—Jim Bartek
CEO of Growth Heroes, a boutique consulting firm

IF THIS IS SOMETHING YOU ARE CONSIDERING, HERE ARE A FEW POINTERS FOR SETTING YOURSELF UP FOR SUCCESS:

1. Do your due diligence.

If you have never worked with multiple clients on multiple projects, do as much research as you can to make sure you actually want to make this transition. Consulting can be high-pressure: After all, you will be working on multiple projects, often with competing due dates, that require differing skills. Remember, too, that you are on the line to deliver solutions to not just one boss, but to many clients. Research the role. Read job descriptions. Ask your friends who are consultants. And, as always, be honest about whether you would thrive in this role.

Essentially, being a successful consultant is more about knowing how to best run a business versus knowing how to best run a system. If you are a wizard at Salesforce, you might know how to run the system the best, but you also have to be a wizard with the processes that make a business successful.

—Jim Bartek
CEO of Growth Heroes, a boutique consulting firm

2. Network.

Having connections will help you secure a job as a consultant, and it will help you draw clients to your firm. You can do this by starting a blog, joining user groups, and participating in the Answers community, a forum on Trailhead that allows users to ask and answer questions about the Salesforce platform.

Rob Kaplan is a senior consultant and engagement manager who says his work as a solo administrator created the foundation for a successful career as a consultant.

"If I could get on board the mothership and be a Customer Success Manager, that would be wonderful, too," he said. *"But I'm not sure I have the breadth and depth they are looking for yet. So the path for me now is consulting."*

Why does he enjoy his current consulting role?

"Varied work," he said. *"I always knew that consulting would be my last gig. With my current employer (CRMD+), my various projects have differing needs, in diverse sectors, led by a range of stakeholders. What they have in common is the desire to increase efficiency, or add a new competitive capability, that really tackles the strategic challenges that face them."*

He explained that working as a solo administrator creates the foundation for a successful career as a consultant.

"If you work as a solo administrator, you don't always get to direct the particular Salesforce clouds you are exposed to—if your employers don't want to do Marketing Cloud, you won't learn that; if they don't want to do Service Cloud, you won't learn that; and if they don't want to do a robust Sales Cloud, your learning will be confined to Trailheads."

(Continued on next page...)

> *"But you can go deep on the internal challenges that you perceive, and if you are doing your job well, you can nominate those areas for future projects where you want to personally grow as well."*

3. Be a specialist and a generalist.

As a consultant, you will be responsible for providing Salesforce-related recommendations and technical solutions to a variety of clients. You need to know enough about the platform to find solutions, which means you need to be a generalist. To this end, getting as many certifications and trailhead badges as you can shows that you have tremendous knowledge across-the-board as a generalist.

That said, if you specialize by industry or by a specific Salesforce technology, you can develop a deeper understanding and become the go-to person for that industry/technology.

My day ranges from practice management to client management and the myriad of other little responsibilities in between the spectrum. The only thing that keeps my day steady is the platform I work on: Salesforce. I must say that, as an organization, Salesforce works meticulously around the calendar to make the lives of all the other Santoshes out in the world steady. Salesforce always releases updates to the platform, works on bugs and resolves them, and conducts webinars for the welfare of the Salesforce community.

(Continued on next page...)

With this in mind, it helps to think of a successful career as a consultant a little like going back to school. You have to:

- Constantly update yourself with what's new and consider how it impacts your existing designs.
- Always pair business consulting and IT consulting to leverage the best of the platform. This is like lab activities in school where theory meets practicals.
- Have a checklist of features that comes out of the box with every Salesforce cloud offering. This is a list that grows as you deepen your knowledge.
- Ask questions that are open ended. Remember that there are two schools of requirements: 1) extrinsic requirements, which is what the client says what they want; and 2) intrinsic requirements, which is what the client believes they want. The role of a consultant is to extract intrinsic requirements. For instance, clients are often looking for ways to automate and reduce their selling time or service time. They might have an idea of how that can happen, and as consultants, we need to understand their intrinsic requirements and suggest options from prior experiences in a similar industry to drive meaningful, profit-driven conversations.
- Keep things simple. Every requirement, and every solution to a problem, stems from simplicity. While designing Salesforce solutions, focus on simplicity.
- Last and the most important: Never forget the big picture. Every client has a motive with respect to their use of Salesforce. Always focus on that motive, and work toward helping your client achieve the outcomes they want.

—Santosh Kumar Sriram
principal consultant

AYMERIC ZITO:
CEO of a Consultancy Firm

Aymeric Zito is the CEO of ProQuest Consulting in Australia.

Aymeric Zito has a bachelor's degree in cellular biology and neuroscience, and a master's degree in computer science. Freshly graduated, he was hired as a Java developer and his career quickly transitioned into the consulting industry, where he progressed to become a trainer and then a senior solution architect in the financial industry.

In 2010, he joined ProQuest Consulting, one of Australia's leading Salesforce implementation partners. ProQuest was among the first companies in Australia to become a Salesforce partner. In addition to support and operations employees, it staffs seventeen Salesforce consultants, ranging from junior consultants to lead consultants.

Aymeric started as a consultant. Today, he is ProQuest's CEO.

He was kind enough to share his story, as well as the process ProQuest uses to advance junior consultants up the career ladder.

Aymeric was introduced to Salesforce when ProQuest made the strategic move to become a Consulting and Implementation partner. The company had within its ranks passionate Salesforce professionals who talked Aymeric into learning the platform.

He was amazed at the speed at which Salesforce could deliver business value, particularly when compared to more typical technology stacks like Java or .Net.

"Salesforce certainly got my attention," he said. *"I was obviously a bit reluctant to start from scratch after a decade of coding experience in Java. It was helpful to realize that Salesforce programming language is not so far from the Java syntax. But there was so much more to learn than just the code. And the closer I looked, the more I enjoyed the platform."*

"I have been working with Salesforce for the past eight years, and I have never looked back."

From consultant, Aymeric's career at ProQuest progressed quickly. He transitioned into a couple of management roles before being promoted to COO and then CEO in 2016.

When asked about the general business skills, technical skills, and soft skills that allowed this career advance, he cited his strong technology background, seconded quickly by his interest in solving business problems.

"I have always had an interest in how a business can improve to grow faster and with better efficiencies," he said. By starting his career with consulting and training, Aymeric developed a natural interest in helping people learn more about technology, and do more with it. His passion for agile methodologies and frameworks to deliver high quality solutions in a very short amount of time was key to transition easily into management and leadership.

"I was able to lead teams to understand customers' problems and design the right solutions, but also coach them on how to deliver it."

What got him to the next level? Aymeric cites a deep interest in the company's culture. He began asking questions like: *"What does it mean to work for a company like ProQuest? How different we are from other companies? How do we articulate our core values in such a way that we can recruit the right talents to join the team? How do we make our core values show up in HR, recruitment, onboarding, performance management, performance assessment, rewards, and career progressions?"*

By nurturing these core values and defining the company's DNA, he was able to demonstrate to potential customers and employees that ProQuest is not your typical Salesforce partner. His technical background, ability to establish trust with customers and inspire employees, and his execution mindset all fed into his ability to be promoted to CEO.

So how do junior consultants in ProQuest move up the ladder?

"When consultants with little experience join our company, they start as junior consultants where they shadow a functional or technical consultant."

The company carefully monitors the junior consultant's progress over the first month, expecting the learning period to take somewhere between three and six months.

While shadowing a consultant, the junior consultant gets to learn the complete lifecycle of a project. The key focus is obviously on learning Salesforce, first how to test solutions and then gradually how to configure it. Trailhead is a great platform to help during this particular phase. Junior consultants participate as well into customer workshops, where they learn how to gather requirements and identify problems that need to be solved.

From there, junior consultants work alongside senior consultants and architects to get to know key solution design skills, including data modeling, architecture, process automation, UI/UX and system integration.

"This is probably the part that takes the longest to learn," said Aymeric. *"The consultant can learn Salesforce capabilities fairly quickly, but will take much longer to learn how such capabilities can be made of use for a particular customer of a certain size in a given industry."*

Again, the consultant's job is to understand where the client struggles and what Salesforce can bring to the table. Once a junior consultant has experience designing and implementing small features, the mentor assesses and gives the consultant feedback. When the junior consultant and mentor both feel comfortable, the junior consultant is given bigger and more complex problems.

In three to six months, when management is confident that a junior consultant has reached a certain level of autonomy to implement user stories once the solution has been designed with their mentor, the junior consultant becomes either a technical or functional consultant.

The consultant moves to senior consultant upon demonstrating that they can provide leadership during the early phases of a project, by facilitating and documenting a process-mapping workshops, solution design and sizing meetings, or integration workshops with stakeholders. They need to possess a deep knowledge of the Salesforce platform and how to design a solution based on the customer's requirements. They also need to have demonstrated mentorship skills, as they will now be assigned a junior consultant to mentor.

ProQuest has programs specifically designed to help consultants grow and move up the career ladder. Every Wednesday at lunchtime, the OneQuest initiative allows consultants to present on specific technologies and projects, receiving feedback from more senior team members. Every Thursday morning, the PQ Academy teaches more advanced consulting and development skills, which is how senior consultants become lead consultants.

Lead consultants play a key role in the solution architecture of projects, taking part in internal coaching activities to help the team on their career path, which might include getting new certifications and Trailhead badges to expand their knowledge.

Once management sees that a lead consultant has been involved in the architecture of various projects, with practical experience covering a wide range of Salesforce products and features, and also has successfully led more junior staff, then the lead is ready for the next stage.

"We look for people who care, who are curious and ask questions. Professionals who don't sit back but step up when they notice something that can be improved," said Aymeric. *"We want to hire people who come up with ideas. Don't think you aren't good enough. Don't wait for someone else to challenge the status quo. Get involved, and give your ideas a try."*

YELENA SLOBARD:
Business Analyst and Consultant

Yelena Slobard is a business analyst who works out of her home office for a small consultancy firm.

When Yelena Slobard was first introduced to Salesforce back in 2015, she was working as a phishing analyst overseeing such things as security education programs. Yelena had previously received her Bachelor of Science degree in business from the State University of New York at Buffalo, and she went on to develop expertise in information systems. When she first began using Salesforce, she thought, *"Finally! A database that makes sense!"*

Her brain naturally understood how the schema worked and how the different pieces are put together. Beyond that, she understood the soft skills necessary to interface with customers, so her next job was a natural fit. Yelena was a project manager for a sixty-person startup. In this role, she met with the departments in the company, gathered their needs, and then converted these business needs into Salesforce features and functionalities.

"Because it was a small startup, I wore fifteen other hats that were not Salesforce-related," she said. *"I realized I wanted to be a full-time Salesforce admin."*

In 2017, she became the only full-time administrator for a public company of more than one thousand users, working primarily with the sales and service teams. Just as she did in her job as a project manager, Yelena converted business processes into Salesforce features.

"I enjoyed being an administrator," she said, *"but I found that it became a bit too routine for me. I like taking on challenges and learning new things."*

Time for another career change.

At the time of our interview, Yelena worked as a business analyst from her home office for a consulting firm located in the San Francisco Bay area. She works on six to ten projects at any given time, spending most of her time in meetings with clients and colleagues.

Her day generally looks like this: Because the consultancy firm's development team is in China, she arrives to a slew of emails that she cycles through. Her priority is to determine what needs to be reviewed or tested that day.

About 70 to 90 percent of her day, though, is spent meeting with her colleagues or with her clients.

"No day is the same," she said, adding that she loves the client interactions as well as the challenges.

Still, she admitted that she does miss building. *"I earned my Platform Developer 1 certification, and I know how to code in Apex. I tend to think of all of my technical skills as a way to eventually reach an architect level."*

Her advice for people entering the workforce is this: "Willingness to network is important. Learn what you can, and find opportunities to get your hands on something real, whether that is through volunteering or helping someone that you know. Get your certifications, but at the end of the day, your success is going to come from what you have experience working on, not a piece of paper."

CARLOS SIQUEIRA:
Salesforce MVP and DevOps Sales Engineer

Carlos Siqueira is a solution and sales engineer who was nominated for Salesforce's coveted MVP award in 2017.

Carlos Siqueira is a solution and sales engineer who, in 2017, received Salesforce's MVP designation. But just nineteen months earlier, Carlos had been unemployed and had no knowledge of Salesforce.

Carlos is scrappy, and he always has been. Many years earlier, on Halloween night in 1988, Carlos arrived in the United States from Rio de Janeiro, Brazil. He did not speak English, and though he had eight years of mainframe work under his belt, Carlos spent the next nine months working as a shoe-shiner at the former World Trade Center in New York City, at McDonald's, and as a messenger while he learned the language, became a resident, and finally qualified for a job as a Mainframe Adabas/Natural Programmer/Analyst.

"I learned very early that in order to succeed in America, I could not perform the same as an American. If you were an employer in the nineties and had to choose between two people who were equally qualified, but one of them was born and raised in the USA, and the other one was a foreigner, you were most likely going to hire the person that was born in the USA. I didn't make the rules, but this was my reality as a foreigner," he said.

"You don't have to feel guilty if you are an American born and raised and living in America, but you should appreciate what you have. I cannot be level with the existing work. I have to be better than the average in order to be accepted."

The short story of how Carlos went from unemployed to Salesforce MVP in just nineteen months is this: In 2015, Carlos was experiencing tremendous pain in his left hand, arm, and shoulder.

At the time, he was working a mainframe contract job that required him to fly back and forth between Tampa, Florida, and Los Angeles, California, every few weeks.

"The job was terrible," he said, so he decided to change his life. He quit his job and, on Thanksgiving Day in 2015, Carlos had neck surgery.

With a titanium plate in his neck, Carlos needed six months of limited physical activity, so on that same day, he started playing around in Trailhead.

This was in November, and by February of the following year, Carlos had his first gig as an intern supporting 85 users, driving 1.5 hours each way and working for free.

He had no team. It was just Carlos, Trailhead, and the Salesforce community.

"I was looking for a mentor, and I couldn't find anyone," he said. When he asked around, he could not find anyone to help him. One day, he asked a question in the forum Salesforce Success Community, and no one was able to help him. Fortunately, he was able to find the answer on his own, so he added the answer to his own question.

He decided to make this a habit. Anytime he had a question and found the answer, he would post the information.

"If I have the question, I am sure a lot of other people have the same question," he said.

A few months later, in July of 2016, Carlos became a Certified Salesforce Administrator, and a few months later, he was hired as a junior administrator—his first paid Salesforce job.

But three weeks later, he realized a hard truth when the company decided to transition him from a full-time salaried employee to a part-time hourly contractor.

"They were after my certification. My certification allowed them to qualify as a Salesforce partner," he said. *"Beware of those companies trying to exploit you."*

When Carlos realized that his now-contract-job was exploiting him, particularly after they failed to provide work to him for several weeks, he quit and took a job driving for Uber. He spent more time on Trailhead, got involved in user groups and the Salesforce community, and did all the networking he could to increase his chance of employment. He helped people on Salesforce Success Community, Twitter, LinkedIn, Skype, in Hangouts, via WhatsApp, on email, and anywhere else he could answer Salesforce questions.

And in February of 2017, he received the Salesforce Platform App Builder certification.

The next week, he was hired as technical support for a Salesforce partner that had clients in Latin America, India, Europe, Asia, and the United States. Then, in August, he started working as a consultant for an emerging cloud company in Brazil.

All this time, he continued being involved in the community.

"On September 17, 2017, I got the big news that I was voted Salesforce MVP. It was a shock when I got the message from Salesforce," he said. *"I had to send several messages back and forth to confirm the fact that I was Salesforce MVP."*

When it comes to the "benefits" of being MVP, Carlos has a different message than you might expect to hear.

"The greatest reward of being an MVP is not the status but the ability to be the channel through which the community gets connected," he said.

Unfortunately, Carlos said that too many people attempt to earn MVP status only because they want the designation. They want to be able to claim they are MVPs and use it to earn celebrity within the community when, in fact, they do not necessarily want to make a positive impact or give to the community.

"I am an MVP not because of my strong technical skills," said Carlos, who has more than thirty years of experience in IT and four years with the Salesforce ecosystem. *"I am an MVP because of my involvement with the community and the immediate 'giving back' I am engaged in. I was given this honor because I am a mentor; because I am a product evangelist, educator; because I am involved in the community; and because I will give back, share, and be humble about my knowledge."*

Since earning his MVP status, Carlos has been to several Dreamforce and TrailheaDX events, and he has been a guest speaker for both events, as well as various Dreamin' events. He has earned six other certifications, including Service Cloud Consultant, Field Service Lightning Consultant, Community Cloud Consultant, Sales Consultant, Advanced Administrator, and Salesforce Certified Instructor.

Today, Carlos works for Copado, which is the top DevOps that is 100 percent native to Salesforce, offering solutions that bring together administrators, developers, architects, end-users, project managers and release managers. Carlos is a sales engineer for the company and a Copado Certified Administrator, and a Copado Certified Developer.

His role involves demos and "product evangelism," meaning he talks to other mature Salesforce developers, administrators, and architects, and shows them how Copado can offer a high-quality DevOps solution for their company.

His advice for people who are new to Salesforce is this:

"Use the community, but be realistic about the people in the community. We have an amazing Ohana, but at the end of the day, there are zebra stripes and tiger stripes. Look for the people who are authentically willing to help, who would do this regardless of what company they worked for because helping is part of their DNA. Be aware that people will tell you that there are millions and millions of jobs out there, and you can get certified and get one of those jobs just by playing around in Trailhead. But that isn't accurate. The platform is your best option to learn for free all that Salesforce has to offer, but you need to put the time and not cut corners or rush for badges and certification. Most people are in the community to help you, and some of them are there to try to promote themselves or win an MVP award."

Carlos has other advice that runs against the grain. Of the common advice to start your career by volunteering, Carlos offers this warning: *"Nonprofits do not have much money, so they cannot afford to have someone new come in and make a big mistake. Make sure that if you are interning for a nonprofit, they have other Salesforce people who can oversee you."*

"My message for those considering Salesforce (or any other career change) is to follow your passion, be active, get involved in the community, ask, talk, post, seek a mentor, start to give back immediately, share, and be humble."

DONNA HUDSON:
From Retirement to Business Analyst and Consultant

Donna Hudson is a business analyst who works out of her home office for a mid-sized consultancy firm.

"I know ladies are not supposed to tell their age," said Donna Hudson, a business analyst for a consulting company, *"but maybe it would be encouraging to someone: I turned 60 years old this past June, and I just restarted my career."*

Donna retired in 2018 after a 21-year career at a private college. She cleaned and organized everything she could get her hands on. Then she took some time to volunteer, but before long, she realized that retirement simply was not for her.

Fortunately, she had an idea. In the five years leading up to her retirement, she had taken on a new responsibility—that of a part-time Salesforce administrator for the private college.

And she loved it.

When she found herself bored with retirement, she began tossing around ideas.

"Salesforce just kept coming back into my mind," she said.

Prior to retirement, Donna had learned about Trailhead, the online re-

source for learning about Salesforce, but she had not fully immersed herself into this abundant free training resource. Upon realizing she wanted to re-emerge as a Salesforce consultant, though, Donna quickly began using the trailmixes, modules, trailheads, and projects available through Trailhead. She trained everyday, enjoying the points and badges used to gamify the training.

Then she began the process of becoming certified. At first, Donna said the process felt "daunting," adding that at her age, she questioned her ability to become certified.

But Donna earned her Salesforce Certified Administrator and Certified Platform App Builder certifications, and within a year of beginning her Salesforce studies, she was snatched up by a consulting firm. As of this publishing, she has earned her Salesforce Sales Cloud Consultant and Marketing Cloud Email Specialist Certifications, and she graduated from the 2019 Rad Women Code Intro to Computing course.

Donna works remotely. Her days consist of meeting with her clients, configuring their Salesforce platforms, and discussing features they would like to have added. She liaises with the development team in India, so some of her day is spent working with these teams on more sophisticated developments in which she needs assistance.

She also spends a portion of her day training new users.

"It's a great mix," she said. *"Everyday is different."*

Donna has this advice for people new to Salesforce: *"You need two traits. The first is you have to be able to overcome the fear of failure. This was probably the biggest thing for me. At my age, I kept wondering:* Can I still learn? Am I capable of learning this new technology? *The other trait was discipline. You will have to show up everyday, whether you are at home or work, and learn something new."*

Day in the life:
MEET DONNA HUDSON

Donna Hudson is a business analyst for a consulting firm in the United States. She works with a variety of clients, from retail to support services companies. Donna works from home, interacting with her clients through Zoom conferencing, with the initial meeting focused on gathering client requirements. As the project progresses, the client and Donna meet once or twice a week. When the requirements do not involve code or custom configuration, Donna completes the configuration work within the Salesforce org.

Donna retired from her previous career a few years ago, but after organizing and cleaning everything she owned, she quickly learned that retirement was not for her, so she reinvented herself as a Salesforce professional.

8:00 a.m.
Donna checks Slack for messages from coworkers and the development team in India and sets her day's priorities. She has three client meetings, two to discuss ongoing projects, and one to train new users.

8:30 a.m.

Via video conferencing, Donna, with the help of a developer who works from India, takes her first meeting with a client, an energy sales provider. The client has asked to have call center integration.

The call takes about an hour as Donna spends time eliciting information from the client and discussing solutions with the developer, all with the goal of making sure the solution the client requested is the best solution that is available. She documents the user stories and requirements using Jira.

9:30 a.m.

Following the call, Donna makes the changes that she can make by meeting with a third-party call center integration provider. She logs into the client's org using the Jira cards from her discovery call and subsequent meetings to begin configuration. Depending on the complexity of the project, Donna may work with her development team in India, or she might work with a third-party provider to coordinate implementation of a call center.

Noon

Donna eats lunch while answering easy emails from her clients. Internal communication and client communication is all done through Slack.

12:00PM

12:30 p.m.

Donna prepares for her second call of the day with an industrial automation company by reviewing the development team's work on the project.

1:30 p.m.

Donna has her second meeting of the day with the client and developer. She takes the lead in demonstrating the new feature of a Visualforce calculator, with the developer answering questions about what can and cannot be done in Salesforce.

2:30 p.m.

Donna and the developer have a quick call to recap the next steps, which requires Donna to test the implementation and the developer to promote the Visualforce calculator to Production.

3:00 p.m.

Yet another meeting, this one with an amusement park client that has hired two new employees who need to be trained. Donna spends an hour walking them through entering new leads, sending emails using Salesforce enhanced email, and running daily activity reports.

4:00 p.m.

Donna pulls her attention back to the energy sales provider, finalizing the third-party call center integration requirements so the developer can begin her work.

5:30 p.m.

On a slow day, Donna ends her workday by about 5:00 p.m., but most days end at about 5:30 p.m.

CHAPTER TEN:
The Entrepreneurial Pathway

In Chapter Six, we spend much time discussing the life of an entrepreneur. If you have not read that section, I encourage you to do so. The chapter dispels many of the misconceptions about the life of an entrepreneur, but it bears repeating: The entrepreneurial life is not one of unlimited freedom. If you are an entrepreneur, you will work longer hours, have fewer vacations, and have more responsibilities. Consider this, for instance: When you embark on your entrepreneurial vision, you will not have a single client. Unless you have a nest of savings that finances your life, you will essentially be working two jobs: the first will be your day-job, which pays the bills. The second will be your weekend, evening, and everything-in-between job as an entrepreneur, which will not pay the bills until you build a client base.

I have loved working for a variety of different clients. I once had a client who was a high-end car manufacturer. The environment was intense, fast-paced, and serious. At the same time, one of my other clients was in the health insurance industry. That client was slow to move and laid back. It was like night and day.

You have to learn to adapt, and then you have to figure out: Can I do this? Am I happy doing this?

—Ken Seaney
Freelance consultant

That said, defining the life of an entrepreneur is impossible. Freelancers, for instance, can take on as many or as few clients as they want, working solo, and defining their workdays. Consultants who own firms are responsible for not only their clients, but also their employees. They worry about paying the bills and making payroll. AppExchange vendors are entrepreneurs as well, though some develop apps that require little management once they are listed. Others turn their apps into a full-time job.

The AppExchange is an online store that offers paid and free Salesforce apps and lightning components. Think of the AppExchange as the Salesforce-specific equivalent of the App Store. Apps have been configured for specific industries, or for specific functionality.

This chapter takes a look at case studies of people who have embarked on an entrepreneurial endeavor within the world of Salesforce.

CASE STUDY

PAT MCCLELLAN:
Full-time AppExchange Vendor

*Pat McClellan is the developer and entrepreneur
behind Proton Text, an app available on the
AppExchange.*

Pat McClellan is a "career changer." He has worked as a video producer, as a macromedia director, as a digital media producer, as a Microsoft account director, and as the Chief Marketing Officer for a marketing agency.

Back in 1982, he even took a single class in computer sciences, which involved punch cards and used a programming language called Pascal, which was popular in the seventies and eighties, but eventually replaced by C programming.

He never trained as a programmer, though.

"This theme comes up a lot in Salesforce," said Pat. *"Frequently, a person works in operations, and they have an aptitude for technology, so they become an accidental administrator and end up setting up users and workflows. Even though these people don't think of themselves as IT people, they end up going down a path that blossoms into bigger things."*

"That's one path," said Pat, *"but it's not mine."*

Though Pat never trained as a programmer, he loved making things, whether they were videos or web media. In his career as the managing director of a marketing agency, though, his days were spent managing projects rather than developing projects.

After fifteen years, he was frustrated. Fortunately, he had used Salesforce at two marketing agencies. When he quit his job, he jumped on Trailhead and started learning Salesforce. He knew he wanted to be a developer and interface with clients, but he wasn't quite sure what that looked like. Instead, he trusted that the answers would come, and he fully immersed himself in Trailhead, earning Trailhead's highest badge, Ranger, in just five weeks. Over the course of five months, he also earned three certifications and double Ranger status.

Upon earning a badge or certification, Pat would post his accomplishment on LinkedIn.

"Each time, I would receive calls from headhunters who asked me to send them my résumé. They would respond with, 'We don't know what to do with you. You've been a Chief Marketing Officer, but no one has ever paid you to write code.' They all said I was a bit of a unicorn, and they could not help me."

As Pat talked to people within the Salesforce ecosystem, he began meeting people who had 400 or 500 badges, but they could not land an interview because they had never been paid to work in Salesforce.

"I had a 33-year career behind me," he said. *"I was a good saver, so I was in a position to spend some time building something for the AppExchange to prove my skills. I decided that instead of getting depressed about my situation, I was going to use my time to get practical. I started building my app during Thanksgiving weekend of 2017."*

Pat's app, Proton Text, is a Lightning component that integrates SMS messaging into Salesforce objects. The app requires advanced programming skills and integrates with another company's technology.

By June of the following year, Pat had made great progress and decided to submit it through security review for the AppExchange. By the end of August, he had worked out all the bugs, and Proton Text was listed on the AppExchange. All said, Pat spent fifteen months studying Salesforce and working on his app before he landed his first customer. Today, he services about 100 customers as a one-person entrepreneur. He has days that are specifically reserved for coding, during which he fixes bugs, adds features, and plans for the second release of the app. He also reserves days for marketing, which involves writing blogs, outreach, and personal networking.

"My story is inspiring to a lot of developers, but most of them cannot afford to quit their jobs and work on an app full time," he said. *"I have an MBA and a business background, so I was able to write my business plan, but my ability to do this on my own largely came down to the fact that I saved a lot of money and could spend time bootstrapping this."*

What do his days look like? *"I love my life,"* said Pat. *"I work from home, and I work a lot of hours because I like working a lot of hours. I work six days a week, and I work long days, but I wake up and am excited to get to work. I start work while I am still in bed. I swim three days a week for an hour, and I think through code that entire time."*

"I get most of my ideas for new features from my customers who ask why the app doesn't do certain things. Oftentimes, within a day, I can push a patch out to them."

"One of the things that appeals to me about this lifestyle is that I can move very quickly. I am very agile. If a customer calls to report a bug, the patch is usually done within that day."

Developers who work for firms don't often have that luxury. Their days are spent in meetings, in more meetings, and then in additional meetings. They code for a few hours a day, whereas Pat can often code for twelve hours because his planning meetings occur with himself, while he is driving or while he is swimming. The rest of his time is spent coding and working with clients.

"Once or twice a week, I get an email or call from a customer who has a question. Perhaps they are receiving an error message or a new employee is confused about the app. My number-one priority on those days becomes servicing my client. Everything else gets pushed. I have to focus on customer service to differentiate myself from the big guys who have technical teams numbering in the hundreds but who do not answer the phone. When customers call, I answer, and I know every single one of them."

Pat went on to say that he was in the midst of replacing a colored icon with a flashing icon. This was at the request of a client who is color-blind.

"Entrepreneur is a French word. As the saying goes, it means: Had an idea. Did it."

He takes a break for lunch and dinner, but Pat continues to work into the evening hours.

"If you work for yourself and you work from home, you only have to work half a day," said Pat. *"Just figure out which twelve hours that is."*

Pat noted two traits that entrepreneurs should have: 1) a sense of urgency; and 2) resilience.

"Having a sense of urgency does not mean that you have to speed through everything, but it does mean that you have to identify a specific goal and wake up every day with a driving sense of, I don't have enough time to do this! The reason I can work sixty or seventy hours a week is because I have to drive to get this done. When I wrote my app, I wanted it out by the end of June. When June came, I knew I had more to do, and it was driving me crazy. I pushed and pushed to get it done."

The sense of urgency, he said, is necessary because the obstacles will otherwise defeat you.

And you will face obstacles, which is why resilience is necessary. "The day before I was planning to package my app and submit it to security review, I found out that another company with a great reputation, more resources, and a huge technical team, was releasing an app that does exactly what my app does. I thought: *I am so screwed. I just wasted 12 months of my life.*

"*But then I took a step back and realized that the integration into Salesforce was not strong. I had four or five other competitors, and I just decided: I am going to compete against the big guys. Resilience is that emotional strength to bounce back even stronger, and I leaned on that. I spent the next 45 days making sure my app does things that the competitors' apps don't do. I thought:* They better release something amazing if they want to beat me. *And I decided to be the best.*"

Today, Proton Text is paying the bills (and then some), and he is looking forward to developing new apps. In fact, his advice for developers who lack the time and financial resources he had is this: Develop a small app that will get you on the AppExchange. For instance, Pat is tinkering with the idea of developing a translation app.

"*It seems like people might want to have a popup in the utility bar that translates up to 250 characters. A developer with a full-time job could create that on the evenings or the weekends, and it would go through security quickly.*"

"*Entrepreneur is a French word,*" he said. "*As the saying goes, it means: Had an idea. Did it. Tons of people have great ideas and don't do anything with them. They can talk themselves out of their ideas. They see that six other people have that app, or they say someone else can do it better, or they say they do not have time and are busy. It's so easy for people to come up with excuses for not doing something.*"

"*You're an entrepreneur if you can go from had an idea to did it.*"

CASE STUDY

KEN SEANEY:
Freelance Salesforce Consultant

Ken Seaney is a freelance contractor currently working to convert a federal agency's systems into Salesforce.

For fifteen years, Ken Seaney ran his own business, 123Stickers, which specialized in custom vinyl stickers, t-shirts, and banners. In this capacity, he managed employees and made all principal decisions for the business's operations, financial, and organizational activities. He developed company policies, procedures, and manuals for various positions and processes; oversaw all digital and print marketing campaigns; managed ecommerce; researched and implemented IT solutions for the firm; and managed all human resources issues.

No one could argue that Ken is not an entrepreneur.

Today, his descriptor is a little more vague. Ken is an independent contractor who works with a recruiting agency that pairs IT specialists with contracting jobs. He is an at-will contractor, so his contract could be terminated at any time. Beyond that, the contract is up in three months. Though the recruiting agency will likely find another job for Ken, he always runs the risk of having no work.

Still, putting his case study in the *Entrepreneurs* chapter was a tough call. He isn't spending his days hustling for work. He does have steady work. He even receives a W-2 rather than a 1099.

Nonetheless, Ken's case study appropriately belongs here. His career path has included many years as an entrepreneur. He can easily compare and contrast employment versus entrepreneurship (versus nonprofit work). As is true of most entrepreneurs, he has happy feet and bounces from one position to another.

"I don't think I would want to work for Corporation X and be on the inside Salesforce team," he said. *"That might be attractive to someone else, but I like having a completely different team with a completely different client and a completely different culture solving a brand new business problem. Having variety is exciting to me, where that might be a little scary for some."*

He isn't sure what he will do when his federal contract ends in March.

"It's a little scary," Ken said, *"But I think I will get placed right away. And if I don't, I can always follow up on LinkedIn. People regularly recruit me, so I imagine the ball will be in my court."*

Ken has government clearance, so the one option is to find other work as a government contractor.

"The U.S. government is going full force into Salesforce," said Ken. *"Across all sorts of agencies, they are converting processes into Salesforce, so there is a huge amount of security in that market."*

"I don't see any end in sight with federal work," he said, adding that a strong career for those with no criminal record and a "clean lifestyle" is to pursue the federal path. *"If you can get clearance, the work is endless."*

All that said, Ken also suggests that those new to Salesforce consider working for nonprofits. Having worked for several nonprofits himself, Ken has a soft spot.

"The most fun I have ever had and the greatest people I have ever worked with have been in the nonprofit world," he said. *"You will get less money working for a nonprofit, but you won't have to deal with the intensity."*

After working for various nonprofits, Ken has found himself inspired by their cause.

"They are trying to help people, so at the end of the day, nonprofit work is fulfilling. One of the nonprofits I worked for converted old parking lots into green spaces. I loved working for them, and even though I didn't get paid a cent, if they called today, I would work all weekend for them."

It bears noting that Ken has contracted with nonprofits that do pay—though the pay has been about 20 percent less than what he earns through other contracts.

Ken reflected on his time as an entrepreneur: *"It's a lot more work. While you think you want to work for yourself, you might not understand that you have to be working on the business all of the time. And as a freelance consultant, you get a 1099, which means no taxes are withheld. You have to set the money aside and pay it at the end of the year, and you will get taxed at a higher rate than an employee. You might think you are making a lot of money, but after taxes, you might not be."*

Due to his long-term contract, Ken doesn't have to worry about when the next client will appear so that he can keep the lights on.

"When you are always hustling for work, and you complete a project, that's when the next shift begins. You start thinking: Where am I going to get the job tomorrow. You spend a lot of time working on your business, but if you aren't working in your business, then you don't get paid."

Though Ken can see the pros and cons of many various Salesforce career paths, he does have one piece of solid advice, regardless of a person's path:

Start now.

"My neighbor's son came home for the holidays, and I found out he was strug-gling to find work. He worked a little bit with Salesforce for one employer, and I said: 'Get your Admin certification now because you will never hurt for work.'"

"If I was younger, I would spend more time on the developer side. I would know more about code. If I had started ten years ago, man, I would not ever look for work."

CASE STUDY

NUMAAN MOHAMMAD:
Developer by Day, AppExchange Vendor by Night

Numaan Mohammad is a developer working at a Canadian consultancy firm and the owner of Big Object Utility, an app available on the AppExchange.

Numaan Mohammad had been working as a Salesforce developer (and then technical lead) in India for several years when he was asked to speak at a Salesforce event about Big Objects. A "Big Object" is what is used to store and manage massive amounts of data on the Salesforce platform, and Numaan had specialized knowledge in Big Object technology.

Numaan had researched the subject so thoroughly for the event that he decided:

Why not create an app that allows users to view, filter, and export Big Object records?

He set about the process, working full-time at his day job as a developer, and evenings and weekends developing the app. After about seven months of what he calls "a joy ride," Numaan's app, Big Object Utility, was ready to be submitted to the Salesforce AppExchange, where it is listed free of charge today.

But that's just the beginning of the story. When asked how the app has helped move his career forward, Numaan has this to say: *"It made me famous in a way."*

Numaan developed connections within Salesforce and outside of Salesforce. He met with the group leader from San Francisco, Daniel Peter, who gave valuable suggestions for Numaan's product.

He has also exchanged tweets with Salesforce's vice president of product management, Andrew Fawcett, and other top techies.

"I think it is because of the app that they hired me," he said. *"The app was my advantage. They knew:* If you hire this guy, he will know how to build your product."

Beyond that, people have offered to buy Big Object Utility, but for now, it remains on the AppExchange free of charge.

"Right now, I don't want to make money off of it," he said. *"I think I have in-spired some people who have started building other apps. They ask me questions on Twitter about how they should do this and that. I want to keep it this way for some time. Maybe I will turn it into something mainstream and sell my product later."*

And what about the process of getting the app listed and approved on the AppExchange? Numaan said that Salesforce was incredibly helpful. *"You have to build your app in such a way that you are following the AppExchange rules, but if you do, it is very easy."*

"I am thankful to the Salesforce community who have supported and helped me during the product build cycle."

Day in the life:
NUMAAN MOHAMMAD

Numaan Mohammad is a developer with more than five years of experience with Salesforce. He recently moved from India to Canada to pursue the next step in his career as a technical consultant at a boutique Canadian Salesforce consulting firm. He is also the owner/developer of the Big Object Utility, an app available on the AppExchange. Numaan is currently working on a very large scale, cross-cloud implementation project that has Sales, Service, and Community Cloud elements and more.

"I am loving the development work and getting the chance to build lots of custom Lightning Web Components that will be used by millions of people around the world. The team was very helpful in my starting days to get adjusted in the project. I like the vibes of the company," he said. "I don't feel stressed out."

6:00 a.m.
Numaan starts the day over a cup of hot tea. He prepares breakfast and gets ready for the office, leaving the house by 7:30 a.m.

8:00 a.m.
Numaan arrives at the office and dials into a scrum call along with his team. Scrum call is a meeting held every morning to set the context for the coming day's work. Because the project contains people from different parts of the world, it has been set to early morning for those in Canada. In the scrum, Numaan gives a report of the work done and the status of the tickets (organized in Jira) that are completed or pending. Today, he focuses on the development of a ticket that lets a user filter the data on a community page.

8:30 a.m.

After the call, Numaan checks all emails and messages in Slack to catch up on messages from internal team members and clients.

He spends the first few hours at the office developing in VS Code (his favorite development tool nowadays) by connecting the Macbook to a two-monitor workstation.

When working on a component, a developer often sees the output on the screen.

By making use of multiple monitors, one monitor can be used for development, another monitor for output, and the laptop screen for messages. Numaan finds that development is more efficient and faster from these types of workstation setups.

11:00 a.m.

Numaan takes a small break with fruit and coffee before attending an internal team meeting to give updates about assigned tickets. The team uses a Jira board that will contain all the tickets with their status. In the meeting, they discuss any technical difficulties that are a roadblock or technical solution for a given ticket.

11:30 a.m.

Back to development. Numaan is currently working on an LWC component that filters the data for a community user based on the selection of input. In the company, help is just a Slack message away. There is a technical channel where getting a solution to any problem is very easy, be it an out-of-the-box configuration, a custom solution, or a workaround.

12:00 p.m.

The company has lunch-and-learn sessions once or twice a week. These are casual sessions that include technical information as well as topics colleagues are excited to talk about, such as new Salesforce release features, how to prepare slides for a presentation, paragliding, new developer tools, and the like.

1:00 p.m.

That said, Numaan usually avoids eating at his desk, so after the lunch-and-learn, he has lunch with his office friends at the building's food court. He eats a light lunch so he doesn't feel sleepy in the afternoon.

1:30 p.m.

Back to work. Numaan spends 80 percent of his time in development nowadays, so he returns to work on the large-scale, cross-cloud implementation project. Today he is working on a LWC component that will be used in a community page to allow a user to export his downline users data, which is appearing on the screen to download a CSV format file.

3:30 p.m.

Numaan goes for a coffee break. "I like sitting on the couch with my coffee and laptop where the sunlight comes from the window and the place is surrounded by plants. It feels more productive to have something like that around you."

4:30 p.m.

Numaan spends the last few hours of the day wrapping up projects, pushing the completed development to the code repository, creating pull requests, and updating the status in the Jira ticket. Pull requests allow him to tell others about changes he has pushed to a repository. Once a pull request is sent, reviewers can review the set of changes, discuss potential modifications, and even push follow-up commits if necessary. Logging the time that is spent on the project with details of the Jira ticket.

That said, Fridays are different. People who have completed their work grab a drink, sit on the couch, have conversations with their colleagues, and play games. Today, Numaan challenges a colleague to a game of Jenga. "This type of culture makes the work environment a better place. I want to spend more time there, so it makes me more productive."

5:00 p.m.

Numaan packs up and takes the Skytrain to reach home. On the train, he checks Twitter for Salesforce updates or news before arriving home, where he relaxes and eats dinner.

8:00 p.m.

Numaan spends an hour or so each evening addressing his own work on the Big Object Utility, an app that he has made available on the AppExchange. He answers questions from users, fixes bugs, and works on the next iteration. This new feature was created when he was back in India, and it shows Big Object records in the related list. For example, if a company is using a Big Object to store archived orders, it can use Big Object Utility to see at a glance those that are related to an account. Currently within Salesforce, related Big Object records cannot be shown on the standard related list. In Numaan's product, though, a component uses the Aura Lightning bundle to simply drag and drop onto the page with some minimum configuration. All the related child Big Object records will appear under the standard Lightning record page.

CHAPTER ELEVEN:
Entering the Salesforce Ecosystem

Time and time again, people working in Salesforce-related careers say that no amount of badges or certifications compares to real-world experience working in Salesforce.

But how can you beat the "chicken-egg" dichotomy? If you cannot get a job without experience, how do you get experience?

Here are a few tips for breaking into the market:

- Volunteer

- Join the community

- Build your portfolio

- Hone your interviewing skills

- Be passionate

My advice for people getting started in Salesforce is this: Jump in. You can't break it.

The typical advice given to people just getting started is to volunteer for a nonprofit, and that is good advice, but keep in mind that you can volunteer elsewhere, too. I bet there are people you know who have a database problem.

For instance, I knew a college freshman with a serious love of rollercoasters. He could name the height, speed, centrifugal force, and years in operation for every rollercoaster in seven different theme parks in the northeastern part of the United States.

I put all of his knowledge in Salesforce for him. It was a way for me to practice, and I knew it would be fun for him. He could add to it, or he could throw it away. Either way, no one's revenue depended on it, and I was able to practice at a very basic level where to put fields, which data types made sense given his knowledge set, that sort of thing.

I also knew a guy who put his entire home beer-crafting knowledge in Salesforce, including the temperature, ingredients, and rotation time for all of his recipes. And why not? This is what I mean by: **Jump in. You can't break it.** *Anything that is a database can be done in Salesforce.*

—Rob Kaplan
Senior consultant and engagement manager

VOLUNTEER

If you become active in the Salesforce community, you will run across opportunities to volunteer at nonprofits. You can use these volunteer experiences on your résumé, and you can solicit letters of recommendation from the nonprofits. Try not to get worked up about the amount of money you are making—or, in this case, the amount of money you are not making. Volunteering pays off in the long run, so think of it as an investment in your future.

> *"I cannot stress enough how important it is to attend Dreamforce because that really does open your eyes to the possibilities. It is a substantial cost, and you do not need to go every year, but going once or twice really does open your eyes."*
>
> **—Neal Lightfeldt**
> **Sales excellence manager**

Volunteering at a Nonprofit

Many opportunities are available for helping nonprofits with their CRM systems, which are often old and hard to use. Through Salesforce's Power of Us program, eligible nonprofit organizations can receive ten subscriptions of Sales & Service Cloud Enterprise Edition, as well as the Nonprofit Success Pack, which includes functionality for managing fundraising programs, donations, volunteers, and supporters. Convincing nonprofits to upgrade should not be hard!

After the initial setup, you would likely be required to help with data modeling and data migration activities. Data modeling is required to customize the out-of-the-box data model for any specific requirements for the particular organization and will put your new Salesforce configuration skills to good use. After the data model is set up, transferring the data from the legacy system will be necessary. This is your chance to get to know Data Loader. There are often integration requirements; however, you will find suitable options on the AppExchange so you can avoid any need for development.

Going live with a new system in three months is not unusual. The nonprofit will be happy to give you glowing recommendations for providing the nonprofit with functionality that they were hoping to implement but never were able to accomplish with their old system—**and all for free.**

Volunteers can wonder where to start and feel challenged when they encounter issues. To address this, look for someone with Salesforce experience who can work with you on the project or be available to answer questions as they arise. If you reach out, someone within the Trailblazer community will be available and will help, usually beyond your expectations!

"In late October 2017, I became a volunteer for a nonprofit who was using another CRM at a remote data center," said one Salesforce newbie who used this strategy. *"The CRM was difficult to use and was not fully implemented. After a couple of weeks, I convinced them to use Salesforce. I helped set it up and did some of the data modeling and data migration. I found an app on the AppExchange that helped with the integration. Within two months, the integration was successful, and it was a major win for this nonprofit. In two months, I was able to help them accomplish something they had been trying to accomplish for two years."*

"Sometimes it felt challenging to get what I needed. As a total newbie to Salesforce, I didn't know where to start. Thankfully, I found my way by using YouTube, Trailhead, and plain brute force. I did reach out once on the Trailblazer community when I was having a data overriding issue during data migration. The support was awesome!"

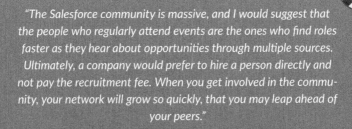

"The Salesforce community is massive, and I would suggest that the people who regularly attend events are the ones who find roles faster as they hear about opportunities through multiple sources. Ultimately, a company would prefer to hire a person directly and not pay the recruitment fee. When you get involved in the community, your network will grow so quickly, that you may leap ahead of your peers."

—Ben Duncombe
Director of Talent Hub, a Salesforce recruitment company

JOIN THE COMMUNITY

One of the stand-outs of the Salesforce community is that it truly is a "community." Just about everyone with a history in Salesforce knows that if they post a question with the hashtag "Askforce," they will get a response within the hour. More than a few Salesforce enthusiasts spend Taco Tuesdays and Salesforce Saturdays together discussing the latest features, opportunities, and challenges. And code is readily available through the Answers forum on Trailhead. (In fact, Neal Lightfeldt, a sales excellence manager, said, "The Answers community has been an absolutely critical part of getting problems solved. I have been able to look so smart so many times thanks to that! I cannot tell you how many times Answers has saved me.")

Becoming part of the community as early as possible is key to getting a job in the Salesforce ecosystem. When you attend your local user group, you will connect with lots of different people including other administrators, employers, and recruiters; they can then put you in touch with people who are hiring or recruiting.

It's never fun going to events where you do not know anyone, but you need to do it. It might be a little awkward to introduce yourself the first or second time, but once you start connecting, the opportunities just don't stop.

My community involvement has led to many benefits. I have the right connections, I am recognized as an expert, and I am seen as worth employing. I have also been invited to Dreamforce and to write a blog for Salesforce. I honestly do not think any of this would have happened if I were not such an active participant in the community.

—Christine Marshall
Administrator, Salesforce MVP, and leader of the Bristol Salesforce Admin User Group

Salesforce is rich with community,
SO GET INVOLVED.

CHECK OUT GOOGLE TO FIND RESOURCES IN YOUR AREA SUCH AS:

- **Your local user groups**
- **Affinity groups, such as:**
  - > Military Trailhead (https://veterans.force.com/s), which helps members of the military;

  - > PepUp Tech (https://www.pepuptech.org), which helps underserved communities pursue careers in technology; and

  - > Ladies Be Architects (www.ladies-be-architects.com), which is run by women in Salesforce and available to all aspiring architects.

- **Salesforce Saturdays**
- **Taco Tuesdays**
- **Trailhead Tuesdays**
- **Salesforce Lunch 'n Learns**
- **Salesforce Dreamin events, which are community-driven conferences**

Remember:

Growing your career includes learning how to manage your career, build your brand, and maximize your earning potential. For a free career assessment, head over to **https://cloudtalent360.com/career-assessment-book-offer/** to learn strategies for accelerating your career.

YOU CAN ALSO FIND ONLINE COMMUNITIES VIA:

- The #Askforce hashtag on Twitter
- The Trailblazer Community on Trailhead, which includes the Answers forum
- Salesforce YouTube channels
- Salesforce blogs

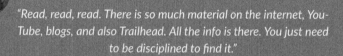

"Read, read, read. There is so much material on the internet, YouTube, blogs, and also Trailhead. All the info is there. You just need to be disciplined to find it."

—Stuart Smith
Director at the Salesforce recruitment company SaasPeople

AND, OF COURSE, SALESFORCE HAS MAJOR EVENTS, TOO, SUCH AS:

- Dreamforce, which is an annual four-day conference that costs about $2,000 to attend (not including airfare and hotel expenses)
- The World Tour, which is a traveling Salesforce event

By spending time with these communities, you will meet people who can point you in the direction of opportunities.

I think a lot of people who are working in IT are probably introverts. I know I am, and the concept of attending a community group was absolutely terrifying to me. I could not think of anything worse than going to an event in a roomful of people I don't know and having to talk about who I am. I have gone to events where I sit in the back row and don't talk to anyone, but when I came to Sydney and decided to go to a user group, I decided: Enough is enough. I am just going to go and make friends.

I walked away from my second or third meeting, and I was asked to revive Sydney's Women in Tech group. That boosted my confidence to engage with more people, and eventually, I realized: Okay, everybody feels like this. Everybody is terrified to come along at first.

I got this sense that we are all in this together. I found my people, and I keep learning that everybody is going through the same sort of challenges I am going through. There is an incredible sense of openness and of being welcomed in the community groups. They are just so accepting. It doesn't matter who you are, or where you are from. It doesn't matter if you have never used Salesforce, or if you have been using it for twenty years. Everybody is the same.

—Lorna O'Callaghan
Platform manager

If you want to work for Salesforce itself, consider this advice from John Conway, a principal enterprise architect for Salesforce. "Get to know some people who work in Salesforce," said Conway. "They will help you understand the culture, advise you on the roles available at Salesforce, and can also act as a referral for you. Whether it's Dreamforce, World Tour, or a local event, I'd encourage people to attend in person or online. It's a great way to network and get to know our teams, solutions, and our values."

BUILD YOUR PORTFOLIO

Build a portfolio that showcases what you can do. Then, put this information on your résumé. This is particularly helpful if you are looking to enter a particular industry and your portfolio shows that you understand that industry.

Interestingly, Ben Duncombe, the director of Talent Hub, which is a recruiter for Salesforce jobs, said that relying on recruiters is not always the only way to find a job.

"There are so many things you can do in your spare time as a Salesforce professional that you can showcase in an interview," he said, noting that he recently built a job-tracking tool that, among other things, automates emails asking for feedback. "If you do not have experience, you can build little apps like that. In an interview, you can then say, 'I appreciate that I do not have any official experience, but this is what I have been doing in my spare time to show that I can build solutions in Salesforce.'"

He went on to say, *"Be smart. Don't sit around waiting for jobs. Be active and do things that help you showcase your skills when you do get an opportunity."*

Of course, if you have the time and expertise, you can always create free apps or components on the AppExchange, which can help you promote your abilities, albeit through a longer and more difficult process.

A lot of your success boils down to discipline and diligence. I had to send out tons of résumés at first. I got sent on more than a few interviews where I got to the second or third interview and never got a call back. Still, I had to get up, head down to my office, hit up people, and take more meetings. And some of those meetings didn't turn into any work for a couple of years.

Sometimes the interviews require practical application. You might have to build in a developer org, and then have the client critique you. Other employers will send a multiple-page spec, and you have to develop a solution and talk about it.

You're not going to talk your way into a Salesforce job. You have to deliver the goods. If you don't get another call, or if they turn you down outright, you have to wake up and hit it hard the next day.

—Ken Seaney
Freelance consultant

HONE YOUR INTERVIEWING SKILLS

Sooner or later, you will be brought in for an interview, assuming you are persistent in your journey. Here are a few tips for acing an interview:

1. Know how to package yourself.

Take stock of your background, whatever it might be, to show a recruiter or employer that your background can be applied to a Salesforce career. It helps to look at soft skills. For instance, if you were the leader of a club or captain of a sports team in high school or college, use this to demonstrate your ability to manage projects or communicate with a diverse group of individuals. If you were a party planner, use this to show your ability to manage stress, time, and competing demands. The point is, if you go deep to show an employer who you are, you can tell the story of how your background can be used to pursue a Salesforce career.

2. Come prepared.

"Treat every interview as your first," recommended Ben Duncombe, the director of Talent Hub, which is a recruiter for Salesforce jobs. "The problem a lot of people have is that there are a lot of opportunities in the market. Therefore, they get a bit blasé about things. There's nothing more awkward than being asked why you are interested in that company or what values of yours line up with the company, and not knowing anything about the company. Go back to basics and prepare."

3. Ask questions.

"A lot of people fail to ask questions," said Duncombe, but there are no excuses for not asking questions.

Don't just ask any old question, said Duncombe. Ask questions that cause the hiring manager to think, *That's a good question. I want this person to ask these sorts of questions to the customers and the user base.*

Particularly if you are applying for a role that demands that you have elicitation skills, ask questions to showcase this ability.

4. "Prepare to educate the interviewer."

This advice ceoms from Stuart Smith, director at the Salesforce recruitment company SaasPeople. "A candidate who knows the platform will have the confidence to discuss not only what they have achieved in previous roles but also what they can bring to the business from innovative ideas or possibly implementing different products related to Salesforce. It is not enough to go into an interview and only answer the questions the interviewer asks. I often recommend that candidates bring examples of things they have produced on the system to improve efficiency, etc," he said.

5. Demonstrate that you are active in the community.

Show the blogs you have written, or talk about meetups you have attended.

6. Be prepared to present and defend your thought processes.

Ajay Dubedi, the CEO of a consulting firm with over 200 employees, still participates in both technical and non-technical interviews and is active in the vast majority of the company's hiring decisions.

Ajay said he likes to ask candidates to solve puzzles during the interview so that he can see their thought process.

"Many times, I ask this question: 'Imagine you have ten match boxes. Each matchbox has ten sticks. Nine of the matchboxes have sticks that weigh ten grams, but one of the matchboxes has a stick that weighs eleven grams. If you have a digital scale, what is the fastest way to find the matchstick that weights eleven grams.'"

"There are multiple ways to solve the problem and multiple answers to this question. I don't really care about the answer, but I do care about who can best explain the thought process and demonstrate presentation skills," he said.

"I want the candidate to talk while thinking out loud," he said. "I am more interested in what is happening inside the person's mind."

There are a lot of soap-opera stories out there about people who didn't have hope, and they were unemployed, and then they found Salesforce (or Oracle, Microsoft, etc.). Those stories are real and compelling. I like those stories. But at the end of the day, remember that the people you work for want ROI. They want a return on their investment in you. They want solutions. There are people out there telling all sorts of stories about their success, but sometimes their stories are not related at all to what the stakeholders want. I lost 20 pounds because of Company X. I met my spouse because of Company Y. That's nice. How does that relate to the business? How does that empower others to be successful? What can you do for the stakeholder?

—Carlos Siqueira
Salesforce MVP and DevOps Sales Engineer

The hardest part is landing that first role. It's a lot like the chicken and the egg debate. You are told that to land that job, you need experience. But you can't get experience without a job. So what's the answer? You have to find every advantage to improve your odds of getting that first job:

1. *Expand your network. This is the most important method for getting an interview. With a good network, you can go further than someone with three times your experience but no network. Referrals go a long way.*

2. *You can't control your work experience, but there are other methods of demonstrating expertise besides work experience. You can show evidence of skills with certifications. You can also build out real-world solutions using Trailhead. During an interview, instead of talking about your work experience, talk about the combination of certification and skills.*

3. *Take any job you can to get actual work experience. Work experience isn't only Salesforce, but the hundred other things that go into being a good team member. You can work as a business analyst at a consulting company, freelance admin/consultant, or even volunteer admin at a nonprofit.*

4. *Another option is to land a Salesforce adjacent role, like in customer success, sales operations, etcetera (assuming the team uses Salesforce). Even though you would be competing for entry-level positions in those teams, if you are a certified Salesforce administrator, you would be at a huge competitive advantage in comparison to other entry-level applicants. You could then transition into an administrator opening from within the company and gain a powerful skill set for any administrator.*

—Moon Algazzali
Administrator

BE PASSIONATE

Ben Duncombe, the director of Talent Hub, which is a recruitment firm for Salesforce-related jobs, said that he is more likely to be able to help someone who is clearly passionate about Salesforce: "People who show passion for the Salesforce platform are most likely to build a successful career in Salesforce as they tend to help themselves by building a network, attending events, and giving back to the community."

In the early days of his career, Dominick DeFazio was given the opportunity to transition from a salesperson to a full-time role in Salesforce at an earlier job.

"I worked as a Salesforce developer and administrator for my old employer for a year on a salesperson's salary without earning any commission, which was terrible," he said, laughing at the memory. *"It's hard enough to survive in New York City, so I was really bare-bones-ing it, but I knew it was a great opportunity. I went to business school, so I wasn't going to get another opportunity to jump into the world of computer science and development. I didn't mind taking the low pay as a first step."*

Even though starting salaries for Salesforce employees are generally above-average, your passion for the role should be enough that allows you to take a less-than-competitive salary for a job that gives you the best shot of pursuing a career plan that you love.

Salesforce has three new releases a year, so if you aren't passionate about Salesforce, you will find it difficult to stay abreast. Do yourself a favor: If you don't feel passion, put down this book and start researching another career!

Day in the life:
BERENIKE KASSAB

Within the course of a few months, Berenike Kassab was divorced, mourned the death of her father, and found herself temporarily homeless and living out of her van as she searched to find her place in the world as a single mother.

This is when she discovered Trailhead.

"I realized that I am not just a mom," she said. *"I am a woman who possesses valuable knowledge and skills. I felt smart, and for the first time in a while, I realized I could pick up new skills, redefine myself, and take care of myself and my children through a job in IT."*

Berenike went on to earn her Certified Salesforce Administrator credential and is working toward Salesforce Platform App Builder and Sales Cloud Consultant certifications.

Today, Berenike is a client experience consultant for Edmonton-based Riva, a Salesforce AppExchange partner. Riva makes enterprise applications interoperable by ensuring customer data is meaningful, secure, and connected. Plus, it keeps clients in compliance by making sure that only the right employees can see customer data by surfacing it to the right screens.

Berenike works from her home in Sydney and is responsible for helping Riva's APAC clients, maintaining relationships, and renewing client contracts. She is the first point-of-contact for tier-one support cases, carries out user training, and oversees new Riva implementations across the APAC client base. She also keeps clients informed about new product developments, latest updates, and features. Berenike consults clients on the best way to integrate their Salesforce instance with Riva. The CX team she works with consists of seven other Riva employees spread out across the globe.

"I think my clients value me because I never aggressively upsell. Rather, I consult, build lasting and real relationships, and actively listen to their needs, always thinking about their business requirements instead of trying to sell more," she said.

Originally from Germany, Berenike holds university degrees in marketing, business communication, and international politics. She is self-trained in SEO and web development and, when her children were babies, she ran her own company building websites for small businesses in Germany.

Berenike credits her career achievement to her continued hunger for new knowledge, adaptability, and resilience. She is also disciplined and self-motivated to stay abreast of changes in technology.

As a quiet and introverted person, Berenike has worked hard to be recognized.

"I was bullied in school," she said, "but instead of retreating to the sidelines, I had a stubborn determination and decided to turn adversity into strength, drown out the noise, and use the failures in my life as turning points."

Today, Berenike has her mind set on becoming a Salesforce developer all while improving her skills and becoming a more valuable asset for Riva. Even without formal coding training or experience, she knows she will get there.

"I believe in dreaming big, setting big goals, and going after them—without compromise," she said. "We only live once."

5:00 a.m.

Thanks to the flexible hours Riva offers, Berenike is often in front of the computer in the early morning hours before her children awake.

The first orders of business are to review the day's priorities, attend team calls with North America, and answer client emails. Today, she has a client whose sync policy is producing an error, so Berenike investigates whether she can help resolve the issue or whether she needs to involve support based in Edmonton.

Berenike finds that the issue is related to a simple "Delete Safety" error, and she responds to the client's email with a solution.

6:00 a.m.

Most of her clients are not in the office until 8:00 a.m. or 9:00 a.m., so Berenike spends the next hour on Trailhead. Many of her clients have questions about custom objects, so the more Berenike knows about Salesforce, the better she can help her clients.

7:00 a.m.

Berenike awakens her children. They eat breakfast together before Berenike takes them to school.

8:30 a.m.

Back to work. But first, a shower!

11:00 a.m.

Berenike usually works from home, but today, she has a meeting with a client in Sydney. Berenike fires up her Salesforce demo to train the Salesforce administrator on using Riva so that he can better administer his teams and users. Berenike walks the Salesforce administrator through the Riva Cloud Dashboard, reviews the sync policy settings, and discusses some common use cases to better utilize Riva in the company. To continue building lasting relationships, she also makes a point to have coffee and chat with the other decision-makers in the office.

1:00 p.m.

Berenike arrives home and eats a quick lunch.

1:00PM

1:30 p.m.

Berenike is back in front of her computer. A client has emailed with a technical question. The client is wondering if Riva can be customized to archive emails in a specific folder in Salesforce rather than at the account level. Berenike calls the client to gather some more information and then opens a support ticket to liaise with the team in Canada for an estimate of cost and timing involved in completing this customization. She hears back from the team straight away and will stay in close contact with the client over the next few days to implement the changes.

2:00 p.m.

A large part of Berenike's job is making sure that clients are happy and prepared to renew their contracts with Riva. Berenike spends a chunk of every day reaching out to clients to make sure no issues have popped up.

Today, she calls on a client she has not spoken with in a while. During the phone call, the client said the company has been looking at alternatives to Riva because it wants to be able to sync custom fields in Salesforce.

A large part of Berenike's job is making sure that clients are happy and prepared to renew their contracts with Riva. Berenike spends a chunk of every day reaching out to clients to make sure no issues have popped up.

Today, she calls on a client she has not spoken with in a while. During the phone call, the client said the company has been looking at alternatives to Riva because the client wants to be able to sync custom fields in Salesforce. Berenike checks the company's sync policy and realizes that with a simple advanced function, she can enable that feature for the client at no additional cost. Berenike reaches out to the team in Canada through Zendesk and is able to adjust the client's sync policy to match their specific needs. The client is so happy that the company now wants to add another fifteen users to its subscription. How great are client phone calls?

3:00 p.m.
It's time to pick up the kids, so Berenike shuts off her computer and heads out the door. After giving them a quick snack, she takes her kids and their new puppy to the park. When they return home, she spends the next few hours with bath time, dinner, homework, card games, and bedtime stories.

8:00 p.m.
With the kids in bed, Berenike has an hour left to work. Because Riva is expanding its client base in Australia and New Zealand, a big part of Berenike's job is to stay involved in the community, both in person and online. She is a member of the local chapter of Women in Tech, and she regularly engages with other community members online and at meetups.

Though helping publicize Riva is part of her job, Berenike would engage with the community nonetheless. *"Can I put my identity into this ecosystem?"* she said. *"If I can, that's the way to become more successful."*

Tonight, Berenike writes a blog post about the challenges and strengths of single working moms before turning off the computer and relaxing with a glass of red wine.

PART THREE

TECHNICAL SKILLS AND CERTIFICATIONS

Ultimately, your ability to move forward in a Salesforce-related career will be determined by two skill sets: 1) Your technical skills, which are based on your training and experience (and can be showcased through project experience and certifications); and 2) your soft skills, which are the unquantifiable attributes that enable an employee to work with others, manage stress, and persist despite obstacles.

Part Four will dig deeper into the soft skills, whereas this section—Part Three—takes a look at the technical skills and ways to demonstrate these skills.

- **Chapter Twelve** guides you on the resources for gaining technical skills.

- **Chapter Thirteen** discusses certifications, why they are important, and what the certification process entails.

- **Chapter Fourteen** helps you proactively manage your Salesforce career.

CHAPTER TWELVE:
Technical Skills

How does one gain the technical skills necessary to enter the Salesforce workforce? Here is the good news: The resources are abundant, and many of them are free through Trailhead, which is Salesforce's robust portal for learning Salesforce (www.trailhead.salesforce.com). If you have the time and are determined, you can learn Salesforce without spending a penny.

Here is the bad news:

The resources are so abundant that it might seem overwhelming. You could spend hundreds upon hundreds of hours just sorting through the many different free resources, some of which extend beyond the actual Salesforce technology to broader business concepts such as unconscious bias, inclusive marketing practices, and trust building. The pathways are abundant, and there is no one-size-fits-all place to start.

The resources on Trailhead have been gamified—learners earn points and badges as they progress—so the process is fun. The Salesforce community is known for being friendly, helpful, and engaging, so more often than not, you will find someone who can point you in the right direction if you are confused about where to start.

Still, some would rather pay for a more directed learning experience, so Trailhead also features several dozen classes through Trailhead Academy, which offers in-person and virtual classes for people who want to master Salesforce.

In this chapter, let's take a closer look at the individual resources available for learning Salesforce. At the time of this writing, these resources included:

- Hundreds of modules

- More than 100 projects

- More than 100 "trails"

- Several dozen "trailmixes"

- A variety of other resources, including the Trailhead Academy and Trailhead Bootcamp

MODULES

Modules are dedicated to teaching specific bite-sized topics and using the related features. For instance, you can work through a 35-minute module that teaches you how accounts and contacts work together in Salesforce.

The modules have interactive challenges, and you will earn points for completing them. Salesforce has around 600 modules, and the numbers are growing as Salesforce releases new updates and features.

Through its Trailhead site, Salesforce has created a gamified method of learning Salesforce, and touting expertise along the way. You start off as a scout, with no points or badges, and work your way all the way to ranger by earning 50,000 points and 100 badges.

PROJECTS

If you want hands-on practice using the Salesforce skills you have learned, check out the Project portal, which allows users to select business-related projects, such as building a conference management app, as well as projects that are lighter in tone, such as the ones for building a battle station and building a bear-tracking device.

As with modules (and all free training resources available through Salesforce), you will earn points when you complete projects. Building an app to manage your lemonade stand will earn you 500 points; learning how to find and fix bugs with Apex Relay Debugger will earn you 400 points.

How do you earn badges on Trailhead?

When you finish any module or project, you will be awarded a badge, which represents your general knowledge of a specific topic.

TRAILS

Trails are guided learning paths that will take you through specific modules and projects based on the Salesforce role you are learning, your level, and the product you want to explore. For instance, as of the time of this writing, if you are exploring the role of an administrator as a beginner, and you want to learn about Service Cloud, Salesforce has six trails for you to explore. If you are an advanced business user wanting to learn about the Commerce Cloud, Trailhead has two trails for you to explore.

Again, you will earn points for these trails. The almost-two-hour "Build Your Career as a Salesforce B2C Commerce Functional Architect" trail will earn you 1,100 points; the eight-and-one-half-hour "Admin Beginning" trail will earn you 9,050 points.

TRAILMIXES

Next comes "trailmixes," which are customized learning paths that other people have shared based on their favorite trails, modules, and projects. There is, for instance, a seven-hour trailmix titled, "Get your company started with Trailhead," which helps companies create a culture of learning through the Trailhead resources. (You'll earn 4,700 points for navigating through this trailmix.) For those who are new to development, you will find a "Build Your Developer Career on Salesforce" trailmix that combines various projects, modules, and trails into a nearly eleven-hour course that will earn you 6,600 points.

Many trailmixes are created by Salesforce, but they also can be created by individuals who curate a list of trails and make public for others to follow.

Then there are "superbadges," which are earned when you complete a re-al-world business challenge. For instance, you can earn the Data Integra-tion superbadge (and 6,500 points) when you synchronize external data systems and Salesforce.

Unlike the general gamification badges (starting with scout and ending with ranger), superbadges are often added to a person's résumé. They val-idate your technical skills and showcase your real-world experience.

> *Superbadges are a great way to test your knowledge of concepts, features, and platform capabilities.*
>
> **—Mariella Brodersen**
> **Success manager**

With all of these available resources, it can be hard to know where to start.

Here are some tips from various Salesforce professionals:

> *I have learned a lot through Trail-head, but I have also done modules that have no relevance to me. Be discerning. There are a lot of options, so find the ones that are most relevant to your career path.*
>
> **—Lawson Teo**, Administrator

> *My favorite parts of Trailhead are the projects. They provide (almost) real-life scenarios and help you consider the available solutions from a variety of perspectives.*
>
> **—Cheri Poirier,**
> **Lead analyst, systems**

I learn best by exposure, so Trailhead didn't help a lot until I was actually in our Salesforce org solving real problems. If you're having a hard time retaining everything from the Trailheads, you're not alone.

—Tim Hage, Junior administrator

Trailhead is a great resource, but I honestly prefer asking more experienced colleagues. For anything development related, I prefer using documentation or blogs.

—Caroline Häming,
Senior consultant

Trailhead offers an overwhelming amount of knowledge, so it is easy to become burdened with unfinished trails and modules which leads to poor retention. Something as simple as setting a fixed time every day for trails (thirty or sixty minutes) and keeping notes (even if they aren't much more than a couple of words) can help keep you on track and boost your retention.

—Jorge Luis Pérez Pratt, Developer

The module materials are like stories, not boring text. Many times, they have a practical real-world exercise or a few questions to cement important principles. I use modules all the time to pick up new skills and keep the skills I don't use in my current job sharp.

—Moon Algazzali,
Administrator

Trailhead may be the best platform for studying in the world. I recommend following the trails instead of worrying about badges and points. Focus on learning what you need to learn.

—Marcos Vale,
Salesforce consultant

Trailhead can teach pretty much all aspects of Salesforce, and more. A word of warning: Once you dive into the more advanced modules, it can be a bit overwhelming. Just have patience. Don't give up. Break it into smaller pieces and keep learning.

—Mildred Morales,
IT and database director

Find the right modules for your needs, and then design and build things in a sandbox so that you are actually thinking about how Salesforce can solve your needs, as opposed to learning a theory without any applicability.

—Miranda Moonilal,
Senior administrator

Create a Trailhead playground for an aspect of your personal life, such as a side business, tracking a list of movies you have seen, books you have read, or trips you have taken. Then create an all point-and-click app with custom objects, fields, process builders, validation rules, quick actions, etcetera. This is the best way to try out new features, random things you think that could be fun or useful, but not necessarily relevant to your company. Also, this is a better way to memorize and enforce knowledge learned than in Trailhead standard generic tests.

—Lorenzo Alali, Administrator and business systems analyst

If you are using a Trailhead for a specific career path, jump to the superbadges and, when you get stuck on a concept you don't understand or a configuration you can't find, work backward.

—Corey Cacananta,
Developer and consultant

Trailhead alone is not enough. It needs to be supplemented with actual use.

—Ben Stokes,
Administrator

> *I love Trailhead, and it is extremely useful. However, beware that Trailhead alone does not sufficiently prepare you for the test. Trailhead gives you an exercise, and you solve it. The test is more general and nuanced.*
>
> **—Eric von Stromberg**, Project manager

OTHER RESOURCES

In addition to the resources available through Trailhead, you can also find additional resources through:

- **The Salesforce YouTube channel,**
- **Salesforce blogs and bloggers,**
- **The #AskForce hashtag on Twitter,**
- **The Trailblazer's Guide to Careers podcast,**
- **The Salesforce StackExchange (www.salesforce.stackexchange. com), which is a Q&A web portal for Salesforce professionals.**
- **The Trailblazers Community on Trailhead, which includes:**

  1. The Answers forum, which is a forum that allows community members to ask and answer questions; and

  2. MVP Office Hours, which is a forum that allows community members to engage with Salesforce MVPs.

Salesforce MVPs are announced annually by Salesforce. Salesforce describes MVPs as "lifelong learners who go above and beyond to share their expertise and help the entire community blaze trails." At the time of this printing, more than 200 people had been named MVPs.

The Salesforce community is unique in that it has so many engaged, active participants who are willing to help one another. In fact, the enthusiasm with which community members help each other is so surprising that an urban legend has sprung forth. According to the tall tale, one MVP answered 10,000 questions in the Answers forum and on the Stack Exchange over the course of six months. The truth is that he answered thousands of questions over the course of two years, but he did so while working a full-time job and raising his family.

We are a great little glee club.

—Rob Kaplan
Senior consultant and engagement manager

The point being:

If you pose a question in any of the forums dedicated to transferring Salesforce knowledge, you will get an answer. In fact, you will probably get more than one answer, and you will get these answers in the first hour. Salesforce professionals are dedicated to helping out their community, and they will find time to help you locate the resources you need, free of charge.

If you go looking, you will find no shortage of resources for getting answers to your questions.

TRAILHEAD ACADEMY

Through virtual and in-person classes, Salesforce offers several dozen classes that are more direct learning experiences. To give you an idea of cost, the five-day (virtual or in-person) class "Administrative Essentials for New Admins" costs will cost some thousands of dollars. It includes everything you need to know to become a Salesforce Certified Administrator. A two-day class specific to Service Cloud Administrators will be less expensive.

Is it worth it?

Check out what some Salesforce professionals have to say about Trailhead Academy.

The Admin 101 course was incredibly valuable to me as a first-time administrator. However, I do think there are a lot of free or less expensive options that can replace that course as long as you are a strong self-starter.

—Emily Duncan, Administrator

Trailhead Academy is much better than Trailhead. The exam preparation is amazing and was critical to my success in getting certified.

—Jared Beard,
Senior solutions engineer

I paid for the System Architect class, and it was fantastic. The investment paid off quickly since there are integration projects currently being undertaken at my company, and we had a few integration issues, which I was able to fix faster thanks to the stuff I learned through the Academy. I would recommend having at least some basic knowledge, depending on which course you attend, before attending the classes. The classes are intensive, so you will benefit more if you already have some knowledge.

—Hao Lu, Database administrator

I understand that people feel compelled to compare Trailhead and Trailhead Academy, but they must be seen as complementary rather than similar. Trailhead Academy aligns with certifications, and the instructors respond directly to your questions. Trailhead aligns with whatever Salesforce is promoting at a point in time, and the catalogue of courses gets larger and larger every month. In the best-case scenario, users respond to your questions via social networks.

—Fabrice Cathala,
Solution architect

TRAILHEAD BOOTCAMP

The Trailhead Bootcamp is a four-day, in-person event that combines expert-led training, on-site help from instructors and fellow attendees within specialized study groups, networking opportunities, and two chances to obtain Salesforce certifications. A participant can choose from one of six tracks including Administrator, Platform Developer, Marketing Cloud Email Marketer, Pardot Digital Marketer, Application Architect, and System Architect. For most of the day, participants spend time with their instructor and group in their chosen track room.

The first chance to take an exam is set at the start of the Bootcamp, and the second chance comes on Thursday, toward the end of the event. So much learning is expected to happen between the two exams that you can take the same exam twice if you do not pass the first try.

The first Trailhead Academy in Australia, held in June of 2019. Our instructor patiently explained oAuth Flows.

But it wasn't all studying! We took time to enjoy great food, music, and even some fire-twirling entertainment

Day in the life:
JOHN CONWAY

Meet John Conway, a principal enterprise architect at Salesforce. Before he joined Salesforce, he worked in management consulting, private equity, and at some start-ups. His first exposure to Salesforce was as a customer. John was impressed by how easy Salesforce was to use and customize. He became an AppExchange partner and built one of the first Lightning components to be listed on the App-Exchange. His next move was to a Big Four consulting firm where he worked on Salesforce implementations and Agile transformation projects. He was then re-cruited by Salesforce from a LinkedIn post made by his current manager.

John generously shared some of his personal thoughts and opinions about a day working as an enterprise architect for Salesforce.

"Every day is different, which is one of the things that I like about working for Sales-force. I get to interact with a wide variety of customers and account teams. The enter-prise architect role is unique in Salesforce in that I am a generalist who covers all the cloud solutions offered by Salesforce and our partners. I use that knowledge to help cus-tomers understand the platform. I also lead Salesforce's Illuminate program in Western Canada. Illuminate is Salesorce's approach to enterprise architecture. During an Illuminate, we help our customers to develop a technology vision with an action plan to implement that vision."

"Salesforce has four core values that touch everything we do. These are trust, customer success, innovation, and equality. When I was interviewed, it was clear that Salesforce was looking for people who can live these values every day."

"As for soft skills, those will vary by role, but in general, I think we are looking for people with emotional intelligence who are strong communicators and can adapt quickly to change."

"The soft skills I use the most are:

1. **Emotional intelligence, to deal with a wide variety of customers and account teams;**

2. **Project management skills, to lead the Illuminate projects;**

3. **Business acumen, to understand what our customers are trying to achieve.**"

"Salesforce is very flexible. I can stay in the enterprise architecture role and progress to a master or distinguished architect. However, if I wanted to try something else I could apply for any position at Salesforce. Salesforce is very generous when it comes to education and provides us with numerous internal learning opportunities as well as an education reimbursement."

"I think that Salesforce's commitment to the community is incredible. Our 1-1-1 philanthropy model is unique. We donate one percent of our time, equity, and products to communities around the world. Late last year, I taught 21 newcomers to Canada how to be Salesforce admins. The total program involved nine partners, 21 students, and 30 volunteers. Without Salesforce's one-percent pledge, we would not have been able to fund the program."

"My favorite thing about working for Salesforce is our ecosystem and how enthusiastic they are about our solutions and Salesforce as an organization. Last time I checked into a hotel, the receptionist noticed I worked for Salesforce and told me how much she and her colleagues loved using Salesforce as it made their work experience so much better."

CHAPTER THIRTEEN:
Certifications

Plenty of reasons exist for getting your Salesforce certification, but this should be said upfront: Certification is not a golden ticket to a job. It should not be the first thing you focus on, nor should it replace actual experience and training.

Certification is like getting a diploma.

It shows that you have passed some courses, but this hardly equates to real-world, on-the-job training. I say this upfront because I want to be clear: Certification alone is not enough to set you up for a career in Salesforce. Just like you would cross-train to run a marathon, you should have a healthy mix of experience, training, and certifications for a strong start in your Salesforce career.

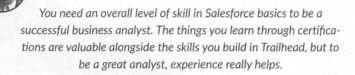

You need an overall level of skill in Salesforce basics to be a successful business analyst. The things you learn through certifications are valuable alongside the skills you build in Trailhead, but to be a great analyst, experience really helps.

—David Beckham
Senior lead Salesforce business analyst

WHY GET CERTIFIED?

Though there are plenty of highly skilled Salesforce workers who do not have any certifications at all, here are some of the arguments in favor of getting Salesforce certifications:

- More and more, employers require certification as a condition of hiring. Certification offers employers an objective way to benchmark and verify a candidate's ability.

- Being certified can help you position yourself for a raise within your existing company.

- Certification helps connect you to others in the Salesforce community, and it increases your reputation (in the same way that badges and superbadges will).

- Salesforce certified professionals have to take certification maintenance exams to retain your credentials. This means you will have to keep up to date with changes and new functionality, which will help you communicate to employers that you are staying abreast of the ongoing releases by Salesforce.

- You will feel more confident, which has several benefits. You will be more likely to attend community events, feel better about engaging these events, and present yourself more favorably during job interviews.

Right off the bat, the second I had a certification, I felt confident in myself. As someone who has never been a developer before, it was really important for me to have a sheet of paper that said, "Dominick, you are a developer now."

But I think the true benefit of having a certification really is for the very reason Salesforce set out to certify people, which is that certification is a rigorous process meant to weed out the people who are not actually qualified for the work they are doing. If you have a certification, you stand out as qualified, and that helped me when talking to clients and when establishing my own credibility when working with people under me.

—Dominick DeFazio
Developer and chief technology officer

CERTIFICATIONS AND THE SALESFORCE CAREER LADDER

The number of certifications Salesforce offers is always growing, but as of the printing of this book, it offered around 30. These certifications include base-level certifications such as Administrator and Advanced Administrator, and more niche ones, such as CPQ Specialists and Marketing Cloud Email Specialist.

CERTIFICATION OVERVIEW

The following diagram groups some of the more in-demand certifications into tracks. Those new to Salesforce, regardless of the role that they will be working in, are encouraged to obtain the Admin certification. Not only is it a prerequisite for some of the other certifications, but it also covers the basics of the platform and point-and-click configuration.

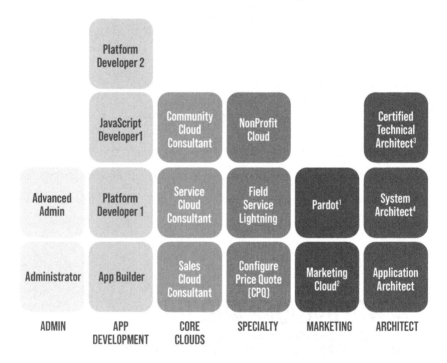

[1] Pardot certifications include Pardot Specialist and Pardot Consultant

[2] Marketing Cloud certifications include Marketing Cloud Administrator, Marketing Cloud Consultant, Marketing Cloud Developer, Marketing Cloud Email Specialist

[3] Application Architect certification will be granted on completion of the following certifications: Data Architecture and Management Designer, Sharing and Visibility Designer, Platform Developer I, Platform App Builder

[4] System Architect certification will be granted on completion of the following certifications: Development Lifecycle and Deployment Designer, Identity and Access Management Designer, Integration Architecture Designer, Platform Developer I

The App Development track is for those that will be involved in building and developing apps, both declaratively and programatically. The App Builder certification covers declaratively application development, the platform developer certifications extend into programmatic development.

The Sales, Service and Community Cloud Consultant certifications cover in detail the functionality and configuration options for these core Salesforce products. Although they are named "Consultant" certifications, you could be an internal consultant implementing one of these products internally dealing with internal stakeholders, or you could be an external consultant implementing the product as part of a consulting company.

The specialty certifications include products that provide niche functionality that are used by segments of the overall Salesforce user base. The usefulness of obtaining these depends on if you will be using these products as part of current or future work and projects.

The Marketing Certifications cover the Pardot and Marketing Cloud products. Pardot is a business-to-business (B2B) marketing automation tool whereas Marketing Cloud is designed for business-to-consumer (B2C). So again, the decision to pursue these certifications will depend on if your organization already uses these products or if you will be exposed to them in future project work.

The Application Architect and System Architect certifications are achieved after a number of prerequisite certifications have been successfully completed. The Certified Technical Architect certification is granted on the completion of Application Architect, System Architect and passing an in-person board review examination.

As someone who helps people with their certification goals, I am often asked the same two questions:

- *"How many certifications do I need?"* and
- *"In what order should I take the certifications?"*

Some people will argue that five certifications or seven certifications is the magic number, but I disagree. The order in which you take the certifications, and the number of certifications you earn, depends upon your career path. If you are an admin, and you do not wish to move beyond this role, aim for three certifications to start with: Administrator, Advanced Administrator, and Platform App Builder. Then you may consider Sales Consultant, Service Consultant, or Community Cloud, depending on which cloud your organization has implemented or is planning to implement. If you are a consultant working with a wide variety of clients, you might need more than seven, including some of the specialty certifications.

The following diagrams show the certification paths that might be necessary for:

- **End-User Functional Careers**
- **End-User Technical Careers**
- **Consulting Careers**

Remember, plenty of people have Salesforce careers and do not have certifications, meaning the certification paths depicted may or may not be mandatory based on your individual employer. If you are just starting in Salesforce and you do not yet have a job, I strongly recommend beginning the certification process as it will open more doors and stack the deck in your favor.

CERTIFICATIONS FOR END-USER FUNCTIONAL CAREERS

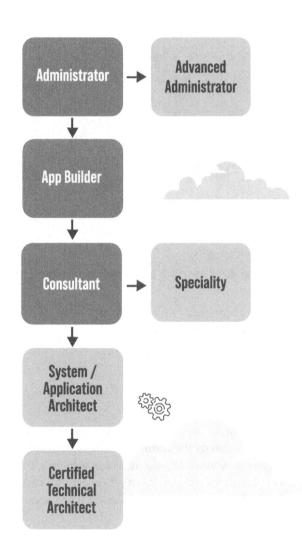

ADMINISTRATOR

People working in a functional role should start with the Admin certification to understand the basics of the Salesforce platform.

ADVANCED ADMINISTRATOR

Advanced Admin covers more advanced configuration platform features. The Admin certification will provide the fundamentals. Advanced Admin topics will dive deeper into advanced application of configuring Salesforce and its features, including security, reporting, and process automation tools.

APP BUILDER

The App Builder certification will allow understanding of declarative configuration capabilities of the platform.

CONSULTANT

Depending on project and organization needs, Sales Cloud, Service Cloud, and Community Cloud consultant certifications will be useful.

SPECIALTY

Depending on the clouds that an organization or project uses, a consultant can study for a specialized certification such as Field Service Lightning, CPQ, or Marketing Cloud.

SYSTEM / APPLICATION ARCHITECT

A solution architect would progress to the architect-level certifications and aim for achieving Application Architect and System Architect certifications. These will provide the required domain knowledge to design appropriate solutions.

CERTIFIED TECHNICAL ARCHITECT

A CTA certification demonstrates the ability to apply knowledge of all Salesforce architectural domains. A candidate must design a solution to a scenario and successfully present to a technical review board.

CERTIFICATIONS FOR END-USER TECHNICAL CAREERS

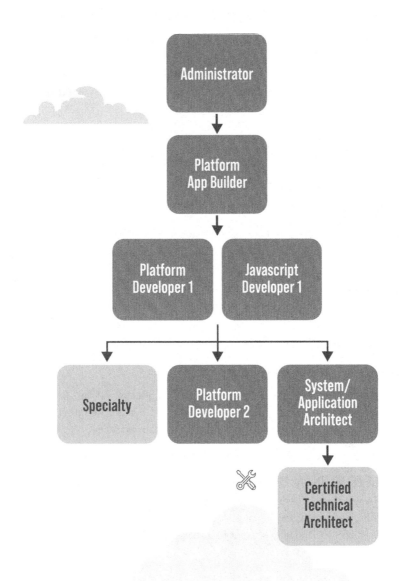

ADMINISTRATOR

A developer should start with the Admin certification to understand the fundamentals of the Salesforce platform.

PLATFORM APP BUILDER

The App Builder certification will allow a developer to understand declarative configuration capabilities of the platform.

PLATFORM DEVELOPER 1

With PD1 a developer will learn and confirm their knowledge of how to develop programmatic solutions using APEX, VF, SOQL, and the Lightning Framework.

JAVASCRIPT DEVELOPER 1

The Lightning user interface and Lightning components use a JavaScript framework, so developers need to have a working knowledge of Javascript.

SPECIALTY

Depending on the clouds that an organization or project uses, a developer can study for a specialized certification such as Community Cloud, CPQ, or Marketing Cloud.

PLATFORM DEVELOPER 2

PD2 certification can be achieved to learn and confirm knowledge of advanced Salesforce development practices.

SYSTEM / APPLICATION ARCHITECT

As a developer progresses to work on solution and technical designs, architect-level certifications, leading to System and Application architect, will provide the domain knowledge required to design appropriate solutions.

CERTIFIED TECHNICAL ARCHITECT

A CTA certification demonstrates the ability to apply knowledge of all Salesforce architectural domains. A candidate must design a solution to a scenario and successfully present to a technical review board.

CERTIFICATIONS FOR CONSULTING CAREERS

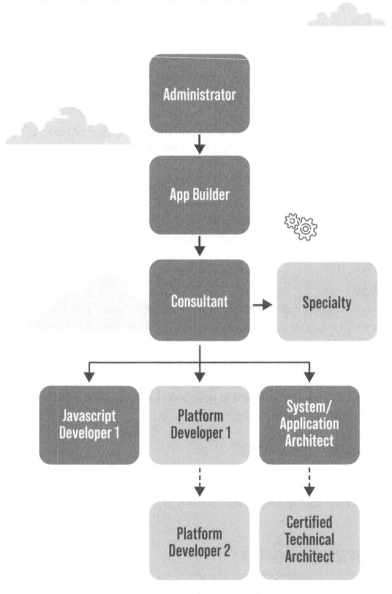

ADMINISTRATOR

A consultant should start with the Admin certification to understand the basics of the Salesforce platform.

APP BUILDER

The App Builder certification will allow a consultant to understand declarative configuration capabilities of the platform.

CONSULTANT

Depending on project and organization needs, a consultant can achieve Sales Cloud, Service Cloud, and Community Cloud consultant certifications.

SPECIALTY

Depending on the clouds that an organization or project uses, a consultant can study for a specialised certification such as Field Service Lightning, CPQ, or Marketing Cloud.

JAVASCRIPT DEVELOPER 1

The Lightning user interface and Lightning components use a JavaScript framework, so developers need to have a working knowledge of Javascript.

PLATFORM DEVELOPER 1

With PD1 a developer will learn and confirm their knowledge of how to develop programmatic solutions using APEX, VF, SOQL, and the Lightning Framework.

SYSTEM / APPLICATION ARCHITECT

As a consultant progresses to work on solution designs, architect-level certifications, leading to System and Application architect, will provide the required domain knowledge to design appropriate solutions.

PLATFORM DEVELOPER 2

PD2 certification can be achieved to learn and confirm knowledge of advanced Salesforce development practices.

CERTIFIED TECHNICAL ARCHITECT

A CTA certification demonstrates the ability to apply knowledge of all Salesforce architectural domains. A candidate must design a solution to a scenario and successfully present to a technical review board.

A word to the wise about certifications:

You might be tempted to cram as many certification tests into the shortest duration of time. Resist this temptation. Remember that it is important for you to have a healthy mix of Salesforce-related information on your résumé. Employers will not care if you have eighteen Salesforce certifications if you have no experience. Instead, take a balanced approach that demonstrates knowledge, experience, and certification:

1. Earn some badges and superbadges through Trailhead (or take course through the Academy),

2. Volunteer for a nonprofit to gain Salesforce experience, and/or create a free app to promote your expertise through the AppExchange, and

3. Pace yourself as you move through the certifications paths consistently and as necessary, but remember that certifications are not golden tickets.

Having the Administrator certification is really the first goal that everyone should have. When it comes time after that to start deciding which certification paths and training paths to take next, start by asking where your own interests are. Then combine your interests with the training and certification that is available, whether that is sales, marketing, service, or some other path.

—Matthew Sutton
Founder of Resonant Cloud Solutions, a consulting firm with offices in Australia and India

Because my company helps people pursue their certifications, I rounded up three people who took their certifications and interviewed them about their thoughts, expectations, and strategies in preparing for the exam. I also interviewed them again after the certification exam to see what they thought of the experience.

The results of this interview are detailed in the chart. For privacy, they are referred to as Admin 1, Dev 1, and Admin 2.

Admin I	Admin II	Dev I
Which certification are you preparing for? Why this one?		
I've been preparing for the Salesforce Administrator Certification. I plan to take on future certifications but the Admin exam is the first on my list. It's a good foundation to get immersed in the Salesforce environment.	I'm preparing for the Admin certification because it will provide a good foundation for Salesforce and also for the other certs I plan to pursue in the future.	Salesforce Platform Developer I. My background is a full-stack developer, and I am going in the direction of becoming a top-notch Salesforce developer or, who knows, even a Salesforce architect! It's free to dream big.
How much time did you spend preparing for this exam?		
I've dedicated a few hours each day over the past 2 months. It's easy since the work that I do serves as a way to review as well.	Hard to say because I didn't prepare in one go. I was studying last year, slowly but surely, but did not have an exact exam date scheduled. Eventually, I stopped. Now that I've booked for the Bootcamp, I've been studying for 1 month.	I learned that I [would be taking this certification] from a company that I just joined. Being new in my company and with so many things to learn and process, I can't really say that I am very well prepared. Studying and being able to contribute at work at the same time is a challenge.

Admin I	Admin II	Dev I

Do you have a system to your exam preparation?

Admin I	Admin II	Dev I
I use Trailhead, [your company's] study guides and practice exams. I also engage in forums so I get different perspectives from others.	Since it's my first time to try to get certified, I'm still exploring all the possible ways to prepare. Learning with Trailhead and then reinforcing what you learned using Trailhead Playground or your dev org really helps.	Going through the study guides, testing the theory in an org, and then taking the practice exams works best for me. I wish I'd run through the trailhead modules thoroughly as well if time permitted me, as I know those are also extremely essential.

What was the most difficult part of preparing for the exam?

Admin I	Admin II	Dev I
Just the breadth of knowledge that is involved. There are just too many things to study.	Since the Admin certification is the most basic of all, the questions can be about anything. Also, the questions can be concept or scenario-based. You really have to know Salesforce thoroughly.	The coverage is really vast. Trying to wrap your head around general basic knowledge, concepts, and features, from declarative capabilities down to the programmatic bits is really a huge task.

What is your checklist or go-to [study] material?

Admin I	Admin II	Dev I
Salesforce Trailhead, [your company's] study guides, practice exams, and forums, Salesforce on StackExchange.	Since the Admin certification is the most basic of all, the questions can be about anything. Also, the questions can be concept or scenario-based. You really have to know Salesforce thoroughly.	The coverage is really vast. Trying to wrap your head around general basic knowledge, concepts, and features, from declarative capabilities down to the programmatic bits is really a huge task.

Admin I	Admin II	Dev I

How were you feeling right before the exam?

Admin I	Admin II	Dev I
I felt nervous especially that I probably pressured myself too hard. I just knew that I had to pass the exam and that time was it.	I was calmer than I expected. I did the best I could do to prepare given the circumstances. I was looking forward to my first cert exam experience and was also curious about it.	On the morning of the first exam, I was feeling giddy. I was just really ready to get started and tested on my Salesforce knowledge.

What was the most difficult thing about the exam?

Admin I	Admin II	Dev I
Definitely the time pressure.	The way the questions were phrased can get really tricky! It may initially seem like it's about a certain topic, but it's something different.	The low-level questions that honed in on very specific programming aspects made the exam most difficult.

What didn't you expect?

Admin I	Admin II	Dev I
Maybe just the sheer number of participants especially for our track.	I didn't expect to have enough time to review the questions I marked.	There were a lot more coding questions than I had expected to answer.

What do you think was the key for passing the exam?

Admin I	Admin II	Dev I
Identifying and improving on areas I found myself I was weakest at, which was made possible through [your company's] study materials, and focusing more on the topics that had more weight was the key to passing the exam.	It is important to know where you stand in each category because that's how you know where to zero in. Also, you need to take the category weightings into consideration. That way, you can be more efficient with the time you have for studying.	Understanding the format of the exam, which questions had more weight, knowing that you have an opportunity to go back to questions you weren't quite sure about the answer to. I only felt the pressure after I submitted my answers and was waiting for the results.

Admin I	Admin II	Dev I

What could you have changed about your preparation?
What could you have done better?

I thought that the 2nd exam was just another opportunity for those who failed the first. When I found out that I could choose another exam, I didn't know which certification to take next and so I didn't get to plan that quite well. [Author's note: Participants took their certifications during the Australian Trailhead Bootcamp, where they were invited to take two certifications.]	I wish I managed my time better and prioritized studying more. I did not get to finish the pre-work given to us and I'm sure that would have helped by a lot. I would have known what I needed to improve on and ask for help from the instructors.	I would want to complete the Platform Developer I Trailmix as I completely missed that in my preparation.

TIPS ON TAKING CERTIFICATION EXAMS

Here are three of the best practices for taking and passing your certification exam.

Create a Schedule

I liken this to marathon training. Most people *can* complete a marathon, but they have to be willing to put in the practice runs. The same goes with passing a certification. Well in advance of the test, create a schedule, complete with time for studying, hands-on practice, and practice exams.

This means that you should select a target date for taking your test. Ninety days is a good guideline for the time required to prepare, but you can and should adjust this up or down based on your existing knowledge, experience, and time available to study.

Once you have a target date, list everything you need to do to meet this date, and then break the big goal into smaller parts by listing your mini goals. Work backward from the target date and schedule time to complete all of these mini-goals, which you can then tick off once you achieve them.

Tracking your progress and achieving your mini-goals motivates you to keep going.

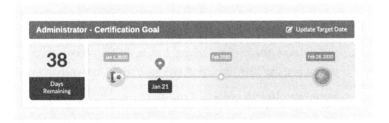

When planning your time, use a traditional calendar or make use of technology to track your progress. Here is a screenshot of our certification-training platform, which shows your progress toward reaching your target date.

Know the Test Objectives

Each certification has an exam outline that details what the test is assessing. Being familiar with the objectives tells you what to study. Again, this is like running a marathon. If the course description says you will face a few gnarly hill runs, you would be certain to have hill runs as part of your training.

Using the objectives, make summary notes and focus on mastering the Salesforce elements you need to achieve these objectives.

Diversify & Practice

The best test-takers use a variety of different platforms and methods for preparing. They complete trailheads. They study course material. They use hands-on experiential learning in their own Salesforce orgs.. They practice by training their minds to visualize themselves taking the test. They take practice exams and use them as a feedback loop to get better each time.

I will liken this to running a marathon: You need to eat well, get a lot of sleep, and use a combination of tempo training and interval runs to best prepare your mind and body.

TIPS ON TAKING CERTIFICATION EXAMS

Create a Schedule	Know the Test Objectives	Diversify & Practice
Select a target date. 90 days out is reasonable.

Then list everything you need to do to reach this target date.

Working backward from the target date, schedule time for reaching all of these mini-goals. | Each certification outlines what the test is assessing.

Use these objectives to make summary notes. Focus on mastering the Salesforce elements you need to achieve these objectives. | Use a variety of ways to prepare. Study course material. Use hands-on experiential learning as well as course preps. Visualize yourself taking the test. And take practice exams. |

Day in the life:
NATALYA MURPHY

Natalya Murphy earned thirteen Salesforce certifications in three years after being out of the IT world for a decade. She has found her home as a developer, choosing to work part-time for a consulting company. For a brief bit, Natalya worked full-time, but she decided to return to part-time work so she could continue to homeschool her children and focus on other personal projects.

Natalya works from home.

7:00 a.m.
Natalya and her husband wake up, take the dog for a walk, then come home and eat breakfast.

Natalya began working from home when her youngest son was born in 2003, so remote work is second-nature to her. Because of the coronavirus pandemic, her husband also worked from home temporarily. And because the couple homeschool their children, they also have the noise of teenagers in the background, meaning they spend a portion of the day closing doors, asking people to lower their voices, and juggling the demands of co-workers, employers, and kids.

8:00 a.m.
Natalya has her first stand-up. This one is to discuss a government project which has three separate scrum teams. Natalya straddles across two of these teams doing prototyping work for possible stories that the client might want to do.

This stand-up looks like a typical stand-up: The team members say what they worked on yesterday, what they will be working on today, and what challenges they encounter. The scrum master makes announcements, and the call ends.

Next, Natalya joins a second call with system integrators from other scrum teams and projects who are also deploying to the same production org. On this call they get a status update from the people who run the deployments for the government agency. At this agency, releases go into production once a month.

After that, she's on to a third standup for the second scrum team she works with.

9:00 a.m.

With the stand-ups out of the way, Natalya looks at what stories need to move up to the next environment. She tries to stay out of the DevOps piece of the process, but she does occasionally step in to help.

Natalya's team makes heavy use of Slack. At any given time, there are at least ten active Slack channels, so she has Slack open all day. If Natalya sees a message pop up, she assesses the urgency, and either replies immediately, tags a team member that is better able to answer the question or, on rare occasion, leaves the question for someone else in the channel to answer.

Today, the QA team is testing work from the team's previous sprint, and they are having a problem with regression testing. The team needs a fast response so they can proceed.

Natalya looks into this particular piece of functionality and responds within the hour with a solution.

10:00 a.m.

A message comes in on Slack asking Natalya to clarify some over-lapping functionality. *"A lot of my day consists of interruptions,"* she says. *"Imagine that you are sitting in an office and forty people are shouting across the room asking for different things. That's what my day looks like, but the conversations are happening online."*

10:30 a.m.

Natalya has taken on the role of "release manager," a self-designated title that she uses to describe the process of making sure all the pieces are in the right place for a release. Do they have their timeline right? Are all the folks doing what they need to be doing? Have they factored all of the quality control issues in? Today, Natalya reviews the document her team needs to provide to the production deployment group and compares it against the team's configuration log to ensure any necessary manual steps such as enabling new Process Builder versions are accounted for.

In preparation for the monthly release, the team is getting ready to push their package into the next-highest sandbox—the first integration point with other project teams. The sandbox was recently refreshed, and Nata-lya spends some time taking care of post-refresh steps, such as updating named credentials and creating supporting test data so the QA team can start testing as soon as the package deploys. She runs an Apex script she wrote to create a group of generic users and another script to reset emails and passwords for forty team members.

11:30 a.m.

Natalya takes a break to take her daughter to the store to pick up some supplies. Her daughter has started an online Etsy shop and needs to pick up more raw materials to make some samples.

Natalya's commitment to her project team is that she will be available to respond to incoming queries from 8:00 a.m. until 4:30 p.m. Eastern time, but she does not have to be physically online.

She lets her co-workers and employer know that she will be stepping out for a bit. While she's away, her Slack notifications keep coming in on her phone, and Natalya responds to them as time allows (but never while driving!).

1:30 p.m.

When Natalya returns, she has some breathing room before her next meeting with an integration team. Today she's working on a Lightning Web Component that will be used on a flow screen to display multiple addresses to end-users and allow them to select one or more addresses for updating. She also works on enhancing an older Aura component that needs to be connected with another Aura component so the UI will flow seamlessly from one pop-up screen to the next.

While working on this component, she notices that the test class for the related Apex controller has some failures so she spends some time troubleshooting it. It turns out a new auto-launched flow is running and is looking for some data that the Apex test isn't currently creating. She updates the test setup method in the test and all is well again.

3:30 p.m.

Natalya is a volunteer instructor for RAD Women, which teaches experienced Salesforce administrators how to write Apex code. She stops her time-tracking app and logs on to her personal computer to review her students' homework assignments and get ready for the next 90-minute session. She isn't doing billable work for her employer, but she does have Slack open in case a query comes in.

There's a problem with a story deployment into the QA sandbox and she offers ideas on how it might be resolved. One of the scrum masters reaches out to her to ask a question about one of her stories. A tester reaches out to ask about one of her stories she's testing.

4:30 p.m.

Family time. Natalya spends some time in the kitchen chatting with her husband while they prepare dinner.

After dinner, the family walks the dog and spends some time reading and watching a couple of favorite sitcoms on Hulu.

7:30 p.m.

Truth be told, it's easiest for Natalya to get work done during the evenings, when there isn't a flurry of Slack messages coming in to interrupt her. Tonight, Natalya works for a couple of hours on the Aura components she was looking at earlier before heading to bed.

CHAPTER FOURTEEN:
Proactively Managing Your Career

So far, this book has provided much information about the career paths available in the Salesforce world, and about entering the Salesforce ecosystem. However, to move forward and grow, keep in mind that once you have entered the world of Salesforce, you must also manage your career proactively.

Your career will grow faster if you have the initiative to take stock of where you are today, plan where you would like to be in the future, and take action.

Together with Jay Sen, an HR expert and my co-founder at CloudTalent360.com, we have developed a program for proactively managing your Salesforce career. Jay breaks a career management plan into eight components:

1. Career situation analysis

2. Career results journal

3. Quarterly performance review

4. Career plan

5. Interview skills

6. Negotiating salary plus benefits

7. Your professional brand

8. Networking via online and physical events

1. CAREER SITUATION ANALYSIS

Start by considering your current career situation. Organize and summarize the key information about your current situation including your current role, salary, bonuses, certifications, public profile, and community contributions. You should also consider aspects of your personality and personal preferences that can have an impact on both your performance and your ability to find and progress in the most suitable career path for you.

2. CAREER RESULTS JOURNAL

A "career results journal" can help you document and organize your efforts and results on a daily, weekly, monthly, and quarterly basis. It can include:

- Daily wins

- Weekly most important result

- Monthly achievements summary

- Quarterly key accomplishments

If you just spend ten to fifteen minutes per day, you can create an ongoing journal of your results. These results can be used to reflect and refer back to when tracking progress toward your goals, to remind yourself of your progress and achievements when presenting during performance reviews, and to update your CV and job applications.

3. QUARTERLY PERFORMANCE REVIEW

Many people dread the performance review and feel unprepared. Instead of scrambling at the last minute to document your accomplishments, you can be fully prepared to present your achievements and maximize the time in the review meeting by following a proactive process that includes:

- Proactively providing a performance review meeting agenda.

- Documenting accomplishments on an ongoing regular basis in a career results journal and having them ready in a structured format for the review.

- Using a template to document and summarise the outcome, agreements and actions agreed to.

Imagine feeling in control and waiting for the performance review process!

4. CAREER PLAN

Set challenging goals for your career to drive yourself forward with focus and motivation. Break your goals down into a plan and actions required to achieve the goals.

Develop a clear one- to three-year plan for where you want to be, how much you want to earn, and the steps to get there. Mapping out a realistic plan will help you move forward in your Salesforce career, getting promoted and moving up to the next levels.

Instead of wishing and hoping to get promoted, taking the time to plan your next steps should include considering what experience is needed for each level, the typical years of experience that you will need, and the actions you can take to progress.

When formulating the plan, you should consider this for the specific career path that you are following:

- The key experiences required for the next level.

- Technical skills required at each level.

- If project management skills are required.

- Which people management skills are required.

5. INTERVIEW SKILLS

Interviewing is a skill that you can develop and improve over time. In fact, strengthening this skill should be part of your career management plan. The skills you can develop include following a structured process to prepare in advance for the interview, practicing your delivery of answers, knowing how to handle difficult questions, and engaging your interviewer to demonstrate and explain your previous experience and your interest and fit for the role.

6. NEGOTIATING SALARY + BENEFITS

Once you have an offer, you need to start the negotiation process. Obtaining the best outcome requires preparation. Negotiation can be a positive experience and a win-win situation for both parties when you are both prepared and come to the table with knowledge.

Remember that there are various parts of the compensation makeup. Be prepared to consciously trade one to get the best mix for your situation, considering:

- Base salary
- Geographic considerations
- Remote working
- Flexibility in hours
- Cost of living
- Bonuses/sign-on
- Benefits (time off, relocation, etc.)

7. YOUR PROFESSIONAL BRAND

Interviewing is a skill that you can develop and improve over time. In fact, strengthening this skill should be part of your career management plan. The skills you can develop include following a structured process to prepare in advance for the interview, practicing your delivery of answers, knowing how to handle difficult questions, and engaging your interviewer to demonstrate and explain your previous experience and your interest and fit for the role.

8. NETWORKING VIA ONLINE AND PHYSICAL EVENTS

Networking is important to meet and connect with people in the community. As Richard Clarke, National Salesforce practice director and principal technical architect at PS+C Artisan said, "People do business with people that they trust and like." Attending events and getting to know people, even online, will set you apart from others and give you the chance to build a relationship that could benefit either party now or in the future.

There are so many events to choose from, so you will need to be thoughtful and strategic and decide which events will help you achieve your goals. Sometimes your goals will not just be about moving your career forward, but helping others.

Set goals for the number and types of events you plan to attend and book them in your calendar.

NEED HELP WITH YOUR CAREER MANAGEMENT PLAN?

Learn how to clarify your goals, create a plan, and develop skills to increase the value of your performance reviews, negotiate better offers, and improve your interview skills. The Salesforce Career Accelerator is provided by CloudTalent360.com, a career management service company founded by Martin Gessner and Jay Sen.

To get started, head over to
https://cloudtalent360.com/career-assessment-book-offer/
for a free career assessment.

Day in the life:
MARC LESTER

Marc Lester is a Senior Salesforce Consultant for a platinum-level Salesforce consultant partner, a community group leader in Jacksonville, Florida, and a planning team member for the Florida Dreamin' conference. Marc and his wife have a fifteen-year-old son. Since Marc works from home and has a flexible schedule, he is able to commit to his full-time job, attend school and sports-events with his family, and volunteer within the Salesforce community.

7:30 a.m.

Marc starts his workday by looking through his emails and responding to his colleagues at work and his clients. Because Marc is heavily involved in the Salesforce community, he has set up alerts so that he receives emails when posts are made in various Salesforce community groups. This morning, he responds to a client asking for help on updating the Log-a-Call page on a mobile device, and he responds to a new Salesforce user asking for advice on resources available to work towards getting certified.

8:30 a.m.

Marc has a fifteen-minute standup call every day with a client in support of its Health Cloud implementation across multiple teams within the organization. Marc is responsible for coordinating the release management process across all the work-streams. Following the call, he spends a couple of hours each day working on requests from a client. Today, Marc is creating reports and dashboards to help support the client's key KPIs for a new implementation that is about to wrap up.

10:30 a.m.

For at least six months of the year, Marc has daily work to prepare for Florida Dreamin' (a Salesforce community conference), and today is no different. Marc is responsible for coordinating sponsors for Florida Dreamin' and takes a break from his consulting work to review the current status of all potential and committed sponsors to determine actions required. Marc sends a few emails to follow-up with potential sponsors and checks in with a fellow team member to share newly committed sponsors on the Florida Dreamin' website and in social media. He also coordinates a quick call with a potential sponsor to provide further details on the benefits of sponsoring the conference and answer any other questions.

11:30 a.m.

Marc has his second client meeting of the day: A project kick-off meeting with a new client to implement a Sales Cloud quick start so they can properly track their leads, opportunities, and existing customers, as well as all the activities related to each of these throughout the sales lifecycle. The meeting lasts about an hour. Following the meeting, Marc has lunch at his desk while he schedules weekly status meetings with the new client and logs into the new client's Salesforce Org for the first time to review current setup, such as Org edition, license types, and available users.

2:00 p.m.

His third and final meeting of the day is with a client to discuss actions that are required to ensure expected data quality across the client's source database, Salesforce, and the client's marketing application. Marc and his client discuss actions required within the integration middleware, as well as the different applications to ensure the expected data quality exists across all applications.

3:00 p.m.

Today, Marc picks his son up from school and takes him to basketball practice. Tonight, his son has practice for a team he is a player on. Later in the week, Marc and his son volunteer as coaches for another team in the league.

5:45 p.m.

Dinner with the family.

7:30 p.m.

Back to work. Because Marc's days are often punctuated with meetings related to his volunteer efforts and time with his family, he often works evenings and weekends. Today, he needs a couple of hours of uninterrupted time to complete the work from his 2:00 p.m. meeting. Marc ensures the proper updates are made within the integration middleware, as well as the different applica-tions, then performs validation to ensure the data quality is as expected across all applications. Lastly, Marc reports back to the client to perform their validation and report back any feedback.

9:30 p.m.

Before wrapping it up for the day, Marc answers emails from clients and responds to Salesforce users in his various community groups and on social media, including Twitter and LinkedIn. Tonight, he finishes up the KPI reports and dashboards for the client that is wrapping up their implementation. He also responds to a LinkedIn request from a Trailblazer who is at the beginning of his Salesforce journey asking for advice on how to determine the best path in the Salesforce ecosystem, including resources to get certified and gaining employment with little to no Salesforce experience.

PART FOUR

SOFT SKILLS

Most of us are given technical-proficiency training. In elementary school, we learn "hard skills," which are those skills that are technical in nature. For instance, we learn how to compute numbers and edit sentences. If we go to college, we may learn engineering, business, and computer science skills.

But from elementary school through college, what we fail to learn are soft skills, like empathy, communication, and conflict resolution. Yet, your soft skills are what allow you to advance. While your technical skills might be enough to help you land a job, your soft skills give you longevity and vertical mobility.

> *You can get all the Trailhead badges and learn Salesforce, but if you are not investing in the soft skills, you are not becoming the best that you can be. If you are not gaining the exposure and experience to be patient, show empathy, and work with a customer, then there are still gaps in your skill set. Those soft skills are not found on Trailhead, so you need to find another way to invest in your personal development and improve the way that you engage with people.*
>
> ## —Ben Duncombe
> **Director of Talent Hub, a Salesforce recruitment company**

.Across the board, employers want to hire and promote people who support the corporate culture, who can manage conflict without creating unnecessary drama, and whose attitudes are easy-going and flexible.

This is even more important today than it ever was.

Due to the changing nature of technology, which disrupts entire industries every few years, the hard skills, abilities, and expertise that you have today will be irrelevant in a few years. Your employers know this, so more important to them than your technical skills are the soft skills you have that make you coachable.

Being coachable means that you make room to learn new skills, to improve upon your existing skills, and to grow as a person. It means you are willing to transform when transformation is necessary. It means you are able to walk away from things that are not working and embrace things that are. Whereas your hard skills determine what you can accomplish today, the degree to which you can be coached predicts your future performance.

Certain soft skills are more important for certain roles. For instance, a business analyst, who is acting as a bridge between IT and the end-user, needs empathy, communication, and conflict management skills all day long. A technical developer, though, has less of a need for these soft skills, though agility is certainly important given that Salesforce releases updates regularly.

Yet, everyone needs to be coachable, particularly if they want to advance in their careers. Developers who want to become technical leads, for instance, might need to improve their communication and presentation skills. Their ability to grow and develop these new skills will depend upon the degree to which they are coachable.

Soft skills, then, are arguably as important as the hard skills you can gain through experience or certification. Certainly, if you plan to move up the ladder, you need soft skills beyond your technical proficiency. The good news is this: Soft skills might seem intangible, but they can be taught, and they can be learned. In this section, we take a look at the five soft skills that are necessary in certain Salesforce roles, and that will always make a person become more coachable.

These skills are:

- **Chapter Fifteen: Agility**
- **Chapter Sixteen: Communication**
- **Chapter Seventeen: Conflict Resolution**
- **Chapter Eightteen: Feedback**
- **Chapter Nineteen: Self-Efficacy**

GENERAL BUSINESS SKILLS EMPLOYERS LOOK FOR:

- Communication
- Writing
- Presentation
- Team Work
- Problem Solving
- Building Relationships

SOFT SKILLS IMPORTANT TO ADVANCING YOUR CAREER:

- Agility
- Communication
- Conflict Resolution
- Feedback
- Self-Efficacy

These are the general business skills that most employers look for, regardless of your role.

In this chapter, we discuss five specific soft skills that can make or break your Salesforce career.

These are the general skills and soft skills that

SALESFORCE PROFESSIONALS SAY ARE THE MOST IMPORTANT ...

WILLINGNESS

When I saw someone struggling in university, I raised my hand, and I tried to help. Sometimes, when I was struggling, I raised my hand and asked them to help me.

I think the most important quality you can have is to be connected to your community and willing to raise your hand. Align with the team. As an individual, yes, you have to learn, master, and grow new skills. At the same time, help others on your team get to where they want to be. Support each other. I think raising your hand to help is the most important trait any organization will look for when hiring someone.

—Vamsi Krishna Gosu, **Founder and director of Techforce Services, an Australian consulting firm**

OWNERSHIP

Ownership of your craft and work is a big thing for me. When you start caring a little bit more and are willing to put in a little bit more extra work, your career will move forward.

—Julian Virguez, **Team lead**

PREDICTING

I am always thinking three steps ahead. If you don't try to see what is coming, you end up doing double the work.

—Mildred Morales, **IT and database director**

CURIOSITY AND ADAPTABILITY

Because new features and products are always being brought into the Salesforce ecosystem, a strong sense of curiosity is important so that you can stay on top of it all. Adaptability is also key because at any moment of your day, you could be pulled into a critical project.

—Daymon Boswell,
Administrator

A THICK SKIN

You have to take negative and positive feedback and not let it impact your motivation and drive. You have to be your own cheerleader. Often no one else will be.

—Jared Beard,
Senior solutions engineer

EMPATHY

Often, the end-users are having troubles, and if you sound stand-offish or cut them off while they are venting their frustration (or nervousness), you will only exasperate the situation.

—Scott Shapiro,
Senior administrator

NEGOTIATION

Often there will be limitations within Salesforce, either budgetary or technical, that result in the desired solution not being possible at the current time. Negotiating an alternative that the customer is satisfied with is key.

—John Polesso,
Administrator

CRITICAL THINKING

You have to be able to think from multiple angles and be flexible in your solution recommendations.

—Kelley Vann,
Solutions specialist

TIME MANAGEMENT

Especially for a consultant, everything comes with a "time price tag." You need to learn how to manage your time and plan for the work that needs to be done.

—Fabrice Cathala,
Solution architect

LOVE OF LEARNING

You will always need to be updated on what is new and what is upcoming. What are the new features? No matter what path you are on, you will need to know.

—Maimoona Shahid,
Senior developer

CHAPTER FIFTEEN:
Agility ←

In the world of live theater, a "swing" is a performer whose job is to fill in for one of many potential primary actors. The leads in the play or musical get the spotlight, but the swings are truly the heroes when the show must go on due to injuries or illnesses. A swing might fill in for one actor one night and a different actor the following night.

In the Broadway production of School of Rock, for instance, nine-year-old Duke Cutler was a swing for four roles: Zack, Billy, Mason, and Freddy. He needed to know the lines, choreography, and musical performances of each of these characters, and sometimes he had almost no notice before being called to the stage.

Many impressive adjectives can describe a swing: Agile tops the list.

The ability to switch directions and be flexible is the most sought after soft skill for Salesforce professionals.

—Prolay Chaudhury
Lead solution/technical architect

The lifestyle of the swing also represents, albeit at an accelerated pace, the future of the workforce. Gone are the days of employees who have one job that they do well for years on end. Instead, businesses change directions at the drop of a dime, and their employees either come with them, or they are left behind. New technologies replace old ways of conducting business—and if companies and their employees do not adapt, they quickly become dinosaurs.

Tech is always changing. You need to love learning new things to adapt and keep up.

—Sebastian Larrea
Administrator

Much can be said about being regimented and orderly, but employers love employees who are agile. Agile employees can respond to new projects and new processes. They can make adjustments without too many growing pains. Agile employees also discover new and better ways of conducting business.

Specifically with relation to Salesforce, agile employees dive into the Salesforce platform updates, eager to see how they can make processes more efficient, and embracing the updates that happen three times a year.

With that said, here are three tips for becoming a more agile employee.

TIP #1:

Replace all know-it-all attitudes with vulnerability.

To be sure, being knowledgeable is great, but there is a big difference between being knowledgeable and being a know-it-all. People who are knowledgeable are an ever-growing well of information. They are always taking new knowledge in. Their doors are open. They are hungry for new bits of information that might change their perspective.

KNOW-IT-ALL   KNOWLEDGE

People who are know-it-alls, on the other hand, are always spitting information out. Their doors are closed to new bits of knowledge. After all, they know everything, so they don't welcome new data.

People who are knowledgeable:

- Seek wisdom from other people. They want to learn, so they are comfortable finding answers from other people.

- Value truth over being right. People who are knowledgeable enjoy being wrong because it means they have learned something new.

- Can collaborate. They realize their pool of knowledge is strengthened when they have insight from people with differing pools of knowledge.

Part of any people-leadership role is adaptability. So often in a leadership role, things get thrown at you, and you have to completely reframe everything you have been working on and rebuild your plan. You can be frustrated, sure, but you have to be able to reset that vision for the people around you.

— Lorna O'Callaghan
Platform manager

In other words, they are vulnerable. They are comfortable opening their doors. They realize that other people might have something valuable to add to their lives.

From time to time, we all have know-it-all tendencies to a greater or lesser degree. Some of us are know-it-alls about a specific subject; others seem to walk around knowing it all, all of the time.

The business world moves faster than ever, and reading where the market goes quite frankly is the difference between having a career and losing it. I fell into Salesforce quite by accident. I quickly realized I could leverage my existing skills and reinvent my career.

—Jorge Luis Pérez Pratt,
Developer

Life is unpredictable, and so is business! Always be prepared for things to change, and have the creativity to think of new solutions. If you have a strong solution, then it will be flexible enough to endure any changes that may come.

—Mariella Brodersen,
Success manager

Regardless, you will know you are being a know-it-all if you find yourself:

1. Offering unsolicited advice about the same subject.

2. Talking more than you are listening.

3. Feeling like you are smarter than everyone around you.

4. Being combative or argumentative a good amount of the time.

5. Accused of having a condescending tone of voice.

6. Embarrassed and even a little bit angry when you are proven wrong.

7. Feeling annoyed when forced to collaborate. After all, other people are useless and a waste of your time, or so you think.

Beyond that, people will probably tell you that you are being a know-it-all!

Being a know-it-all makes you rigid. It means you cannot change directions. You spend so much time trying to prove that you are right that you cannot shift course with the rest of your team. You might feel righteous indignation when your team travels in a direction you think is misguided, but it matters not: After all, you have been left behind.

If you want to be an agile employee, you will need to leave your rigid ways behind. If your doors are closed, you will be unable to see the many doors opening in front of you, and you will be unable to walk into unchartered territory.

Technology is changing with a pace faster than ever. As technology and tools are evolving, so are the nature of requirements and approaches. Being nimble has become a necessity in this world. Feed your inquisitiveness and keep on learning. And remember, learning new things, starting something fresh, can be an enjoyable experience.

—Amey Kulkarni, Consultant

You can plan your day to the best of your ability but there will always be things that come up and may require immediate action. Sometimes that is what makes it fun, but sometimes, it is nice to stick to the plan.

—Miranda Moonilal,
Senior administrator

One of the best mantras I can think of for embracing agility comes from Sir Arthur C. Clarke, who was the science fiction writer known for penning *2001: A Space Odyssey:* "The only way of discovering the limits of the possible," he wrote, "is to venture a little way past them into the impossible."

Open your doors. Consider that new information might change your perspective.

Ask questions, and have an open system. A person who is learning will be able to gain more and more experience by asking questions. Many times, people think they know everything, and they stop asking questions, so they are a closed system. Nothing new can get in. A person learning and growing will be sure to experiment, ask questions, and be open to new information.

And this is important because Salesforce is always changing technologies and coming up with new features. Sometimes, top-notch consultants lag behind in terms of knowing what can and cannot be done. When you have an open system, you stay relevant and updated, which makes you seem like you are ahead of the game.

—Ajay Dubedi
CEO of Cloud Analogy, a consulting firm with 200 employees

> *Business needs change on an ongoing basis, so it is important not to get too attached to one way of solving a problem. When I have had to undo something that I thought was one of my most brilliant solutions for a past need, I look at it not as a loss or waste of time, but as great practice and a learning experience, not to mention job security. If solutions were permanent, eventually I would run out of work! Constant change and flexibility mean my job stays interesting.*
>
> **—Abby Tusing,** Administrator

TIP #2:

Prioritize feedback over perfection.

Chapter Eighteen is entirely committed to feedback, but feedback deserves a shout-out here as well. Agile employees prioritize the importance of soliciting feedback from other people. They understand that although changing direction might be difficult, it might also make the product, service, or process better.

Rather than working in silos, hoping to impress everyone with their perfect solution, agile employees intentionally solicit input from other people. This allows them to see different perspectives and identify pieces they might be missing.

TIP #3:

Run sprints instead of marathons.

Rather than setting your sites on a far-out goal that will take months or even years to realize, try breaking your work into tiny sprints. This allows you to change course when something breaks down, or when you realize that a different course of action might make more sense.

When you break your work into short sprints, you can ask for feedback along the way, take time to reflect, and base your next steps on the progress you have already made.

We get really attached to our work. However, we live in an agile world, and sometimes what you have been building for weeks can change at the drop of a hat. Nobody wants to walk away from that project, but trying to breathe life into a fire that is out makes you look bad in the long run.

–Moon Algazzali,
Administrator

Day in the life:
KEN SEANEY

Ken Seaney is an independent consultant who works from his home office. To help him find work, Ken worked with Gridiron IT, a recruiting company that pairs IT specialists with government agencies, federal contractors, and commercial clients.

For the past fifteen months, Ken has been working as a contractor with the United States government as it transitions one of its departments into Salesforce. Because he is an "at-will" contractor, he could be removed from the project at any time, a fact that he said comes with a fair share of stress.

4:30 a.m.

Ken lives in the western part of the United States, making his colleagues in Washington D.C. in a timezone with a three-hour difference. As a result, his day starts before the sun rises.

Ken works from home, but he said he "goes to work, like anyone else." His commute is downstairs to his home office, which he treats with the same boundaries as he would any job.

"I can't let my home life interfere with work. I have to keep it completely separate. The only difference is that my commute is shorter."

After making his ninety-second commute, Ken starts his day by catching up on emails and messages.

5:00 a.m.

The team conducts stand-up meetings each morning. (A "stand-up" is a team daily meeting organized so that people can provide updates to all a development team's members. This  allows them to raise questions or concerns, consolidate and synchronize efforts, and brainstorm solutions to challenging or time-consuming issues.)

During the stand-up, Ken explains where he is in the schedule, what he did the day prior, and what he is going to do today. Most often, he discusses the tasks and issues that have been assigned to him for the current sprint.

The second part of the meeting is reserved for solutioning, whereby team members bring up challenges with development work, troubleshoot issues discovered in testing, and solicit input from the rest of the team. Today, Ken and the team discuss a validation rule error occurring on a Process Builder process.

He also demonstrates a few new features that have been developed so that he can mark them as complete and ready for deployment.

6:00 a.m.

After the meeting, Ken is left to complete the tasks for the day, which includes user stories, small jobs, and specific tasks. User stories are simple write-ups of what the user would like to see with the feature or enhancement, written from the user's point of view. User stories also include acceptance criteria, but usually do not include a detailed approach or solution. Before each sprint, the stories are refined and discussed by the team, prioritized by the client, and assigned to the developers.

These stories can range from simple to very complex. In some instances, the stories may be simple configurations of fields, formulas, workflow rules, or validation rules. In other cases, a story may be something that takes days to develop and test, such as a new custom object, complex Flow or a Lightning Component.

The overall solution is broken down into multiple subtasks by the person doing the development with progress and comments within the main story. When all tasks are completed the feature is ready for deployment to another development org for testing.

The job has stringent requirements and high expectations.

Ken is under a contract that prevents him from disclosing his specific duties, but he said that the vast majority of his day is spent completing pre-defined tasks, keeping to a strict schedule.

There's no overtime on this contract, but there is an expectation that things get done no matter what. In fact, a year prior, Ken spent his Thanksgiving working.

"We had a deadline to meet, so we made it happen," he said.

9:00 a.m.

A developer on Ken's team conferences with Ken via Skype. She needs support executing one of the tasks of her to-do list, so she and Ken discuss the best solutions.

9:30 a.m.

It's a good time for a quick snack. Ken heads to his kitchen for a break and brunch.

10:00 a.m.

Back to work executing the day's priorities. A typical day includes both configuration and development.

Configuration includes creating custom objects, fields, page layouts, Lightning Pages, permission sets, custom permissions, workflow rules for email alerts and field updates, validation rules, email templates, reports and dashboards, community pages, Process Builder processes, and Flows.

Development work includes writing custom Lightning Components for use in both the public community pages and internal user side for use on Lightning Pages and in Flows, Apex triggers, and test classes.

1:00 p.m.

Because of his early start time, Ken enjoys an early closing time. He takes a quick catnap before eating a proper lunch and tending to his personal life.

Ken occasionally has side work as a Salesforce consultant on other orgs, which he tends to in the afternoon. Otherwise, he does a few chores around the house, has dinner and spends time with his wife, and works on one of his hobbies, which include 3D printing, music, and motorcycles.

Today, he watches a movie with his wife before going to bed at 8 p.m.

CHAPTER SIXTEEN:
Communication

Most every employer wants employees who have good communication skills, but what exactly does this mean? The irony of the phrase "good communication" is that it is too vague to precisely define what is required of you.

> *Here is something that can cause your career to come to a halt: Being skilled in the tech side but not the communication side.*
>
> **— Ben Stokes**
> **Administrator**

As such, this chapter boils **"good communication"** down to three essential skills:

- **Essential #1: Be an active listener.**
- **Essential #2: Provide clarity.**
- **Essential #3: Give and assume benevolence.**

> *Poor communication is the number one reason projects fail.*
>
> **—Caroline Häming,**
> Senior consultant

Let's talk about these one at a time.

ESSENTIAL #1:

Be an active listener

Most people are not active listeners. Most "listening" can be better defined as "waiting." That is, people are waiting for the talker to take a breath so they can interject with their own story, their own knowledge, or their own thoughts.

How can you solve a problem if you do not understand the problem?

— Dan Angiu,
President of A2B Nexus Inc., a consulting company

> *Keep communications as brief and possible while being as technically accurate as you can for the given audience. Especially when giving technical comments, break it up using bullets in a laundry list. When requesting feedback, number the requests (1, 2, 3, 4, etc.), and keep each question extremely brief.*

—Moon Algazzali,
Administrator

A person who is *actively listening* is listening with the intention of gathering information. Whereas much of the time, other people are trying to push their own agendas, people who are active listeners are asking questions to elicit additional information. They are more interested in what other people can contribute than they are in what they have to say.

Think of it like this: You already know whatever it is that you have to say, but you probably do not know what the other person has to say. When you are an active listener, you are able to expand the scope of knowledge that you have. This allows you to understand other perspectives, learn from people who are more knowledgeable than you, and demonstrate that you are interested in other people.

An agenda-driven "listener" looks like this:

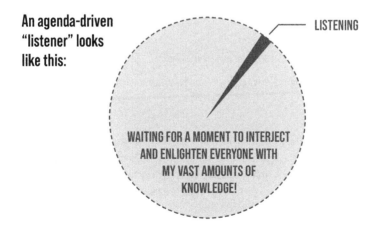

LISTENING

WAITING FOR A MOMENT TO INTERJECT AND ENLIGHTEN EVERYONE WITH MY VAST AMOUNTS OF KNOWLEDGE!

Talking is, of course, an important function of life. It is also likely an unspoken requirement of your job, so I do not intend to imply that you should simply sit back silently and refrain from speaking your mind. Rather, as you go through your interactions, pay attention to whether you are actively asking questions and trying to pull more information from the speaker, or are you waiting for your turn to talk.

> *You will not be able to respond appropriately if you are too busy waiting for your turn to talk.*
>
> **— Kelley Vann,**
> **Solution specialist**

ESSENTIAL #2:

Provide clarity

People with strong communication skills are able to say what they need to say:

1. In as few words as possible; and

2. Leaving no uncertainties as to what is expected.

We all know people who leave us scratching our heads, wondering what is expected of us. Despite a long rambling monologue and many, many spoken words, they failed to give specific direction. It leaves us feeling insecure as to where we stand and confused as to what to do next.

Other people are afraid to ask for what they want, so they sugar coat it and hope that people get the message. Unfortunately, more often than not, this method fails. If a message is open for interpretation, you have no idea how it will be interpreted, but it will most likely be interpreted in a way that best suits the listener, which might not be your intention.

> *Communications need to be short and structured. Use bullet points or an outline. Ambiguous comments can lead to false expectations, which can be fatal. Say what you mean. Mean what you say, and do exactly what you said you were going to do. Customers hate surprises, so don't give them any.*
>
> **—Eric von Stromberg,**
> **Project manager**

> *To quote Brené Brown: "Clear is kind. Unclear is unkind." Clear communication is necessary so that the business, IT, and end-users are all aligned.*
>
> **— Christi Kane,**
> **Administrator**

And still others simply do not know how to speak concisely. In any case, the solution is this:

Don't "bury the lede."

In journalism, the word lede refers to the introductory section of a news story. The goal of the lede is to emphasize the main point and let the reader know what the story is about. Starting the story with the lede is important because writers know they have only a split second to grab a person's attention. If the story is confusing or vague, the reader won't keep reading.

Regardless of how you are communicating—either in writing or verbally—the same advice holds true: Don't bury the lede. Start with the most important takeaway, the action items you want the team to take, or the request you are making for information.

Here are two examples so that you can see the difference:

Subject: **Scope of work**

Hello all! I hope you are having a beautiful Monday morning. It has been such a pleasure working with you, and I look forward to continuing to work on your project.

It's important to me to let you know how we work. We want to provide your team with processes that meet your goals. At times, you might ask us for something specific—let's say a red button—and we might push back by asking you to explain why you want the red button. This is because we want to make sure that a red button is truly the best instrument we have for making your processes efficient. When we ask you to justify the need for something, it is because we might know that a yellow button will actually work better than a red button.

With this in mind, could you please tell me the top five needs that your team has with respect to managing contacts? When we have this information, we can start discussing the best possible solutions for these needs.

Once again, it truly has been a pleasure working with you.

This email is perfectly polite and well written, but I argue that the communication skills could be improved upon. Why? Because it isn't crystal-clear and evident what the reader is supposed to do. Note that the subject line is vague, and the request for information does not happen until the third paragraph. People who are on the go might not even read long enough to see the request for information.

Let's look at how this changes when you present the lede upfront.

Subject: Your top five contact-management needs

Hello! At your convenience, could you please tell me the top five needs that your team has with respect to managing contacts?

A little bit of background with respect to this request (and future requests): We want to provide your team with technology that meets your goals, so it is important to us that we start by identifying the outcome/goals and work backward from there.

At times, you might ask us for something specific—let's say a red button—and we might push back by asking you to explain why you want the red button. This is because we want to make sure that a red button is truly the best instrument we have for making your processes efficient. When we ask you to justify the need for something, it is because we might know that a yellow button is actually better suited for improving your business's outcomes than a red button.

With respect to your contact-management needs, once we have your top five needs, my team can start discussing the best possible solutions for these needs.

With all that said, I hope you are having a beautiful Monday morning. It has been such a pleasure working with you, and I look forward to continuing to work on your project.

Notice that the request for information is included in the subject and in the first paragraph, meaning it will show up in the preview pane of a smart phone. There is no chance that the reader will be confused as to what is expected.

This is what I mean by clarity.

> *You have to listen not just to what is being asked, but what the need is. What is trying to be solved? Keep in mind that the people coming to you for solutions do not understand Salesforce the way you do. Open yourself up to learning their processes and their terminology. Ask questions.*
>
> **—Jennifer Garman,**
> **Business Operations Analyst**

> *Finding solutions right away is not important. Understanding the problem right away is important.*
>
> **—Vishal Shelar,**
> **Technical consultant**

The same goes for making requests in person. Explain what you want first, and then explain why you want it. If the request is lengthy, complicated, or a deal-breaker, follow up with an email that outlines what you want. This way, you leave no uncertainties as to what is expected.

This brings me to my next point: At times, you will be required to deliver bad news. This can be in the form of a project update that includes less-than-desired results, or it can be in the form of feedback to a team member.

In either case, you have probably heard that the best course of action is to use the Feedback Sandwich, which looks like this:

SAY SOMETHING POSITIVE!

THEN DELIVER THE BAD NEWS.

THEN SAY SOMETHING POSITIVE AGAIN!

The Feedback Sandwich sounds something like this:

"You know, I really appreciate Sharon's energy. She is always so happy and kind to everyone, and the whole office just loves her. Unfortunately, she has missed a few deadlines, and we need her to work on that. But the good news is that her attitude is amazing."

Or:

"The good news is that we have fixed all of the bugs that were reported from user acceptance testing. Unfortunately, we are a little bit behind schedule, so we are working double-time to catch up. Thankfully, everyone on the team has been extremely cooperative, and I think the dynamic is in our favor."

The Feedback Sandwich is supposed to lessen the impact of bad news, which is why I argue against it. Though there might be a time and a place for sugarcoating, more often than not, employers and businesspeople appreciate brutally honest straight-talkers. Skirting issues rarely results in the best process. It also jeopardizes relationships. After all, the strength of any relationship you have is based on the strength of the conversation. If your conversations are evasive, timid, or tinted by white lies, the relationships will be ambiguous, apprehensive, or dishonest.

Instead of using the Feedback Sandwich, try using the Open-Faced Sandwich, which looks like this:

DELIVER THE BAD NEWS STRAIGHT AWAY

EXPLAIN THE NEXT STEPS/SOLUTION

> *Understand why something is asked instead of what is asked. Oftentimes, users or businesses ask for X, but what they really want it Y, which can be done with Z in Salesforce.*
>
> **—Lorenzo Alali,**
> **Administrator and business systems analyst**

> *Repeat back what you heard to ensure that you are in alignment. Express gratitude and appreciation to customers as often as you can, thanking them for feedback. Be transparent, even in difficult conversations. Don't be afraid to challenge a customer. Always share out what is being done, by who, and when.*
>
> **—Mariella Brodersen,**
> **Success manager**

The Open-Faced Sandwich puts everyone on the same page as to what the problem is. Reality is out in the open. This might feel uncomfortable, but when the facts are on the table, you can start discussing solutions more easily.

Here are some examples of an Open-Faced Sandwich:

"Sharon has missed a few deadlines. The rest of the team is relying on her, so when she does not deliver her work, the entire project falls behind. I have had a conversation with her, and she has given me her word that she will put in the time this week to get back on track and then stay on track. The good news is that her attitude is fantastic, so I do believe she will make good on her word. I will follow up with you in three days to let you know where we stand."

And:

"The most important update I should give you is that we have run into some issues with configuring the sales process. We have completed the lead management and opportunity management, but we hit some road bumps with quotes and contract management. I think the problem is that our understanding of your process is a little bit insufficient. Would you mind scheduling some time so that I can ask you some questions? For instance: It is not clear what should happen once a quote is accepted and when a contract should be created automatically. Once I understand these variables, we will be able to work efficiently to make sure we get back on track."

When you communicate openly and honestly about successes and failures, as well as solutions and next steps, you develop a reputation for being a straight shooter. The truth is, when you attempt to sugarcoat, you compromise not only your ability to speak clearly, but also your reputation.

You have to communicate in a variety of ways: in-person group trainings, one-on-one coaching, feedback and brainstorming sessions, release emails. The list of ways to communicate with your end-users is endless. I find that the best thing to do is to mix things up—sometimes I'll do a video demo, sometimes a flow chart, and, when the communication is especially important, I will do a user guide and team trainings.

—Emily Duncan, Administrator

Set clear expectations. When things are vague, expectations can spiral out of control.

—John Smoak, CEO of MyOnlineAdmin.com, a Salesforce remote administrator support company

ESSENTIAL #3:

Give and assume benevolence

A person who is benevolent assumes that other people are well meaning. They present themselves as having thicker skins, better attitudes, and more strength in the face of feedback. This does not mean that they are doormats to be walked upon, nor does it mean that they fail to assert themselves when necessary.

Rather, being benevolent means that if you have a positive and a negative interpretation for something, and you have equal amounts of evidence for both, you default to the positive interpretation.

A benevolent person assumes that people are behaving in a way that makes sense to them. When a benevolent person does not understand behavior, they refrain from assigning negative qualities to the person participating in the behavior. Rather, they either seek information with a commitment toward understanding the person, or they simply move on and focus their thoughts elsewhere.

Why does benevolence make for better communication skills? We can give you five reasons.

1. Benevolent people spend less time complaining.

Because their "default mode" is optimistic, they are not as bogged down with negative thoughts, frustrations, and complaints, which makes them more pleasant to be around.

2. Benevolent people bring out the best in their team members.

They believe in other people, which means they naturally communicate in a way that elicits other people's strengths.

3. Benevolent people look for solutions.

By not getting bogged down by problems and complaints, they can focus their energies on troubleshooting.

4. Benevolent people think outside the box.

When the world and the people in it are good, there are endless opportunities for growth and success.

5. Benevolent people are easier to talk to.

Because they believe that other people are trying their hardest, they forgive mistakes and move past upsetting situations.

> *You are the conduit for translating existing processes into Sales-force processes. Listen actively, and ask many, many questions so you do not disappoint your audience when presenting solutions.*
>
> ## —Cheri Poirier,
> **Lead analyst, systems**

You might argue that a person is either born benevolent or not. I am not a behavioralist, so you might be right, but I argue this: If you can make yourself just five percent more benevolent, why not do it? You will be more pleasant and have greater success.

So how can you build this skill? Simple: When you find yourself feeling critical of someone, take a step back and ask for clarity.

Let's imagine, for instance, that your colleague Devin never responds to your emails. You interpret this to mean that he does not believe that your requests are worthwhile, and that he is trying to undermine you. You might be right, but it might also be that your colleague is terrible at responding to emails and prefers to communicate by text.

You have no evidence for either, so why not ask?

> *"Devin, I have sent you a few emails without getting a response. What's going on?"*

Rare will you find a true schmuck who really is trying to undermine you. More often than not, you will find something more reasonable, or something that is at least understandable.

Devin might say,

"Honestly, your emails feel overwhelming. They are really long, and it's hard for me to read them because I have so much on my plate that I never seem to find the time. Oftentimes, it would take me an hour to read and respond to everything, and I feel like my time is better directed by working directly on the project, so I usually wait to talk to you in person, which is quicker and more efficient."

This might not be the answer you were looking for, and it might even ruffle your feathers a bit, but it will help you begin to collect evidence that the world is not quite as malevolent as you think.

Develop relationships by being clear and concise, which eliminates ambiguity. When there's no ambiguity, you become a trusted advisor. People have confidence in what you are bringing to the table.

—Frank Mamone,
Application architect

Day in the life:
ROB KAPLAN

Rob Kaplan is a senior consultant and engagement manager for CRMD+, a consultancy firm based in Boston, Massachusetts in the United States. Rob previously had a successful career as a Salesforce administrator. He was kind enough to share the generalities and a graphical representation of his work for a regional consultancy, as well as tips for helping other consultants along their Salesforce career path.

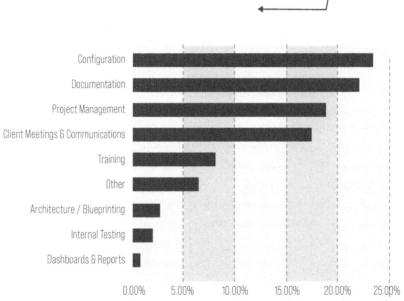

Though there will always be variability based on segmentation, projects, and consultants, this is a good representation of how a senior admin or project manager at a consultancy would spend their time on medium-sized projects, though Rob's workload is admittedly a little light on integration and programming work.

- "Within the **Other** segment, expect to perform various internal sales and marketing activities, as well as external and client testing and user acceptance testing, on-site working sessions, creating and styling custom pages, and code review."

- "In the **Project Management** hours, expect internal meetings about the project with other resources, and the time tracking itself for a given project."

- "A word about **Documentation** as it is meant here. What you see is what you get, and in consulting, it is absolutely critical that a deep understanding of the client's expectations for the completed solution are clearly agreed to in advance. Scope creep—and all the ill-will and financial hardship that ensues—is nearly always the result of poor early documentation of what the client expects. Use mock-ups to project page layouts. Use flow-charts to depict logic trees and automation processes. Having trouble teasing out the solution expectation? Try asking the client to help you craft a set of user acceptance tests for the solution before configuring begins. Uses Sandboxes if a fast mock-up makes sense."

CHAPTER SEVENTEEN:
Conflict Resolution

Teams with high amounts of conflict do not perform as well as those that are cohesive. When employers need to spend time resolving relationship issues, they have lost time that could have been spent developing the company's product or service. And when divided teams cannot lean on each other for support, the company's offerings suffer.

> Conflict is bound to arise. It is never easy or pretty, but in my opinion, conflict is important for growth. It is imperative to never take it personally and to always behave in such a way that you are able to look the other person in the eye. In the end, take stock of what the conflict actually achieved. Most times, when you identify the underlying issue, you can pinpoint the opportunity to learn and grow.
>
> **— Caroline Häming**
> **Senior consultant**

It's obvious that employers would rather hire people who are experts at conflict resolution. With this in mind, consider one general rule when it comes to conflict resolution:

Exchange your desire to *convince* with a desire to be *curious*.

CONVINCE 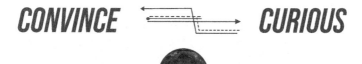 *CURIOUS*

> Being an active listener is important no matter what, but particularly in conflicts. Without it, we cannot understand other perspectives and views. The middle is where the magic happens, but it can't happen if each voice is not listened to.
>
> **—Christi Kane,** Administrator

Remember that for the most part, both parties are working toward the same goal. Use that goal as the foundation for starting a conversation.

—Dorian Gammons,
Senior administrator and strategist

Listen, express your opinion, but ultimately, be open to being wrong.

—Adrian Rubio Martinez,
Consultant

Most conflicts look like this: Both parties are trying so hard to make their points that they cannot hear the other person's point. It's the same closed-door analogy we discussed in Chapter Fifteen. There is no room for growth when you have closed the door and are simply throwing things your neighbor's way.

The more things thrown your way, the more you escalate, which causes the other party to escalate. Soon enough, you have both thrown so many metaphorical eggs that it's hard to recover. And because neither of you feels heard, the voices get louder and louder.

Think of conflict as a benefit. Conflict is oftentimes the result of an absence of another person or department's full perspective. When you can recognize that a company has issues that have not been addressed, this is a productive discovery. It gives you information, and it gives you a problem to solve. As a consultant, I don't need to focus on the emotions behind a conflict. I don't need to be bothered or own the emotions. Instead, the conflict is giving me a lot of information that I otherwise would not have.

—René Görgens
Senior architect and consultant

The best tip I can give for improving your conflict-resolution skills is this: Instead of trying to convince the other party of your perspective, start by becoming extremely curious about what the other person is experiencing. This will naturally diffuse the situation as the other party will feel understood and will, therefore, not need to throw additional eggs your way.

When demonstrating curiosity, take a deep breath, mute your own defensive voices, and ask questions:

- *"What are you experiencing in your relationship with me?"*
- *"From your perspective, what is creating the conflict?"*
- *"What do you need from me?"*

You might not like the answers to these questions, but when you give the other party room to speak first, you will gather information that can help you formulate a response. You will also notice that the tension de-escalates, which will allow the other party to feel less defensive and more open to hearing your perspective—but only after you have listened to the other person's perspective.

Share facts, and gently remind everyone of the desired outcome.

—Harry Silverstone,
Consultant

Keep your cool. Understand that we all have good days and bad days. Put yourself in the other person's shoes, and aim for a win-win.

—Dan Angiu, President of A2B Nexus Inc., a consulting company

> Conflict management is not about pointing fingers or proving someone wrong, nor is it about finding a way to agree on everything. Conflict management is about finding common ground so you can move forward and get the job done.
>
> **—Jennifer Garman,**
> **Business Operations Analyst**

> If you are brought into an uncomfortable situation, contain your responses and your body language. You cannot control what anyone else says or does, but you can control your own response. Count to five before speaking, if need be. Your emotional maturity will reflect on you as a person and color your peer's opinion of you.
>
> **—Kelley Vann,**
> **Solutions specialist**

> When conflict arises, do not wait until it escalates. If anything is pending or up in the air, figure out the root and try to solve it as soon as it arises.
>
> **—Justyna Krajewska,**
> **Administrator**

Once everyone's voice is on the table and both parties feel heard, you will have an easier time finding a solution that takes both people's perspectives into account.

Here is an example from the world of Salesforce. Oftentimes, a client or an employer needs a solution to a business challenge as soon as possible, but the client/employer does not want to wait for the IT department.

Let's imagine, for instance, that a client needs an industry-specific, complex quoting solution that is available on desktop, iPad, and mobile. The sales director has found a niche vendor that can deliver 90 percent of the requirements, and the director and would like to move ahead with the solution immediately.

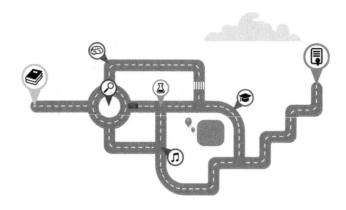

The IT department, though, has analyzed the application and concluded it does not fit with the longer-term technology roadmap, will require complex integration, and is relatively expensive. The IT director proposes to develop the solution on the Salesforce platform, which will require time to develop, cost less, have less integration requirements, and will fit with the IT strategic direction and roadmap.

The sales director, though, does not want to wait for the solution to be developed and is threatening to escalate the issue to the CEO. The IT department is standing firm on only cooperating with solutions that are approved and in alignment with the future direction and skills in the team.

> *Instead of focusing on the conflict, concentrate on the task that needs to be done. Everyone is different, but in the end, what matters is that the team delivers and maintains high-quality work.*
>
> **—Carl Stobie,**
> **Configuration analyst**

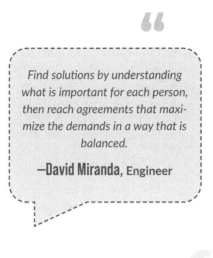

> *Find solutions by understanding what is important for each person, then reach agreements that maximize the demands in a way that is balanced.*
>
> **—David Miranda,** Engineer

To move forward in this situation, each side should take the time to understand the situation from the other's perspective and be curious of why they hold such a strong belief.

The IT director would discover that the sales department is under pressure as the department has been behind target for a number of quarters. The department's inability to efficiently generate quotes on the road is a contributing factor to its failure. Hitting sales objectives is a key organizational priority. In fact, when the sales department does not hit targets, the entire business is at risk (including the IT department).

On the other hand, the sales director would learn that the IT department has faced such situations multiple times before. When the business proposed a stand-alone solution that appeared to offer a quick fix, it resulted in projects that failed due to complex integration requirements.

The ability to empathize is equally important to any Salesforce professional. There will always be challenges when new technologies are adopted, and users will have hesitations. It is important, then, to understand not just the business process and the technology, but also how the users feel about the changes being made to their daily life.

Keep in mind that implementing Salesforce is not the same as implementing other technologies. Salesforce evolves with a business, and it routinely takes over and automates processes. This can threaten some people because a technology is taking work away from them. We want to have the emotional intelligence to assure them that their jobs and livelihoods are not being threatened and that the systems will free up their time to work on other tasks.

— Matthew Sutton, Founder of Resonant Cloud Solutions, a consulting firm with offices in Australia and India

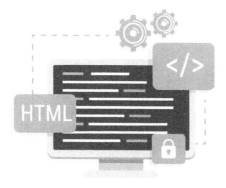

By putting aside their desire to convince the other side, and becoming curious instead, the sales and IT departments can find common ground. Obviously both departments are committed to the long-term success of the organization. Once the IT department understands the priority and urgency, the IT director might propose an alternative that includes a phased approach to delivering the solution with the functionality gaps filled by temporary manual processes.

Occasionally, things will break. When something goes wrong and people get upset, stay positive and solve the problem. Understand that the conflict is not a personal attack. People vent when they are under stress. When someone is upset, imagine that you are a pilot. Let people know in a calm, collected voice that you know what you are doing.

—Moon Algazzali,
Administrator

Day in the life:
PROLAY CHAUDHURY

Prolay Chaudhury is a dedicated IT solution/technical architect Trailblazer and senior developer evangelist with about sixteen years of experience in IT. He holds a postgraduate diploma in computer programming and five Salesforce certifications, as well as an Oracle certification, a Microsoft certification, and a Java certification. He has certifications from the University of Alberta, the University of London, and the University of Toronto. He is a Salesforce Trailhead Ranger.

Though he has worked worldwide, Prolay lives in Bengaluru, the capital of Karnataka in India.

Prolay was kind enough to share a day-in-the-life of an architect while he was working as a technical architect on a particularly difficult project: A network service provider wanted their supplier performance evaluation process to be migrated to the Salesforce platform.

Prolay's team was using the Salesforce Unlimited Edition, which has the Sales Cloud and App Cloud licenses for enhancing and building new applications. As part of the project, Prolay's team was responsible for capturing and crunching billions of records—yes, billions!—and evaluating the key performance indicators (KPIs), as provided by the network service provider's business units of its thousands of suppliers.

This required analyzing best practices in extreme data loading and large data volumes in Salesforce Architecture documents. The data loading process was done via asynchronous batch-processing using Bulk API 2.0.

The team faced several technical challenges. For one, the user was not doing data cleansing before loading the data. Instead, they simply selected an Excel file and began the upload process. Therefore, the team needed to make sure that data was cleansed on their end.

Beyond that, the team's early failures to understand the requirements, as well as an insufficient data model, caused the project to be over budget and behind schedule. Prolay attempted to make sure the client did not continue to make drastic changes to the requirements, but establishing a Salesforce govern and change-management process based on the changing requirements and the ongoing creep in the scope was most difficult. The client was demanding, and the difference between the original scope of work and the final requests were major.

8:30 a.m.

After waking, showering, and eating breakfast, Prolay makes the ninety-minute commute to the office.

10:00 a.m.

Prolay, as well as the developers, program manager, and project manager, meet via Skype for an internal communications call to discuss progress. The client has asked for billions of records to be loaded in the production org such that data can be evaluated and suppliers can be given scorecards, as well as instructions to rectify any scores that fall below the company's benchmarks. The changes in the requirements have created a bottleneck, and the team is troubleshooting.

Part of Prolay's job is to document all of the different ideas discussed during the brainstorming session and communicate these too.

11:30 a.m.

When the call ends, Prolay takes a fifteen-minute break before typing and circulating the ideas discussed during the meeting, as well as the decisions and directions to the various team members.

12:30 p.m.

Before heading to lunch, Prolay takes a call with the development team to discuss the details of specific solutions. Unfortunately, the project is running behind schedule and over budget for several reasons: The team charged with bidding the project underestimated complexity and did not consult with Prolay during the object model and architectural artifacts creation.

Unfortunately, the person who provided the client with a proposal did not have a strong Salesforce or process management background, and therefore underestimated complexities. Beyond that, the client has added several change orders.

Prolay and the project developers discuss what can realistically be done and create a revised schedule.

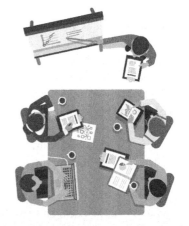

2:00 p.m.

Prolay takes a lunch break with some colleagues before heading back to the office.

2:45 p.m.
From an architectural point of view, the project is not particularly difficult, but it is functionally tedious.

Prolay's team used Visio, Lucid Charts to create architectural artifacts like object model, Systems Landscape, swim lane diagrams, process flow diagrams, system environment, as well as migration flows, roles, hierarchies, and org charts to create a high-level and low-level design. The broad scope of the project is: 1) Define the business-relevant KPIs in the tool and link the data source; 2) Create the ability to define new KPIs or modify existing KPIs, as business needs emerge; 3) Plan, schedule, manage and track supplier evaluation globally; 4) Extract scorecards and reports to view all KPI results of the evaluated suppliers, and 5) Manage the consequences for suppliers with limited ability.

The suppliers whose data is being evaluated are in different regions of different countries, and they are all using different systems to capture data.

Beyond that, the KPIs used to evaluate each supplier differ based on region, and they also differ based on the various departments within each supplier. Prolay spends part of the afternoon helping the development team write rules to help crunch data from a, particularly complex region.

4:30 p.m.

It's time for the stakeholder meeting, which Pro-lay has been dreading. The client has representatives from India, Germany, the United States, and Singapore who join the call, along with Pro-lay and the program manager.

Because of the diverse perspectives of the various stakeholders, finding common ground has been a struggle during nearly every client meeting, with the stakeholders often disagreeing about the goals of the project.

In this meeting, Prolay and his team are attempting to elicit an understanding of the fields that are required for a custom object to display information and to perform underlying functionalities. Because the stakeholders do not agree, Prolay and his team have little success, eventually suggesting a compromise.

The program manager explains the revised timeline from a functional and business perspective, but Prolay is charged with explaining the technical aspects of the delay. Because the project was based on a waterfall framework, the entire project is behind schedule due to the complexities of capturing data.

Prolay is prepared with a PowerPoint presentation that walks the client through the technical solutions and revised timeline.

4:45 p.m.

Unfortunately, an important stakeholder is called from the meeting to attend a work emergency, so the call is rescheduled for 7 p.m.

Prolay makes the ninety-minute commute to his home, arriving in time to eat dinner before the call.

7:00 p.m.

Prolay calls into the conference call, which is tense. The expectations for the development team are high, and Prolay is charged with being up-front about what can and cannot be done.

He and his program manager explain that certain requests simply cannot be accommodated given the cost and time bid: The entire project was on a fixed-bid, and the costs have increased to double the bid price. Prolay loves challenges, but this particular project has given him a continuous headache. For instance, there were various reporting and processing functionalities that could not be delivered.

Fortunately, Prolay has a knack for his ability to accommodate differing perspectives and focus on solutions. Prolay, his program manager, and the stakeholders end the call by agreeing on the next steps.

8:00 p.m.

Prolay is studying to become a Certified Technical Architect, so he spends an hour on Trailhead before calling it quits for the day.

He is studying the architect's journey, which includes application architecture and system architecture of the Salesforce ecosystem. He is also learning advanced Javascript, HTML5, and CSS concepts to master Lightning Web Component Framework. Apart from that Prolay is concentrating on self-paced learning of MuleSoft Anypoint Platform to build APIs and integrations.

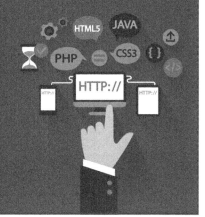

CHAPTER EIGHTEEN:
Feedback

Any employer you have will want you to get better at whatever job you are performing. After all, upping your game, be it in terms of proficiency or efficiency, will only help your employer become more successful. To do this, you need to be able to ask for and accept criticism, also known as feedback.

Taking feedback well mandates that you set aside your defensiveness so that you can listen, incorporate the feedback, and improve for the betterment of the entire team.

> *Being able to listen and take feedback is becoming more and more important in the last few years given the number of people we are able to communicate with thanks to digital technologies. The dynamics of communication, of listening, and of taking feedback: These are and will become more and more important.*
>
> ### — Veronika Peycheva,
> **CRM change analyst**

This is much, much easier said than done. It's human nature to defend ourselves, so most of us become defensive when other people pass judgment on our efforts. This is particularly when the judgment feels unnecessarily harsh.

If you have ever been a high-performing athlete, you know that coaching styles come in all shapes and sizes. You know that some coaches yell, some are respectful, and some are downright rude. The best coaches know that some athletes will bring their best to the game if they are yelled at, and others will fold. They know when to turn on the anger, and when to turn on the kindness.

> *I have learned to take feedback less personally and to turn it into goals. Early in my career, negative feedback would bring me down, but as I have grown, I look at it as a way to learn.*
>
> ### —Cheri Poirier,
> **Lead analyst, systems**

> *Be a sponge for advice and feedback from colleagues and people with more experience.*
>
> ### —Bob Sheridan,
> **Solution architect**

> The Salesforce ecosystem is a fantastic community. You will hear tons of great feedback from other users just like you. Being able to honestly accept and learn from the feedback definitely benefited my career. But a word of warning: Don't let feedback hold your imagination back. I always describe my work as both scientific and artistic. I like to be creative at my work by building out elegant solutions, and sometimes the feedback isn't as imaginative. So my advice is: Take feedback, look at it critically, and then use your best judgment.
>
> —**Hao Lu**, Database administrator

But coaches who differentiate their style based on what the athlete needs are rare. Most coaches—and bosses, for that matter—have one style that they apply to all their team members. Some criticize rather rudely. Some sugarcoat such that you never quite know where you stand. Some are passive and prefer not to say anything critical, only later to explode in a knee-jerk reaction when they have finally had enough.

The truth is that *giving feedback* can be as uncomfortable as receiving feedback, particularly when it involves a problem or a concern. It is very likely that your boss has never been trained to give feedback. As a result, your boss would probably rather avoid it. When it is necessary, it likely feels uncomfortable for both you and your boss, making it that much more difficult to refrain from feeling defensive.

The good news is that you can circumvent all of this—from your own defensiveness to the undesirable coaching styles to your boss's discomfort. By implementing just one technique, you can become great at receiving feedback in a way that feels non-threatening and creates an easy conversation between you and your boss.

The secret is to ask for feedback so often and so eagerly that the back-and-forth between you and your boss with respect to your job performance feels calm and collaborative.

HERE'S HOW THIS LOOKS IN PRACTICE:

1. Start by asking for feedback in small ways.

Ask for feedback in ways that you know you can accept gracefully, and ways that you know your boss can give easily. Try something like this: "On Friday I completed a solution design document, which I have never done before. I felt okay about it, but I also know I can improve with your guidance. Can you let me know what I can do better next time?"

2. Ask open-ended questions.

Questions that demand a judgmental answer like, "How am I doing?" will put your boss on the spot. Instead, ask things like, "Can you please give me one thing I can improve upon this week?" Or, "If I were to magically have one skill that I do not have now, what would it be?"

3. Ask follow up questions.

Ask follow up questions if you do not understand what your boss is saying.

4. Thank your boss.

This shows your boss that he or she is doing you a favor by providing you with instruction, and it reminds you that you should be grateful for the feedback because it allows you to grow and develop skills that will allow your career to advance.

5. Lather, rinse, repeat.

> *Feedback is the only way one can improve. While not always easy to hear, it helps identify weak points in performance and solutions, as well as strengths to hone in on. That said, not all input is intended to be helpful, so reflect on feedback before internalizing it.*
>
> **—Kelley Vann,**
> **Solutions specialist**

AND THAT'S IT.

When you create a habit out of initiating feedback, your boss (or client) will feel more comfortable providing you with instruction, and he or she will likely do so more calmly, which will make it easier for you to receive. As well, you will create a relationship that feels collaborative. When you seek feedback, you show your boss that you understand that you are all of the same team and working toward the same goals—goals you are committed to doing your best to deliver. It also alleviates any tension that might otherwise arise. When your boss feels comfortable giving you feedback, he or she will be less likely to avoid otherwise uncomfortable conversations, only to later explode in frustration.

> The secret to being great at receiving feedback is to ask for feedback so often and so eagerly that the back-and-forth between you and your boss with respect to your job performance feels calm and collaborative.

> *No one is perfect. We all learn by making mistakes and learning from those. Feedback is just another way to learn and grow. In my younger years starting out, I had trouble accepting feedback but I learned quickly that good or bad, there is something to learn from it. Accepting feedback has helped me grow and develop as a business analyst and trusted leader in my company.*
>
> **—David Beckham,**
> **Senior lead business analyst**

One word of caution:

You do not want to overdo it such that you appear to need constant hand-holding. Unless you have been told that your written skills need some work, you probably do not need feedback on the wording of the email you sent to your colleagues to schedule a meeting. A good rule of thumb to follow is this: Ask for feedback at least weekly, until the back-and-forth becomes a natural part of the relationship you have with your boss. Then, unless you feel unsure of something, you can stop asking for regular feedback because you will get it without solicitation.

The tremendous byproduct of asking for feedback is that you can use the feedback that you receive to improve your skills—both hard and soft—and advance your career.

> *I am the type to constantly ask for feedback. I ask those around me: "What can I be doing better? What should I stop doing? What should I start doing?" Then I take time to assess the feedback and understand context. From there, I decide what changes I should make, if any.*
>
> **— Miranda Moonilal,** Senior administrator

Day in the life:
YELENA SLOBARD

Yelena Slobard is a business analyst who works for a consulting firm in the San Francisco Bay area. On most days, she works from her home office, which is rare for business analysts, who normally need to be in front of clients. She also documents her journey in the Salesforce world on her blog: www.sf9to5.com.

At any given time, Yelena is working on six to ten projects, with most of her time spent in meetings with clients and colleagues.

On Tuesdays, Yelena commutes into the city to work from her firm's office. This is a typical Tuesday in the life of Yelena Slobard.

7:15 a.m.

Yelena wakes up, eats breakfast, and drinks her first cup of coffee before heading out the door to catch the 8:12 a.m. train into the city. Although Yelena works primarily from home, she goes into the office every Tuesday to meet with teammates and have face-to-face time with her managers.

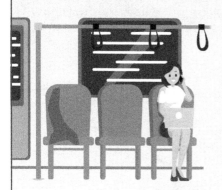

She also uses this time to brainstorm and plan more complex projects where the in-person element helps.

She uses the time on the train (50 minutes!) to chat with her teammates and listen to her favorite podcasts and audio books.

9:15 a.m.

Fortunately, the train arrived on time, which means Yelena has time to grab a small Americano at the local coffee shop, where she checks her email and scopes how to use the day in the office in the most efficient manner.

She uses this time to handle the quick tasks (those that take two minutes or less) before heading into the office.

9:30 a.m.

Today is going to be a great day.

Yelena has a surprise for her office-mates: She brought homemade Oreo cookies to the office, which her colleagues enjoy during the daily sync to review the status of all the clients. During today's sync, she goes through each client's project, updating the previous and next meeting dates, and identifying the next steps and to-dos. She also discusses a technical issue she is having on one project, and receives suggestions from the company's other consultants.

10:00 a.m.

First client meeting of the day. Yelena is the strategic lead on this project, but today's meeting is reserved for discussing the technical and implementation aspects of the project.

11:00 a.m.

Yelena blocked an hour in her schedule to work on a Powerpoint presentation for her 4 p.m. meeting with a client. This is a "catch-up" presentation requested by the client to onboard a new person joining the client's team.

Noon

Lunchtime! Yelena and a colleague grab a sandwich at a coffee shop and chat about sewing.

12:00PM

"I'm the kind of human who gets hangry if you don't feed me," she said.

1:00 p.m.

The second part of the day is an internal strategic meeting with one of the partners to discuss the design of a project and prepare for an upcoming meeting with the client.

3:00 p.m.

The third meeting of the day is a weekly meeting with a client to review questions the client has about implementation of a CPQ project.

4:00 p.m.

Showtime! It's time to walk the client through the Powerpoint presentation Yelena finalized earlier in the day. The presentation goes smoothly, though one attendee got sidetracked on a small technical issue. Yelena was able to steer the meeting back on track.

"This is where patience and good communication skills come into play," she said.

5:00 p.m.

Though she has the occasional evening meeting with developers, Yelena's workday ends at 5:00, which is when most of her clients are done with their days. On her 5:15 train back home, she jumps on a resourcing call with the developers to discuss prioritization of projects.

CHAPTER NINETEEN:
Self-Efficacy ←

Self-efficacy is the ability to create change or accomplish goals in your own life. It is the soft skill that allows a person to take initiative. Employers like employees who have self-efficacy because they are action-takers. When someone needs to jump in and get the job done, people with self-efficacy are the ones who raise their hands.

TIPS FOR INCREASING YOUR SELF-EFFICACY:

- **Tip #1:** Collect evidence
- **Tip #2:** Act "as if"

Self-efficacy is a soft skill that is based on a belief—the belief that you have the power to impact results. Those who lack self-efficacy have an opposing belief—the belief that they will fail. If you want to develop and demonstrate self-efficacy, you need to adopt the first belief.

Changing a belief, though, is easier said than done, so this chapter provides you with two tips for changing your beliefs such that you can increase your self-efficacy and be a more attractive candidate for jobs.

If you want to move into other areas, you have to be willing to raise your hand. You have to be willing to take on tasks that aren't necessarily your tasks to take on so that you can show you have the willingness and, just as importantly, show you have the facility and capability of moving into other areas successfully. Those two things build confidence with leadership that you can move into other roles.

— Neal Lightfeldt, Sales excellence manager

'Fortune favors the bold,' as they say. Taking an active role in the direction of your career rather than being just a passenger is the difference between working just to work and actually being fulfilled with what you do and the role your contributions play in the world at large.

—Jorge Luis Pérez Pratt,
Developer

Let's be clear here: Speaking up and being bold doesn't equate to being cocky or boisterous. It just means taking chances.

–Scott Shapiro,
Senior administrator

TIP #1:

Collect evidence.

Surely, you have accomplished goals in the past, whether these are job-related goals, academic goals, or fitness goals. And most certainly, your journey was not entirely smooth sailing, yet you persisted nonetheless.

The trouble with doubting your own self-efficacy is that it begins a self-fulfilling prophecy. You believe you cannot effect change or reach goals, so you put in minimal effort, and you fail.

> *Managers love self-efficacy. Employees who don't need to have their hand held for everything can reduce managers' headaches. Your job security improves if you can be known as the person who takes charge and solves problems.*
>
> **—Moon Algazzali, Administrator**

The way out, then, is to collect evidence to the contrary by reminding yourself of what you have already accomplished. The evidence helps you overcome your negative way of thinking.

Likewise, set yourself up for success by creating small, doable, mini-goals. Oftentimes, looking too far into the future seems overwhelming and undoable. When you shorten your focus and tackle one small task at a time, you build your belief in your own self-efficacy.

TIP #2:

Act "as if."

Even if you honestly do not believe that you are capable of meeting whatever goal is placed in front of you, act as though you are. Fake it, and the reason is this: The actions that people take when they have self-efficacy are far more desirable than those that they take when they do not believe the goal is attainable.

The degree to which you have self-efficacy will determine:

1. The amount of effort you put into your job.

2. The degree to which you can tolerate obstacles standing in the way of you and your goal.

3. Whether you are successful.

If you do not believe you are capable of accomplishing your goals, you will likely not even try. If you are forced to try, your effort will be minimal, and you will quit when you receive pushback.

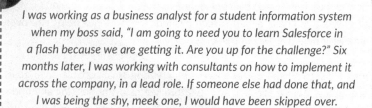

I was working as a business analyst for a student information system when my boss said, "I am going to need you to learn Salesforce in a flash because we are getting it. Are you up for the challenge?" Six months later, I was working with consultants on how to implement it across the company, in a lead role. If someone else had done that, and I was being the shy, meek one, I would have been skipped over.

— Scott Shapiro, Senior administrator

People who have a high degree of self-efficacy—or who act "as if"—are the ones who find their way around obstacles. When one solution does not work, they back off and try another solution. They persist in the face of failure because they believe they are ultimately capable of accomplishing whatever it is that they set out to accomplish.

In other words, acting "as if" will help you collect the evidence necessary to actually change your belief.

If you don't have self-efficacy, someone else will, and not always to your benefit. I worked at a place for eleven years and was a subject-matter-expert in systems and processes, but I was still made redundant. Luckily, I was in the driver's seat. I had already started my Salesforce journey, so I continued to concentrate on developing my skills and became a CPQ consultant.

—Ben Stokes, Administrator and former CPQ consultant

The best way to grow is being unafraid to take new responsibilities, which opens up more possibilities for you to grow in your career. For example, I was asked to present at Dreamforce a week before Dreamforce started. I could have said, 'No,' but I accepted the challenge and spent tons of time preparing for the presentation. It turned out to be such a good presentation that I was asked again by Salesforce. org to present at a local conference in NYC. I'm so glad that I took the opportunity and believed in my ability. When opportunity comes, grab it. It could change everything.

—Moon Algazzali, Administrator

Day in the life:
NEAL LIGHTFELDT

Neal Lightfeldt has worked for the same company, which manufacturers controls for industrial applications, for twenty years. He started as a graphic designer but grew into different positions within the company. Several years back, the company began a new initiative focused on applying OpEx principles to the front-end of the business. Part of that initiative included implementing Salesforce, and because Neal had previously managed the company's old CRM system, becoming the Salesforce administrator was a natural next-step. Neal's official title is "Sales Excellence Manager," and he is the sole administrator dedicated to helping the 76 users in the United States and Germany. Neal generously shared a snapshot of how he spends his days.

20%
1. Maintenance

"This involves troubleshooting and fixing problems. Maybe a report is suddenly not supplying the expected information. Sometimes a user thinks there is a problem, when they just need retraining. Sometimes there are issues with the integration between Salesforce and our backend system. There could be changes to sales territories, which could require reconfiguration. The issues are varied and on any given day I might spend half my time on a single issue. But in general I would estimate I devote 20 percent of my day on maintenance issues."

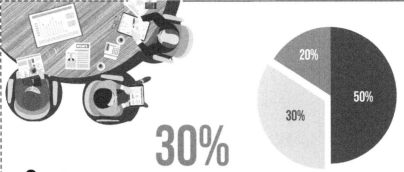

30%
2. Coaching/Training

"This includes training new users or retraining existing users on specific areas. I meet with our Germany plant once or twice a week and provide support/training for the sub-admin there. I monitor the system daily and identify users who are not using the system regularly and target them for coaching/additional training. We periodically have group training as well to demo/promote new features/functions. Continual coaching/training is a critical component to a successful implementation."

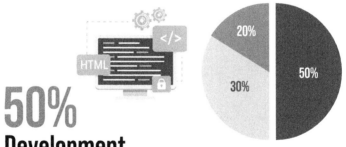

50%
3. Development

"This includes identifying opportunities to develop new apps based on meetings/discussions with users, implementing new applications driven by process-improvement efforts internally, and implementing third-party apps to meet specific needs often driven by executive management. Much of my work in this area involves rolling up my sleeves and doing the work, but it also involves managing outside developers as well. When it comes to actual Apex coding, I will bring someone else on to do that."

CONCLUSION

The University of Wisconsin-Stout is a four-year university in a rural community in the Midwestern United States that enrolls a little under 10,000 students each year. As one of two special-mission universities in the University of Wisconsin system, the University of Wisconsin-Stout is a polytechnic university.

"We are not what would be considered a traditional college," said Professor Evan Sveum, who heads the university's Information and Communication Technology program. "We have an experiential learning component, which basically means we want to give our students experiences so they can start working. The experiences they have plus their credentials will open the door when looking for a career, so we want to make sure they have experiences."

With that in mind, a few years back, the University of Wisconsin-Stout's Information and Communication Technologies (ICT) department made a choice that might seem surprising: It replaced its Microsoft curriculum with a Salesforce curriculum.

Part of this change, said Professor Sveum, was that Microsoft was not as good at providing updated learning systems and learning tools. Beyond that, Salesforce not only has a curriculum for colleges, it also has free supplemental training resources in the form of Trailhead.

Students in the ICT program might, for instance, practice being consultants who need to engage with clients from the perspective of a consultant group. Students are assigned different roles: project manager, technical subject-matter-expert, business analyst, and the like. They interview the "client" and build designs.

"We have found, over and over, that hands-on experiences, along with conceptual insight, matter in the big picture perspective," said Professor Sveum.

By the time students are sophomores or juniors, the University of Wisconsin-Stout helps place them in internships. And by the time they graduate, students have a 100 percent success rate in finding degree-related jobs right out of the gate. (Compare this to one report that found that 43 percent of recent college graduates work in jobs that do not require college degrees.)

Beyond that, they are making what Professor Sveum calls "obscene amounts of money."

"We are sitting in a sweet spot right now," said Professor Sveum. "The demand for effective history teachers is not quite as high as the demand for IT professionals. Don't get me wrong: I like history. But we can say, 'Hey, eighteen-year-olds, if your endgame is to start a career, then let's take a look at the statistics.'"

Here are some of those statistics:

- There are four times as many Salesforce developer positions as there are actual developers

- The number of technical jobs that require Salesforce skills outpace the talent pool by 10 to 1.

- Jobs that require Salesforce skills are growing faster than the overall job market.

- Jobs that require Salesforce skills pay more than jobs that don't require Salesforce skills.

The empirical evidence is also strong. Within the pages of this book, you have read about successful Salesforce professionals from backgrounds that run the gamut. It's not just young college grads that are beginning their careers in Salesforce. In fact, Professor Sveum, whose grown daughter is a Salesforce admin, wonders about his future in Salesforce.

"Every once in a while, I ask: *What will I do next?* And then I remember Salesforce, and I think: *I haven't been on Trailhead for a while. I really like going on Trailhead. Maybe I should go earn another badge.*"

> *I wish I would have started with Salesforce when I was younger. I have been working with this now for about ten years, and only in the past few years have I started getting more certifications. I feel like there is a world of opportunity available to Salesforce professionals. Had I started earlier in my career, who knows where I could be now?*
>
> **— David Beckham,** Senior lead Salesforce business analyst

Professor Sveum is not the only person with a successful career under their belt to consider a Salesforce career.

A year ago, Jim Vineyard had a little understanding of computers. His background was in customer service for nonprofit and for-profit sectors, and he had worked with digital electronics in the military reserve. That said, when he was hired a year ago as a first-tier help-desk agent, Jim knew nothing about CRM in general, much less Salesforce in particular. He was encouraged to become familiar with Salesforce.

Over the course of the next year, Jim earned two certifications—Administrator and Advanced Administrator—and plans to earn others.

"I'll see where my interests and employment options take me," he told me.

"If an older guy who hasn't had a career in IT can start in Salesforce, and, in less than a year, go from know-nothing to being a certified Advanced Administrator, then anyone can do it, if they are willing to do the work."

REFERENCES

Introduction

Global Challenge Insight Report. The Future of Jobs. Employment, Skills and Workforce Strategy for the Fourth Industrial Revolution. World Economic Forum, January 2016, http://www3.weforum.org/docs/WEF_Future_of_Jobs.pdf

Kalil, Tom and Farnam Jahanian. "Computer Science Is for Everyone!" The White House. 11 Dec. 2013. https://obamawhitehouse.archives.gov/blog/2013/12/11/computer-science-everyone

IDC White Paper. *The Salesforce Economy Forecast: 3.3 Million New Jobs, $859 Billion New Business Revenues to Be Created from 2016 to 2022.* Salesforce.com Inc, Oct. 2017.

Columbus, Louis. "Salesforce Now has Over 19% of the CRM Market." *Forbes*, 22 June, 2019, https://www.forbes.com/sites/louiscolumbus/2019/06/22/salesforce-now-has-over-19-of-the-crm-market/#5931d08b333a

2019 Annual Report: Celebrating 20 Years of Salesforce. Salesforce.com Inc, 2019, https://s23.q4cdn.com/574569502/files/doc_financials/2019/Salesforce-FY-2019-Annual-Report.pdf

Part One

Gantz, John F. IDC White Paper. The Salesforce Economic Impact: 4.2 Million New Jobs, $1.2 Trillion of New Business Revenue from 2019 to 2014. Salesforce.com Inc, Oct. 2017, https://www.salesforce.com/content/dam/web/en_us/www/documents/reports/idc-salesforce-economy-report.pdf

Part Two

https://trailhead.salesforce.com/career-path/admin

Conclusion

Cooper, Preston. "Underemployment Persists Throughout College Graduates' Careers." Forbes, 18 June, 2018, https://www.forbes.com/sites/prestoncooper2/2018/06/08/underemployment-persists-throughout-college-graduates-careers/#60bf198b7490

10K Advisors. *New Research Indicates the Salesforce Ecosystem May Be Innovating Faster Than Talent Can Keep Pace, Resulting in Great Career Opportunities but Challenges for Customers.* PR Newswire, 18 Sept., 2018. https://www.prnewswire.com/news-releases/new-research-indicates-the-salesforce-ecosystem-may-be-innovating-faster-than-talent-can-keep-pace-resulting-in-great-career-opportunities-but-challenges-for-customers-300714441.html

ABOUT THE AUTHOR

Martin Gessner is a Salesforce solution architect and the founder of a company that has helped thousands of Salesforce professionals learn Salesforce, develop their careers, and prepare for certifications. He discovered the Salesforce platform over ten years ago and delighted in the possibilities of delivering cloud solutions quickly and efficiently compared to traditional IT on premise projects. He has worked with the Salesforce platform in various roles including business analyst, project manager, consultant, solutions designer, and solutions architect. He holds twelve certifications and enjoys helping others learn Salesforce and succeed with their careers.

To learn more about how you can manage and develop your Salesforce career, head to **www.cloudtalent360.com**.

If you enjoyed
The Salesforce Career Playbook,
would you leave a review for
the book on Amazon?

Made in the USA
Middletown, DE
09 November 2020